the Unofficial Guide™ to Hiring and Firing People

Alan S. Horowitz

Macmillan • USA

8-20-99

Macmillan General Reference
A Simon & Schuster Macmillan Company
1633 Broadway
New York, New York 10019-6785

ISBN: 0-02-862523-4

Manufactured in the United States of America

10 9 8 7 6 5 4 3 2 1

First edition

To my parents, Sophia and Paul Horowitz, and aunts, Betty Padowitz Martin and Sadye Padowitz Schwartz, for their wisdom and encouragement.

Acknowledgments

Many thanks for those who listened to my musings about this book, and generously gave of their support and expertise, including Ray Carlson, Tom Probert, Natalya Rapoport, William Sargent, Marnie Sears, and Tom Vitelli.

Contents

The *Unofficial Guide*
Reader's Bill of Rights

We Give You More Than the Official Line

Welcome to the *Unofficial Guide* series of Lifestyles titles—books that deliver critical, unbiased information that other books can't or won't reveal—*the inside scoop*. Our goal is to provide you with the *most accessible, useful* information and advice possible. The recommendations we offer in these pages are not influenced by the corporate line of any organization or industry; we give you the hard facts, whether those institutions like them or not. If something is ill-advised or will cause a loss of time and/or money, we'll give you ample warning. And if it is a worthwhile option, we'll let you know that, too.

Armed and Ready

Our hand-picked authors confidently and critically report on a wide range of topics that matter to smart readers like you. Our authors are passionate about their subjects, but have distanced themselves enough from them to help you be armed and protected, and help you make educated decisions as you go through your process. It is our intent that, from having read this book, you will avoid the pitfalls everyone else falls into and get it right the first time.

Don't be fooled by cheap imitations; this is the *genuine article Unofficial Guide* series from Macmillan Publishing. You may be familiar with our proven track record of the travel *Unofficial Guides,* which have more than three million copies in print. Each year thousands of travelers—new and old—are armed with a brand new, fully updated edition of the flagship *Unofficial Guide to Walt Disney World,* by Bob Sehlinger. It is our intention here to provide you with the same level of objective authority that Mr. Sehlinger does in his brainchild.

The Unofficial Panel of Experts

Every work in the Lifestyle *Unofficial Guides* is intensively inspected by a team of three top professionals in their fields. These experts review the manuscript for factual accuracy, comprehensiveness, and an insider's determination as to whether the manuscript fulfills the credo in this Reader's Bill of Rights. In other words, our Panel ensures that you are, in fact, getting "the inside scoop."

Our Pledge

The authors, the editorial staff, and the Unofficial Panel of Experts assembled for *Unofficial Guides* are determined to lay out the most valuable alternatives available for our readers. This dictum means that our writers must be explicit, prescriptive, and above all, direct. We strive to be thorough and complete, but our goal is not necessarily to have the "most" or "all" of the information on a topic; this is not, after all, an encyclopedia. Our objective is to help you narrow down your options to the best of what is available, unbiased by affiliation with any industry or organization.

In each *Unofficial Guide* we give you:

- Comprehensive coverage of necessary and vital information

- Authoritative, rigidly fact-checked data

- The most up-to-date insights into trends

- Savvy, sophisticated writing that's also readable

- Sensible, applicable facts and secrets that only an insider knows

Special Features

Every book in our series offers the following six special sidebars in the margins that were devised to help you get things done cheaply, efficiently, and smartly.

1. "Timesaver"—tips and shortcuts that save you time.

2. "Moneysaver"—tips and shortcuts that save you money.

3. "Watch Out!"—more serious cautions and warnings.

4. "Bright Idea"—general tips and shortcuts to help you find an easier or smarter way to do something.

5. "Quote"—statements from real people that are intended to be prescriptive and valuable to you.

6. "Unofficially…"—an insider's fact or anecdote.

We also recognize your need to have quick information at your fingertips, and have thus provided the following comprehensive sections at the back of the book:

1. **Glossary:** Definitions of complicated terminology and jargon.

2. **Resource Guide:** Lists of relevant agencies, associations, institutions, web sites, etc.

3. **Recommended Reading:** Suggested titles that can help you get more in-depth information on related topics.

4. **Important Documents:** "Official" pieces of information you need to refer to, such as government forms.

5. **Important Statistics:** Facts and numbers presented at-a-glance for easy reference.

6. **Index.**

Letters, Comments, and Questions from Readers

We strive to continually improve the Unofficial series, and input from our readers is a valuable way for us to do that. Many of those who have used the *Unofficial Guide* travel books write to the authors to ask questions, make comments, or share their own discoveries and lessons. For lifestyle *Unofficial Guides*, we would also appreciate all such correspondence, both positive and critical, and we will make best efforts to incorporate appropriate readers' feedback and comments in revised editions of this work.

How to write to us:

Unofficial Guides
Macmillan Lifestyle Guides
Macmillan Publishing
1633 Broadway
New York, NY 10019

Attention: Readers' Comments

The *Unofficial Guide* Panel of Experts

The *Unofficial* editorial team recognizes that you've purchased this book with the expectation of getting the most authoritative, carefully inspected information currently available. Toward that end, on each and every title in this series, we have selected a minimum of three "official" experts comprising the "Unofficial Panel" who painstakingly review the manuscripts to ensure: factual accuracy of all data; inclusion of the most up-to-date and relevant information; and that, from an insider's perspective, the authors have armed you with all the necessary facts you need—but the institutions don't want you to know.

For *The Unofficial Guide to Hiring and Firing People*, we are proud to introduce the following panel of experts:

The Unofficial editorial team recognizes that you've purchased this book with the expectation of getting the most authoritative, carefully inspected information currently available. Toward that end, on each and every title in this series, we have selected a minimum of three "official" experts comprising the "Unofficial Panel" who painstakingly review the manuscripts to ensure: the factual accuracy of all data; inclusion of the most up-to-date and relevant information; and that, from an insider's perspective, the authors have armed you with all the necessary facts you need—but the institutions don't want you to know.

For *The Unofficial Guide to Hiring and Firing People,* we are proud to introduce the following panel of experts:

Syl Tang   As Editorial Consultant, Syl Tang provided us with an insider's perspective on workforce planning, with a particular emphasis on the latest in executive recruiting and the legal issues surrounding hiring and firing.

Ms. Tang currently heads up Global Resource Planning for Global New Business Models at Andersen Consulting. Previously Ms. Tang structured the Executive Recruiting Function for the Americas Technology group supporting Andersen's financial services clients. Ms. Tang's recruiting experience began at Ward Howell Int'l, a "Top Ten" retained search firm where she placed CFOs and CEOs in health care and financial services internationally. Her work has included compensation analyses, hiring tools, and the development of retention programs. Ms. Tang graduated from Cornell University with a BS in Industrial and Labor Relations. In her spare time she is a committee member of Inwood House and enjoys travel writing and salsa music.

Elisabeth Alter Elisabeth   Alter has over 10 years of experience in professional banking, 5 of which are in a managerial role. She is currently

Branch Manager and Vice President at Republic National Bank in New York City. In this capacity, she supervises a staff of 20 and is responsible for all aspects of branch sales, staffing, and operations. A graduate of the University of Hartford, Ms. Alter lives in New Jersey.

Lori Bethon Lori Bethon has worked in Human Resources for more than eight years. Currently the Associate Director of Human Resources for Macmillan Publishing USA, Ms. Bethon graduated with a Master's Degree in Organizational Psychology from Columbia University.

Introduction

Hiring and firing are to business owners and managers what knee surgery is to an injured athlete: time-consuming, painful, and absolutely essential if he or she is to make the most of the opportunities life provides. If you don't master the skills needed for effective hiring and firing, your business will run like a car with nearly flat tires—it will go, but never as efficiently as if it were operating in peak condition. Few managers or business owners enjoy hiring, and no one likes to fire, yet almost all of us have to do it at some time. But the processes can be made more effective and less painful. My goal for this book is to help you be the best you can be at hiring and firing, so that your business will be the best it can be.

Hiring an employee is expensive, more so than you might think. A lot of time and money is wasted by poor hiring decisions. Once a person is hired, it's not easy to reverse the choice if it proves to be a mistake. A common attitude to hiring was recently expressed by Gail I. Johnson, a computer reseller in Fairless Hills, Pennsylvania: "We're looking to hire a couple of people, and my experience with hiring is so bad, I'm depressed thinking about it."

Even more emotionally troubling is firing, which has to be one of the most stressful responsibilities anyone has in business. The person you fire will probably feel animosity toward you, while his colleagues may turn against you. When a person loses a job, his career and family life may suffer. This is a responsibility many managers find difficult to live with. Then, too, there are important legal considerations, as well as a firing's possible effects on employee morale. *The Unofficial Guide to Hiring and Firing People* gives you the tools you need to keep your sanity when hiring and firing. With this book you can considerably improve your personal effectiveness and the performance of your entire organization.

How to Use This Book

You will benefit most by reading this book from beginning to end. But you can also use it as a quick reference when facing a particular hurdle. Here is an example of how this book can be used for quick reference: If you have placed a want-ad for a job opening and your desk is now piled above eye level with resumes, Chapter 11, "Screening Applicants," will give you immediate, easy-to-follow advice on what to look for in resumes. Or, if a job applicant is coming for an interview tomorrow, see Chapter 12, "The Interview."

Throughout the book are short notes, or sidebars, that give you quick pieces of information:

Bright ideas are tips and shortcuts that provide an easier or smarter way to do something.

Timesavers are shortcuts that save time.

Moneysavers include tips and shortcuts for saving money.

Watch out! items warn of potential dangers.

Unofficially... items are extra bits of information you may find interesting—usually definitions, general explanatory text, case histories, or food for thought.

Quotes are stimulating remarks people have said about the topic at hand.

There are other books on hiring and firing, but this comprehensive guide, written for small business owners and managers, touches on all aspects of the hiring and firing process, including how to write a job description, how to prepare for conducting a job interview, and how to fire someone as painlessly as possible. This guide is truly practical, with plenty of lists and specific pieces of advice, rather than generalities or theories. But perhaps the most important reason to read this book—and what sets it apart from other books about this topic—is that it not only makes the hiring and firing processes less costly and worrisome, but easy to understand and easier to implement. All the best advice in the world is wasted if not used, so think of *The Unofficial Guide to Hiring and Firing People* as a motivator that is specifically designed to help you do things more efficiently and in a more informed manner, and to shift to these new practices as easily and quickly as possible.

I hope that in reading this book you will learn sensible, efficient new practices that will make your job—and your employees' jobs—easier and more rewarding. If you find a few good pointers that you use over and over again when hiring and firing, I will consider that I've done my job well.

Before You Get Started

GET THE SCOOP ON...
Hiring mistakes to avoid ▪ The price you pay for
hiring mistakes ▪ The good things that come to
those with good hiring practices ▪ The current
job market ▪ Making good employee/job matches

PART I

Hiring: The Key to Your Success

Chapter 1

Hiring is often the orphan of good management practices. It is left until the end, after "more important" management responsibilities are finished. Only then does it get some—and not necessarily enough—attention. All too often, an applicant arrives at an interview, only to find the interviewer reading her resume for the first time as she sits waiting. Managers like this do not give the hiring process its due. Disregarding the importance of careful hiring is a costly mistake, for people are a business's most important, most valuable asset.

This chapter will point out some of the common hiring mistakes people make, the trends in the marketplace and how they affect your hiring ability, and the costs of poor hiring practices.

Hiring mistakes people make

When I was editor-in-chief of a small newsletter publishing company and needed to hire someone to do research, financial analysis, and write articles, I expected to base my hiring decisions on finding the best writer. Therefore, I placed an ad in the newspaper for "Writer."

When the job candidates started coming through my door, the interviews regularly ran 45 minutes or more, with easily two thirds of the time spent with my explaining to the candidates what the company was, what the newsletter industry was about, and what the job's responsibilities were. Competent writers were readily available, but what I didn't find—and needed most—was a writer who understood business, including how businesses operate, how the stock market works, how to read financial statements, how to interview corporate management, and how to separate what's important and accurate from the public relations fluff every company throws out.

I made some mistakes along the way. One person I hired was an MBA student who thought she knew a lot about business, but didn't. Another hiree could write, but I never did figure out what her real interests were. They certainly had nothing to do with business. The one person I hired during this time who worked out well was a lucky accident: Not only could she write, but she also had an MBA and a fair amount of business savvy. From her, I learned what I really wanted and needed.

Hiring mistakes

I could have been a poster child for the manager who does not know how to hire. Here are some of the mistakes I made.

Mistake: Not knowing what I needed. I thought I wanted a writer, but what I really needed was someone who understood business. After several disappointments, I finally learned my lesson, and it changed my whole approach to hiring.

Lesson: Know what you want. Think about what you really need most. It was easier for me to turn poor prose into good prose than it was for me to re-research poorly researched articles. Therefore, I began listing the job under "Financial Analyst" rather than "Writer." Job seekers attracted to ads for financial analysts were very different from those who came as writers, and they worked out much better.

Cost: The costs were considerable, including the costs of advertising, lost productivity, missed opportunities, and wasted time.

Mistake: Not knowing what to look for in the resumes I received. Newsletter writing and financial analysis were so obscure that no candidate had any direct experience with the job, and so all were a compromise. But I couldn't tell which were more likely to work out than others, leaving me to choose largely on guesswork.

Cost: Because I didn't know what I really wanted, I ended up interviewing far more candidates than I needed to. Needless interviews not only wasted my time, but it confused me because I had too many similar people to choose from.

Lesson: Know up front what qualifications and experience you want the employee to have. Choose to interview only those who most closely match this profile. Use the classified ad to explain in detail what you want.

Mistake: Talking too much in the interview. No manager can learn a thing about a job applicant when he is talking, only when he listens. When candidates left my office, they knew far more about me and the company than I knew about them.

Cost: Again, a waste of time.

Lesson: Talk only enough to set the applicant at ease. Describe the company and job concisely, but mainly listen.

Consequences of poor hiring decisions

The result of all these mistakes was that I frequently messed up my hiring decisions. The consequences were not trivial. At least three significant results followed from my inexperience and lack of effectiveness:

1. Tens of thousands of dollars were wasted—the result of wages paid to unproductive employees and weeks of my time lost to hiring and working with the wrong employees.

2. My department was never as productive or creative as it might have been. As an example, introducing new newsletters was an important part of the company's growth strategy, yet not one of my employees ever came up with a viable idea for a new newsletter or other product we could sell. It never occurred to me to ask them during the interview to come up with an idea for a new product. We were limited in our ability to create new opportunities because of my poor hiring decisions.

3. I got a lot of unwanted experience in firing folks.

Talk to anyone with hiring and firing experience, and they will likely regale you with tales of disastrous interviews, poor judgment, ineffective employment agencies, legal problems, and other missteps. The business landscape is a treacherous legal and emotional terrain for those who hire and fire; this book will help you traverse this route without getting blown up by any landmines hidden in your path.

The importance of effective hiring

Southwest Airlines has the same Boeing 737 air-planes that many of the world's airlines use; it flies into the same airports as its competitors, uses the same fuel, serves the same peanuts; and it has to compete for customers the same way its competition does. Yet, it regularly has the lowest costs in the air-line industry, the most productive workers, and the highest customer satisfaction. *Fortune* magazine recently cited it as the number one company to work for in the United States. Its competitive advan-tage is not equipment or fuel or scheduling or mar-keting, but its people.

Lots of companies have labs, but it was AT&T that had perhaps the most renowned, Bell Labora-tories, which was responsible for the transistor among other inventions. It's not Bunsen burners or computers that make one lab more productive than another, but the people in the lab.

Until the 1960s, the supermarket chain, The Great Atlantic and Pacific Tea Company (A&P), was for many years not only the largest supermarket chain but the nation's largest retailer. Today, A&P is large, with sales of $10 billion, but is less than half the size of the largest supermarket chain, Kroger, whose sales top $25 billion, and is only one-tenth the size of the largest retailer, Wal-Mart, whose sales are $105 billion. All of these companies have well-established names, access to plenty of financial backing, and the money to afford to hire top man-agers; and they frequently even sell the same mer-chandise. Why have companies like Kroger and Wal-Mart prevailed over their competitors? Because of the people they hire.

Bright Idea
If you don't think your employees are your most important asset, consider the following:

■ How badly would your busi-ness be hurt if your best employees left?

■ Would you be much better off if all employees were as good as your best?

■ Are you miss-ing opportuni-ties because you don't have enough employees?

■ Do ineffective or incompetent employees hurt your bottom line?

■ Do poor employees out-right *damage* your business?

Trends in the labor market

Employers today are facing a market for workers that is arguably more fluid, dynamic, and difficult to predict than any within memory. This new labor market will affect you directly and profoundly by hindering your ability to find qualified workers, forcing you to pay your workforce more than you otherwise would have, and changing your hiring practices. The tighter labor market can even affect your ability to fire because unproductive workers may be better than no workers, and many positions are currently going unfilled because of a lack of candidates. Ultimately, though, the most important consequence of today's labor market is its ability to affect the success of your business. You may well find it harder to grow your business and make it more effective because it is difficult to attract the qualified people you need.

Here is a list of some of the more important workforce trends today:

Watch Out!
Pay attention to the media's coverage of your market. For example, if you see a competitor moving into town, recognize that it will be harder for you to hire new people and that you may lose some of your present employees.

- **A labor shortage.** The unemployment rate today is lower than it has been in more than a generation. Nationally, it's below 5 percent, and in a number of states it has dropped below 3 percent. Tight labor markets make it difficult to bring on board the number and types of people you need. And the lack of workers is affecting virtually all types of businesses.

Consider, for example, the owner of a small downtown restaurant who placed an ad in the local newspaper for a table server. He ran the ad every day for two weeks but was unable to hire anyone, even though he was paying the going rate, had an attractive restaurant in a good part of town, and was not being especially picky. Why couldn't he hire anyone? Quite simply, he never got a single response to the ad. No one wanted the job. So don't think that only highly skilled positions are going begging—the labor market today is tight for just about all employers in almost every part of the country, and this situation is likely to remain unchanged for the foreseeable future.

■ **Special situations.** The Information Technology Association of America estimated in 1998 that 346,000 information technology jobs were unfilled in the United States. Special situations are fueling this shortage. "Year 2000," the problem of getting computers to recognize dates in the new millennium, is a special situation. So is the *euro,* the coming single currency that 11 European nations will begin using starting in 1999, and all the attendant computer software changes that the new currency will require. These two unusual situations promise to maintain today's severe shortage of skilled computer programmers for years to come.

Special situations don't just affect high tech. Construction workers are likely to be in high demand for years to come because Congress is earmarking billions of dollars to rebuild the nation's highway system and to expand mass transit. Watch out for these special situations, as they can directly affect your ability to get the people you need.

The important legacy left by recent fluctuations, such as the wave of downsizings, has been the breaking of the bonds between employer and employee. No longer can employees expect to spend their entire careers with one employer.

Unofficially...
Average number of jobs that an American worker has held by age 40: eight.
From *What Counts: The Complete Harper's Index*

And now that those bonds have been broken, they can never be restored, which means you now have to deal with a labor force more willing than ever to move to greener pastures. And you have to operate within a society that is more accepting than ever of those who move from job to job. Job jumpers are no longer thought of as flakes or unreliables and, in fact, are often viewed as shrewd. Not since the Industrial Revolution began attracting those living in rural areas to the cities has labor been more willing to change jobs. The phrase "employee retention" was hardly known a few years ago, but today it's a vital concept as employers fight to hold on to their workers and not incur the costs and disruptions that result from heavy employee turnover. (Chapters 3 and 4 cover ways to reduce your employee turnover and retain the employees you have.) You may never have downsized or fired anyone, but you will have to live with the consequences of the actions of others for the foreseeable future.

- **More sensitivity to employee needs.** Roger E. Herman, head of the Herman Group, strategic business futurists in Greensboro, North Carolina, says that companies wanting to attract and retain employees will have to provide more than just good pay. They will need to be more family centered. For example, they will have to adjust to the needs of single parents, who are looking for such amenities as flex time, job sharing, child care, telecommuting, and maternal and paternal leave. Even environmental awareness and other social issues are becoming important elements when workers decide which job they take. When hiring, you will have to be more of a salesperson than in the past, and what you will be selling is what your company is like and why the potential employee would want to work there.

If potential employees don't think yours is a progressive, responsible organization that cares about more than the bottom line, then they won't agree to work for you—or, if they do come on board, chances are good they will not stay for long.

- **The age of the entrepreneur.** Perhaps at no time in history has it been easier or more socially acceptable for people to go off on their own, either by starting their own business or becoming independent contractors. A recent estimate put the number of independent contractors at 8.5 million, or close to 7 percent of the labor force. Many articles have been written about those who in one form or other become successfully self-employed. This has encouraged many in the labor force to at least dream of going off on their own, with quite a few actually doing it. When workers begin to think they can do it on their own and don't need a job, employers have a tough time motivating workers and keeping them on the job as full-time employees. The attitude of workers has changed, with many now believing they don't need The Corporation. As an employer, you must deal with this new perspective every day.

- **The Internet.** Not only is the labor force changing, but so is the way employers look for employees. A revolution in hiring practices is already happening, and it involves looking for prospective employees online. Until the mid-1990s, this employee-search technology did not exist. Now it promises to become a major means by which employers find employees and advertise that they have job openings available. (See Chapter 10.) Unless you learn to effectively use the Internet for your hiring efforts, you will fall behind your competitors who do.

Bright Idea
Collect resumes, even if you are not hiring. Tell friends and associates that you are always interested in having a copy of the resume of a good worker. This practice extends your pool of potential employees and gives you access to people who may be available when you need them.

- **Continual recruiting.** Conventional wisdom says you look for workers when you need them. Most employers wait to begin the hiring process until either someone leaves their employ or they have expanded enough to justify creating a new position. This is a reactive strategy—the employer reacts to a changing situation.

While this reactive approach worked for many years, it is decidedly less effective now. The tight labor market and the need for specialized skills means that most employers cannot afford to wait around until the need for a worker arises.

There are two compelling reasons for a proactive approach:

—The search process will likely take longer than you expect.

—Because you know the labor market is tight, you should plan for growth in your business *ahead of time.* Being actively on the lookout for good talent is a new trend that, as yet, few managers appreciate. If you want to improve your hiring practices, you must learn to become proactive.

- **Training programs.** Your hiring practices must take into account a new kind of workforce with rapidly changing skills suited to the Information

Age. You may want to incorporate skills training for your employees, something employers rarely had to do a generation ago. Think carefully about the types of skills your workers will need, and plan accordingly.

- **Need for "Renaissance" employees.** "Renaissance man" is a term describing a person who knows about a lot of things—the arts, science, business, athletics, and so on. He or she is skilled in a variety of disciplines. For many companies today, the ideal worker is a Renaissance employee, someone capable of doing a variety of tasks and able to take on a variety of responsibilities. The downsizing that gripped corporate America starting in the 1980s not only threw many people out of work, but it changed the organizational structure of many companies in fundamental ways. Companies now are flatter and leaner and, as a result, employees need a wider variety of skills. Even on the factory floor, the use of teams has changed the nature of work so that workers are less likely to do the same job over and over. They need the skills to do a variety of jobs. This trend changes how you hire because you must now look for versatile workers who either have a broad range of skills, or are trainable and flexible enough to learn a lot of new things.

Watch Out!
The most common reasons why managers make poor hiring decisions are: poor analysis and description of the job's functions; vague understanding of the job's goals; insufficient interviewing techniques; inadequate initial screening of applicants; "overselling" the company to the job applicant; and inadequate reference checks.

Benefits of effective hiring practices

Good hiring practices are absolutely necessary for your success. Here are a few of the benefits that come from knowing how to hire effectively.

- Your company becomes more competitive.
- Efficiency improves.

- Employee turnover declines.
- Costs decrease.
- Profitability increases.
- Organizational creativity climbs.
- Quality escalates.
- Management's time and efforts are more focused on direct business issues rather than employee hiring and termination issues.
- Employee morale rises.
- Training time and expenses are cut.
- Your employees work better as a team.
- Employees' willingness to support corporate strategies increases.
- Your career gets a boost up the corporate ladder.
- Your business reaches its full potential.

Can you afford to ignore these benefits? Can your business be at its best without them?

A good match: a suitable person for the job

What does it mean when someone says, "Christine is really suitable for that job," or "Larry just isn't cut out for that job"? Is Christine a better person than Larry? Of course not. What we're really doing when we measure people against jobs is comparing the demands of the job with a person's capabilities.

To be effective at hiring, a manager must think about two things:

- The demands and requirements of the job
- The person's abilities and experience

While these do not have to be in perfect sync, they certainly need to match up fairly well. Here's a graphic representation of what I am talking about. It comes from Tom Probert, smelter manager at Kennecott Utah Copper:

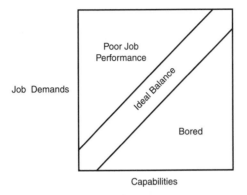

As you move to the right along the bottom of this graph, the more capable is the person. Sure, it's desirable to have talented, capable people—but only to a point. Capabilities must be balanced against the demands of the job. If the person's capabilities outrun the demands (measured along the left axis), you have one bored employee. This is the triangle area of the box in the lower right. Bored employees are unhappy, unproductive, and even disruptive employees.

The other side of having employees whose capabilities outrun the demands of their jobs is when employees have limited capabilities but relatively heavy job demands. They may try hard to perform well, but they just don't have the skills, abilities, or experience to do a good job. This area of poor job performance is seen in the triangle at the upper left of the box.

The ideal balance between capabilities and job demands is the area between the two parallel lines.

Watch Out!
If you over-stretch your employees by asking them to do too much or take on responsibilities beyond their capabilities, expect them to become hesitant, indecisive, almost paralyzed in their decision making. If your employees are inadequately challenged, you are likely to see hasty, ill-thought-out decisions, poor attitudes, and lack of commitment.

Here, the employee's capabilities closely match what the job requires. The employee is sufficiently challenged to remain interested in the job, while having the wherewithal to do good work.

Keep this graph in mind when creating job descriptions and choosing among job candidates.

Examples of job/employee matches and mismatches

Example 1: You pay a low wage for a job requiring a fair degree of skill. The applicants who will apply are likely to have capabilities below those necessary to do an acceptable level of work. The result: Poor job performance. You have a mismatch.

Example 2: You need workers for a menial job. You advertise the position in a college newspaper. Bright, aggressive college students become your applicant pool. You hire them and they quickly turn into a pool of bright, aggressive, very bored employees. The result: High turnover, low productivity. You have a mismatch.

Example 3: You have a lower-level supervisor job available. You're paying the going market wage rate. Education isn't too important, but supervisory experience is. You advertise by listing the job with your state's job service. Those who have worked as supervisors but lack much education apply. The result: A good balance between employee capability and job demands. You have a match.

Match the person's goals with job potential

There's more to matching people and jobs than capabilities and job demands. One of the more frequently overlooked aspects of job/employee matching is the relationship between a person's goals and the job's potential. If the person is very driven but the job lacks much potential for development, there's a conflict. Once the employee understands the job's limitations, she is likely to perform poorly—or leave. Some people are very content to stay at a job for years and are challenged by continually improving their performance or that of their team. This is the type of person you want in a position with limited upward mobility. When hiring, consider an applicant's growth potential, and try to match that potential with a position that can accommodate his or her growth.

Costs of bad hiring decisions

If you hire an employee who does not work out, you can always fire that person and hire another—or so the thinking goes with many employers. Let's ignore for the moment whether acceptable replacement candidates are available for the job. Bad hiring decisions cost you in many ways.

I once hired a writer who submitted a very competent sample article but ended up staying for only six weeks before I had to fire her. Within her first couple of weeks, it became obvious she knew little about business. I still wonder whether she wrote the sample article herself.

You can never be too careful when hiring. It's easy to be wrong, and a mistake will cost you dearly. This woman earned about $2,000 per month, so her six weeks on the job cost about $3,000 in salary. Add in other costs, such as Social Security and overhead, the time I spent on the hiring process, and the time I spent working with her, and the cost of my poor hiring decision was probably $6,000. And this does not include the costs of missed opportunities resulting from her lack of productivity. Such losses can be especially devastating, and they make the cost of an ineffective hire far higher than you ever expected.

Bright Idea
To match a candidate to the job, you must know the applicant's long-term goals. During the job interview, be sure to ask: What do you want to achieve with this job? If the job can satisfy the candidate's goals, by this criterion, you have a match.

One of the hidden costs of poor hiring decisions is lost customers. If an employee annoys your customers, you can lose those customers for life, and you may never know it.

For years, I went to the same dry cleaner. The employees knew me by name. One day when I picked up some shirts, I found that one had been torn during laundering. The manager, whom I had never seen before, said it was not the dry cleaner's fault; the shirt was simply worn. True, it was an older shirt but not threadbare, and the shirt was torn in the middle of the back—not a typical type of wear and tear. I had to argue with her for 15 minutes before she reluctantly agreed to give me a $10 credit. Had she offered this credit immediately, I would have accepted it and come back again. Instead, they lost me as a customer. I used up my credit and never went back—all because of an employee who should never have been hired in the first place, or should have been better trained in customer service.

It has been estimated that someone who likes a business's products or services tells 4 people about how good the business is. But when she does not like the product or service, she will spread the bad news to 18 people. These figures may not be scientifically verifiable, but there is no doubt that people are decidedly more likely to tell their friends and colleagues about bad experiences than good ones. You have to figure into the cost of poor hires the potential of losing some of your customers.

Another cost is lost opportunities. Until I learned from my mistakes that I should hire only people who knew business and investing, the writers I hired didn't think to recommend new product ideas or marketing approaches; they simply didn't think that way. Our lost business opportunities cannot be quantified in dollar terms, but they must have been considerable.

Don't forget the cost of replacing a failed, or lost, employee. Advertising expenses, your time, disruption of your business or department—these all hurt your effectiveness and the productivity of your employees.

If you have invested in the lost employee, such as in training or travel, this money is gone. The productivity lost while you search for a replacement is another significant expense.

A study by the Saratoga Institute of Santa Clara, California, as reported in *Workforce* magazine, found that the average cost to hire exempt employees (those not entitled to earn overtime pay) was $8,300 apiece, not including training costs. If you hire six employees a year who for some reason do not work out, you waste about $50,000 annually. In fact, according to the Saratoga Institute, the cost of turnover for employees earning $82,000 a year is about $108,000 apiece, or approximately $1^1/_3$ times the employee's annual wage.

According to an article in *HR Focus*, the Basic Industry Division of NALCO (a specialty chemical company in Naperville, Illinois) estimates that the cost of replacing a sales representative who has been with a company for six months is about $50,000, while replacing a seven-year veteran can cost in the neighborhood of $250,000.

Another view comes from AEtna, the life insurance company, as reported in *HR* magazine. AEtna figures the cost of turnover to be 93 percent of a person's outgoing salary. This figure includes hiring and training a new person, plus lost productivity

Moneysaver
Set a goal for yourself that the cost of hiring a new employee should range between 8 and 15 percent of the employee's first year's salary. Most employers exceed this. If you use search firms or hire high-tech workers, your costs are likely to be in the range of 25 to 30 percent. Senior staff are always more expensive than juniors.

and the supervisor's time, to which is added the current salary. To figure the cost of turnover for a person earning $25,000 a year, for example, you take 93 percent of $25,000, which is $23,250, and add the current salary of $25,000, for a total of $48,250 in turnover costs.

Gary Cluff, an employment expert based in Reston, Virginia, does an annual survey for the Society for Human Resource Management. His 1997 survey found that in 1996 the average cost per hire was $9,390 for exempt employees and $5,404 for nonexempt. The average cost to relocate a new hire was $18,311.

Roger Herman of the Herman Group says you can count on the cost of a lost employee being at least twice his annual income. Someone earning, say, $60,000, will cost at least $120,000 to replace. He says the cost can go much higher if you've engaged an executive search firm.

Behavioral Technology, Inc. estimates the cost of a bad hiring decision for a position paying $25,000 per year as follows:

COST FORMULA: SALARY × ESTIMATE

Cost Factor	Amount of Expense
Inefficiency/customer costs prior to the person leaving	$25,000 × 10% of salary = $2,500
Inefficiency/customer costs while a replacement learns the job	$25,000 × 10% of salary = $2,500
Cost of new hires, recruiting fees, interview travel, etc.	$25,000 × 5% of salary = $1,250
Indirect costs such as low morale, loss of customers, abuse of equipment, frustration, etc.	$25,000 × 10% of salary = $2,500
Total estimated cost of a bad hiring decision	**$8,750**

Using these numbers, a bad hiring decision will cost you about one-third of the employee's annual salary. If you make a bad choice in hiring a middle manager at $50,000 a year, expect that decision to cost you about $17,500.

No set formula exists for determining the cost of turnover, which is the cost of having to replace an employee. But as these various measurements show, losing an employee is an expensive proposition, no matter which formula you use and regardless of the position and the salary. A few bad hiring decisions a year can easily cost you tens of thousands of dollars, and it's not unreasonable to figure you could be out money in six figures.

Think of hiring as investing. Good hires will produce for you for years and years. Bad ones can cause you to lose your business. Poor choices in employees can drag you down as surely as poor quality control, poor customer service, poor financial controls, and poor marketing.

Hiring and firing are too important to you and your business's success—and too risky—to do by the seat of the pants. The remainder of this book will show you how to steer clear of the landmines and to create a clear path to success based on having a productive, creative, efficient workforce.

Just the facts

- Just because you have experience hiring and firing, don't think you can't do them better.

- Hiring mistakes cost you thousands of dollars in out-of-pocket expenses and often much more in lost opportunities.

- The market for good employees is changing dramatically. You must recognize the trends and

Timesaver
When calculating cost-per-hire, here's a quick model recommended by the Employment Management Association that says you should include the following: internal costs (salaries, benefits, etc.), external costs (travel, fees for outside recruiters), company visit expenses (candidate travel, interview expenses), direct fees (advertising, job fairs), and supplemental data (average annual salary of new hires, time-to-fill, number of interviews versus number of hires). From *HR* magazine

change with them or risk losing the good people you need to be successful.

- The benefits of good hiring practices include
  improved competitiveness, higher efficiency,
  lower costs, better quality, and more efficient
  use of management's time.

- Match a person's capabilities with the job's
  demands, or your partnership with that employee will not work for either of you.

Hiring and the Law

Chapter 2

Hiring and firing have been compared to a battlefield laid with landmines, and sometimes that's no exaggeration: If you don't watch where you step, bad things can happen. Of all business activities, personnel issues are perhaps the most fraught with potential mistakes. Many relate to legal issues, others are more management-oriented. In this chapter, I will address some of the major legal considerations a manager must understand when hiring and firing.

Careful background checks

In chapter 13 I will discuss how to check references. Of course, you want to check references to ensure that you have an accurate picture of the person. But there's another reason: If you don't check references thoroughly, and the employee commits a crime, even when off-duty or not on company business, your company could be held liable.

"In more than 30 states, courts have held that a company can be held liable if one of its employees goes on a crime spree even after-hours. Employers tend to lose the cases if they failed to do

23

a background check that would have turned up evidence of previous misconduct," write Kim S. Nash and Julia King in *Computerworld* (October 27, 1997). And employees committing crimes in the workplace are not uncommon. As reported in article by James W. Fenton Jr., et al., in *SAM Advanced Management Journal* (Autumn 1997), "statistics show that one million individuals are subjected to workplace violence every year, and that homicide is the number one cause of death on the job."

One thing you have to protect yourself against is deceptions by applicants, which unfortunately are quite common. As an example, an article in *Personnel Journal* (December 1995) reports that, in an effort to determine the extent of falsification of experience, the Port Authority of New York and New Jersey advertised for electricians experienced at working with a Sontag connector. The Port Authority received 170 resumes—an impressive number, considering that the Sontag connector doesn't exist.

An employer should also be prepared to conduct a background check to uncover lies of omission—the deliberate withholding of important (and possibly disqualifying) facts. Background checks not only help assure an employer that he has chosen the right person in terms of ability and experience, but also protect the company and its employees and customers. If someone lies in his application, the employer hires him without conducting a background check, and that employee later commits a crime, the employer may be held liable. Unfortunately, examples of such criminal actions are legion. A suit was brought against a major restaurant chain for an assault on a three-year-old boy by an employee with a previous conviction for child molestation.

Employment tests

Employment tests are those that test a person's technical expertise, knowledge (such as math skills), and personality. Tests should be relevant to the job, or you can get into trouble. If the job requires typing on a computer, then the applicant should take a typing test. If writing skills are important, then give applicants a test of writing something similar to what they would write on the job. The tests you can most easily get into trouble with are personality tests where it's hard to show a relationship between scores and job success.

Discrimination

Discrimination is a major concern for employers with regard to hiring and firing. There are quite a few laws relating to discrimination, and they contain enough nuances and "fine print" that the average business owner or manager will want to consult with an experienced personnel attorney to be sure all rules are being followed. You should consult with an attorney before you begin the hiring process, to be sure your procedures and practices will not get you into trouble. There are some important antidiscrimination laws that you should be familiar with.

The following discussion of antidiscrimination laws is drawn from the U.S. Equal Employment Opportunity Commission (EEOC). The EEOC enforces the federal laws that prohibit employment discrimination on the basis of an individual's race, color, religion, sex, national origin, age, or disability. The following highlights select issues of particular interest to small businesses.

Employers who come under the jurisdiction of EEOC-enforced laws

- Title VII of the Civil Rights Act of 1964 (Title VII) prohibits discrimination on the basis of race, color, religion, sex, or national origin. Title VII applies to employers with 15 or more employees.

- Age Discrimination in Employment Act of 1967 (ADEA) prohibits age discrimination against individuals who are 40 or older. The ADEA applies to employers with 20 or more employees.

- Title I of the Americans with Disabilities Act of 1990 (ADA) prohibits employment discrimination against qualified individuals with disabilities. The ADA applies to employers with 15 or more employees.

- Equal Pay Act of 1963 (EPA) prohibits wage discrimination between men and women in substantially equal jobs within the same establishment. The EPA applies to *most* employers. More specifically, the EPA applies to employers with two or more employees and, according to the law, "does not apply where the employer has no employees who are engaged in commerce or in the handling of goods that have moved in commerce and the employer is not an enterprise engaged in commerce or in the production of goods for commerce."

- The sections of the Immigration Reform and Control Act (IRCA) that relate to national origin discrimination prohibit the hiring of any person who is not legally authorized to work in the United States. The IRCA's citizenship discrimination provisions apply to all employers with at least four employees.

IRCA makes it unlawful for an employer to hire any person who is not legally authorized to work in the United States, and requires that employers verify the employment eligibility of all new employees.

IRCA also prohibits discrimination in hiring and discharge based on national origin (as does Title VII) and on citizenship status. IRCA's antidiscrimination provisions are intended to prevent employers from complying with the Act's work authorization requirements by discriminating against "foreign-looking" or "foreign-sounding" job applicants.

IRCA's national origin discrimination provisions apply to employers with between 4 and 14 employees (who would not be covered by Title VII).

How employees are counted

All employees, including part-time and temporary workers, are counted for purposes of determining whether an employer has a sufficient number of employees. An employee is someone with whom the employer has an "employment relationship," which is most readily (but not exclusively) indicated by a person's appearance on the employer's payroll. Independent contractors are not counted as employees because the work they perform is based on an independent contractual relationship, not an employment relationship.

Issues of particular concern to small businesses

A number of issues under the Title VII, ADEA, and ADA are of particular concern to small businesses. These include the following:

- **Sexual harassment**

  Sexual harassment is a form of unlawful sex discrimination. Sexual harassment includes unwelcome sexual advances, requests for sexual favors, and other verbal or physical conduct of a sexual nature that are made a condition of employment, that unreasonably interfere with work performance, or that create an intimidating, hostile, or offensive work environment.

  Employers are responsible for maintaining a workplace free of sexual harassment, and they may be liable for the unlawful conduct of their agents, supervisory employees, employees, and, in certain circumstances, even non-employees, such as customers or salespeople, who sexually harass employees at work.

- **Racial and ethnic harassment**

  Harassment on the basis of an individual's race or national origin violates Title VII. Racial or ethnic slurs, jokes, offensive or derogatory comments, or other verbal or physical conduct based on race or nationality are unlawful if the conduct creates an intimidating, hostile, or offensive work environment, or if it unreasonably interferes with an employee's work performance.

  Employers are responsible for maintaining a workplace free of racial and ethnic harassment, and they may be liable for unlawful conduct by their agents, supervisory employees, employees, and, in certain circumstances, non-employees who harass employees at work.

- **Pregnancy discrimination**

  Under Title VII, discrimination on the basis of pregnancy, childbirth, or related medical conditions is unlawful sex discrimination. Title VII's prohibition against pregnancy discrimination applies to all terms and conditions of employment, including hiring, firing, promotion, leave, and benefits. For example, discrimination based on pregnancy is illegal under both the California Fair Employment and Housing Act (FEHA) and the Federal Title VII laws. And, from the court ruling on the *Johnson Controls* case: "The Court properly holds that Johnson Controls' fetal protection policy overtly discriminates against women, and thus is prohibited by Title VII . . ."

■ **Religious accommodation**

An employer is required to provide an accommodation for employees' sincerely held religious observances or practices unless the accommodation would impose an undue hardship on the employer's business. Examples of religious accommodation could include granting time off for religious observations or permission to wear certain clothing or religious symbols.

Undue hardship can be claimed if an accommodation imposes more than "de minimis" cost, generally meaning more than ordinary administrative costs. Undue hardship can also be claimed if an accommodation requires violating the terms of a seniority system (for example, by denying another employee's job or shift preference).

■ **Age Discrimination in Employment Act**

The Age Discrimination in Employment Act (ADEA) prohibits age discrimination against

Bright Idea
The Immigration Reform and Control Act is enforced by the U.S. Department of Justice. For information on IRCA's antidiscrimination provisions, contact the United States Department of Justice, Office of Special Counsel for Immigration-Related Unfair Employment Practices; (800) 255-8155 (Employer hotline/voice); (800) 237-2515 (TDD); Web site at www.usdoj. gov/crt/osc.

workers 40 or older in all aspects of employment, including hiring and benefits. You generally cannot ask what a person's age is, though it is allowable to ask about a person's age if age is a bonafide occupational qualification, which it is for public safety—drivers, for example. You can, of course, ask about many other things, such as education. And an employer can discriminate based on non-age factors, such as scores on tests that are relevant to the job, and on seniority.

To avoid violating the ADEA, employers should carefully avoid basing employment actions— particularly hiring, firing, and promotion decisions—on assumptions or stereotypes based on age. Such assumptions include, for example, notions that older workers are inflexible, set in their ways, unable to learn new procedures, unable to perform certain jobs safely, unable to work for younger supervisors, and likely to retire. Employment decisions regarding older workers—just as those regarding younger workers—should be based on their individual skills, abilities, and merit.

To avoid unlawfully deterring older job seekers from applying for advertised jobs, help-wanted notices and job advertisements should not include terms or phrases such as "young," "recent graduate," "boy," "girl," or "age 25 to 35." Instead, use terms like "energetic" or "entry-level."

An employer is not required to provide equal health insurance, life insurance, or disability benefits to older workers if it costs more to do so. An employer may provide older employees with lower health, life, and/or disability benefits as long as it spends the same amount on both older and younger workers. Because of the ADEA's cost exception, small employers can hire older workers without concern about additional expenses for such employee benefits.

■ The Americans with Disabilities Act (ADA)

The ADA prohibits employers from discriminating against qualified individuals with disabilities. An individual with a disability is defined as someone who has a physical or mental impairment that substantially limits one or more major life activities, or has a record of such an impairment, or is regarded as having such an impairment. (See Appendix D for more information on ADA.)

It is seldom costly for a business to determine whether an individual has a disability for ADA purposes. In many cases, the nature and extent of a disability and the need for accommodation will be apparent.

If the need for accommodation is not obvious, an employer may lawfully require an applicant or employee who requests an accommodation to provide documentation—for example, from the individual's doctor or rehabilitation counselor—regarding his or her disability and functional limitations. An example of a functional limitation would be color blindness in a job that requires the ability to distinguish colors.

The documentation, particularly a doctor's statement, will generally contain the information needed for determining whether the individual has a disability, including: what the

Bright Idea
Small employers can often get assistance with funding accommodations from state vocational rehabilitation agencies. For information, contact: State Vocational Rehabilitation Services Program at (202) 205-8719 (voice); (800) 877-8339 (TDD); Web site at www.ed.gov/offices/OSERS/RSA/rsa.html.

Bright Idea
The Job Accommodation Network (JAN) is a free national consultant service that provides information on ADA, as well as how someone with a disability can be accommodated in an existing workplace. For confidential information, telephone them at (800) 526-7234 (voice/TDD), or visit their Web site at http://janweb.icdi.wvu.edu

condition/impairment is; how the impairment limits the individual; and what treatment has been provided and for how long (unless the diagnosis is recent).

The ADA requires an employer to provide a reasonable accommodation for the known disability of a qualified applicant or employee unless it would impose undue hardship on the employer's business. Generally, an applicant or employee must request an accommodation. Studies show that most accommodations involve low cost and are relatively easy to provide. Reasonable accommodation might include moving furniture or other obstacles out of the way so that a worker in a wheelchair can have clear access to a location, and providing signage pointing to a bathroom equipped for the handicapped.

What do these regulations mean?

From a practical point of view, these regulations and laws mean that when it comes to a hiring interview, for example, there are topics you cannot ask about, such as the following:

- *Age:* About the only thing you can ask in regard to age is if the applicant is 18 years or older.

- *Disability:* You can't ask a candidate if he or she is disabled. However, once the fact of a disability has surfaced (and the candidate is supposed to tell you of a disability that is not obvious and for which you may have to arrange accommodations), then you can ask about the applicant's ability to perform certain job functions. *Focus on the needs of the job.*

- *Religion:* Don't ask, unless the job requires work on Saturday or Sunday and you have to know if the candidate is willing to work those days. Be tactful. You might say, "This job requires you to work every Sunday morning. Is that acceptable?"

- *National origin:* Don't ask, though you can ask if the candidate is a U.S. citizen or has a green card or visa documenting the right to work in the United States.

- *Marital status:* Don't ask.

- *Race:* Don't ask.

- *Criminal history:* Don't ask about arrests, although you can generally ask about convictions.

- *Education:* You can ask for details about educational history, though not, "Have you graduated from high school?" Instead, ask "Tell me about your educational background."

- *Military background:* Do not ask what type of discharge he or she received, but you may ask whether the candidate has had military experience if such experience is needed for the job.

- *Height and weight:* Do not ask unless it relates to the job (law enforcement, for example, has established a valid need to know about candidates' heights and weights).

Stephen Sheinfeld, chairman of the labor and employment department at the New York law firm of Whitman Breed Abbott & Morgan, says the things that you should focus on, whether on an application or during the interview, are the job functions and what it takes to succeed in that job. "It's none of an interviewer's business whether somebody is married or has kids, whether somebody years ago had some type of physical ailment, whether someone ever had a worker's compensation claim, whether someone had people in their family who spoke a foreign language, what their national origin is, or what their sexual orientation is. These are all examples of things that are not permissible. Why are they not permissible? Because the law says so. And why is that? Because they have nothing to do with the job."

What do you want to focus on? Focus on their prior job experience, places of employment, responsibilities and accomplishments on the job, salary or wage. You can ask if they've been convicted of a crime.

In addition, be careful what you promise. Promises not kept can cause major problems down the road.

The best policy, the best legal protection, notes Sheinfeld, is to be honest and fair. He also warns: When hiring, don't make promises you can't keep because that's just going to lead to both disappointment and possible legal claims of breach of contract or misrepresentation.

When firing someone, you also have to be careful. These things can get pretty tricky. James Essey, president of TemPositions Group of Companies, gives an example of the care that an employer must take when facing the necessity of firing. "Let's say you're in the firing discussion and the individual has never come on record saying that they were depressed or anything like that, or had any other disability, and it now comes out that they had this disability. If you were to say, 'Well, you know, I noticed that you had that and as a result, you couldn't do your job, and so we have to terminate you,' you've then discriminated against her because she has a disability. You probably were just saying or affirming that disability because you were trying to make her feel better at the time, but by discussing it in any way, you could leave her grounds to come back and say, 'Well, they knew about this and they should have accommodated me and they didn't.' It would have been better not to get into the discussion at all."

Who files suit, and why?

Lawsuits brought by workers against their employers can come from many directions and for various reasons, but many legal actions arise from fairly standard (and avoidable) issues. Richard A. DuRose, leader of the employment group in the national law firm of Foley & Lardner, says there are a few "themes" he finds among people who file lawsuits when they are fired:

- If a firing is unexpected, an employer increases the likelihood of a lawsuit being brought, or at least seriously contemplated and possibly threatened. If the employer has been giving warnings and spelling out opportunities to correct problems, employees can accept being let go much more readily than if they feel "blindsided." When taken by surprise, the reaction is to get revenge, so those fired look for ways to file a lawsuit or complain about various violations.

- In addition to employees who feel blindsided, those lacking the confidence they can find another job are good candidates to sue you. This kind of employee is often one who has been with a company for a long time and has not been in the job market for many years.

Instead of looking for work, he will apply his energies to getting revenge on the company.

- Lawsuits can also arise when an employee is terminated as a result of downsizing or reorganization. If the department has to reduce its "head count" by one or two persons, a boss may determine which two employees he wants to get rid of and then develop a reason to let them go. The legally and morally correct approach is to create an objective test and subject all people in that department to the same test.

Non-compete agreements

Non-compete agreements are contracts an employee signs (generally when beginning work at a company) stipulating that if the employee decides to leave the company, she will not go to work for a competitor for a specified period—often two years, but sometimes as short as one year or as long as five. The duration of noncompetition depends on what the employer wants and what the employee is willing to agree to. The non-compete agreement might also state that the employee will not start a competing business. The value of non-compete agreements is often hard to calculate. They may sound good on paper and yet not stand up in court.

The purpose of the non-compete agreement is to protect valuable but intangible assets that employees may take with them when they leave the company, such as proprietary information, intellectual property, customer information, manufacturing techniques, management plans, and the like.

Different states have different views of noncompete agreements, and you need an attorney to tell you what you can and cannot do in your state with regard to these agreements. At the least, your non-compete agreement must be in writing. It's not uncommon for states to require limitations to the agreement; most states won't let you stop an employee from competing everywhere, forever. Keep in mind that the reason many courts are not big supporters of noncompete agreements is that they limit a person's ability to make a living, a limitation the courts are not eager to uphold.

If you think you might benefit from having employees agree to a non-compete agreement, contact an attorney to have one drawn up. This is not a do-it-yourself project.

Just the facts

- All your hiring efforts should be informed by the knowledge that many types of discrimination are largely illegal, including discrimination based on age, race, and handicap.

- Job-related skill tests can be helpful—but beware the personality test.

- Don't ask about a person's arrest record—though you can generally ask about convictions.

- Non-compete agreements sound good on paper, but many don't hold up to judicial review because many state courts restrict them or largely do away with them altogether.

- In a hiring interview, marital status, ethnic background, sexual orientation, and other personal matters are not appropriate for an interviewer's inquiries. Focus on the needs of the job.

GET THE SCOOP ON...
The pros and cons of full-time workers ▪ How to
determine whether you need to hire ▪ Overtime:
When it's good, and when it's bad ▪ Low-cost
ways to boost productivity ▪ How to identify
your productivity problems

Do You Really Need Another Employee?

Chapter 3

The automatic reaction of many business owners and managers when short of staff is to add full-time, permanent employees. Often that is a good idea, but it's not always necessary. There are alternatives to hiring full-time workers that may make more sense—and cost less money. In chapter 8, "Outsourcing Your Hiring," I talk about the use of contingency workers. In this chapter, you will learn about some workable alternatives to hiring new employees—such as by asking workers to work overtime, outsourcing certain functions, and redistributing workflow.

Full-time employees

Before diving into the alternatives to hiring full-time employees, consider some of the advantages and disadvantages of bringing in new workers on a permanent, full-time basis.

Watch Out!
Five signs that
you need full-
time workers:
(1) employees
are having to put
in excessive
overtime;
(2) employee
turnover rate is
high; (3) absen-
teeism is going
up; (4) quality
is declining;
(5) there's more
than the usual
amount of bick-
ering between
employees, sug-
gesting a height-
ened level of
stress.

Advantages

- *Reliability.* Full-time workers focus full-time energy on the job, and are more likely to be loyal and diligent than a part-time employee.

- *Availability.* Full-timers are there when you need them.

- *Higher motivation and skill level.* Because full-time workers are focused on the job full-time, they tend to be more motivated than temps or part-timers. And because they work 40 or so hours a week, they typically know the job better and are therefore better prepared for promotions and expanded responsibilities.

- *Growth-oriented.* Full-timers are more likely to be committed and motivated to training and upgrading their skills.

- *Good investment.* Full-time workers also save money for the employer. Because they have a *career* and not just a "job," each year they are with you, the cost of bringing them on board amortizes.

Disadvantages

- *Overhead costs.* The principal disadvantage of full-time workers is the overhead cost involved, an expense that does not vary with the demands of your business. As with rent, you pay your full-timers no matter how busy they are or how much money you are making. You generally have no employees who are more expensive than full-timers. They are paid for the most hours, receive the most benefits (medical insurance, sick days, vacation, unemployment insurance, retirement accounts, bonuses), and cannot be brought in and put out as business demand waxes and wanes.

■ *Training costs.* If full-time employees need training, you have to provide it and pay for it, whereas for temporary workers, the employment agency provides the training.

Now let's look at some of the alternatives to hiring. It may not be necessary to hire, after all.

Alternative #1: Overtime

Having your employees work overtime, in place of adding employees to your payroll, is admittedly a doubled-edge sword, but it is one that, in the proper circumstances, can be an effective way of reducing your need for more workers.

Of course, some employees, typically hourly workers, get paid extra for their overtime work, usually time-and-a-half, and sometimes double-time or more for work during weekends and other special circumstances. Salaried employees may be asked to work overtime and not be paid directly for the time, though employers will often provide perks in consideration for the additional work, such as "comp" (compensation) time, or days off.

Overtime provides the employer with a number of advantages over hiring additional workers. One advantage is that, often, current employees appreciate the opportunity (within reason) to work overtime because it boosts their incomes. In some companies and industries, overtime is so common and consistent that workers count on it—they expect it. So overtime can be a nice boost to your workforce's morale.

Overtime is also advantageous because it means that those working for you are experienced, proven

"
You can be totally rational with a machine. But if you work with people, sometimes logic has to take a backseat to understanding.
—Akio Morita, cofounder of Sony, quoted in *The Ultimate Book of Business Quotations* by Stuart Crainer
"

employees. Current employees are also immediately available; if you have a sudden surge in demand, you can ask current workers to put in extra hours rather than having to hire new ones.

There are disadvantages, however, to using overtime as a way of avoiding hiring additional full-time staff:

- Workers may not want to put in overtime, for family or other reasons.

- The stresses of working overtime may affect your workers' health and attitudes, even if they want to put in the time.

- Too much overtime can negatively affect quality. When people are tired or stressed, the quality of their work is likely to suffer, and your business—and customer relations—will suffer too.

If you decide to use overtime as a strategy for limiting your need to hire additional workers, you can help minimize the negative aspects of overtime in a number of ways. Help take care of your workers' personal needs. If they have young children, provide child care. When possible, be flexible. You might need your employees to work extra hours, but it may not matter much what time of day they put in the extra hours.

Give your employees a say in how overtime is to be organized. When employees lack any control or influence, the level of stress increases dramatically. Allow your employees to collectively schedule overtime, who gets it and when.

Alternative #2: Redistribute work

Rather than hire new workers, consider redistributing existing work more efficiently. First I'll discuss studying your company's workflow to determine needs and possible restructurings, then I'll cover the advantages to organizing your workers into teams.

Survey your company's workflow

To enhance productivity, you must first understand the workflow of your organization. To gain this understanding, you might consider hiring an employment consultant to help you redesign your workflow to improve productivity without having to add employees. (See Chapter 8 "Outsourcing Your Hiring.")

Another technique is to draw a diagram of how work flows through your company or department. Writers will often create an outline of a book or article they are writing because it helps them see how well the project is organized, what's missing, and where things do not flow well from one subject to another. A workflow diagram can be used to trace lines of communication and how things move from one person to another. Or, instead of drawing a diagram, you can list the steps involved in your office or factory, and see how well the pieces fit together.

Let me illustrate with an example based on the experience of Mountain West Stagecraft, a scene shop that designs and builds sets and displays for theaters and trade show exhibits, as well as in-store displays. The process is as follows:

1. Design the set or display.

2. Gather the materials needed to build it (paint, wood, metal, glass, nails and screws, etc.).

3. Build the set.

4. Deliver the set to the customer's site.

5. Assemble the set for the customer. (If the set is not permanent, there is a sixth step, which is tearing down the set.)

Mountain West often had trouble meeting its deadlines, and the owners thought the problem was that they did not have enough help. They started looking to hire an additional one, maybe two, workers, but every time they considered hiring someone, they could not figure out where the new employee would work. That was a giveaway that the problem was probably not a shortage of help. If it is not obvious how an extra pair of hands can help, then you probably do not need an extra pair of hands.

Finally, they sat down and analyzed their workflow. They found that they had a "bottleneck" in the delivery of the sets to customers' sites. They had one truck, and some sets took several trips to deliver. And sometimes the site was an hour or more away. Hiring another person would not have solved this problem. Their solution was to rent one or more additional trucks when a set was to be delivered, and use existing employees to drive the trucks to the customer site (these employees were needed to assemble the set anyway). Renting a truck or two for a day, every once in a while, was much cheaper than hiring full-time help. Plus, sets were delivered much more efficiently, and employees were not tied up for hours or days going back and forth.

A careful analysis of your workflow may reveal opportunities to eliminate some of the labor you are requiring of those already on your payroll, thus freeing them up to do other, more productive tasks. For example, an employer may require a great deal of paperwork that takes hours of employees' time and produces little of value. Or, a boss may require workers to be at work at 8:00 a.m. and permit them to leave at 5:00 p.m., when, as shown by a workflow study, the busy time is from 3:00 p.m. to 6:00 p.m. This employer could boost productivity simply by shifting workers' hours to 9:00 a.m. to 6:00 p.m.

Time for teamwork?

A workflow study might indicate favorable conditions for organizing your workforce into teams. Teams often are more efficient and better able to cover for one another than workers who function individually. Therefore, if you have a situation where a worker is out sick or there's a substantial increase in the workload, a team often can handle such contingencies better than a group of individuals.

Here are some essential points about managing a team:

- Keep the team focused on its goals. It's as easy for a group to go off on an unproductive tangent as for an individual (this might be a good time to create a mission statement to further define your goals).

- Make sure team members communicate and share. Instill a teamwork ethic within your employees if you are to redistribute work in such a way as to make this a workable alternative to hiring additional workers. Communication and sharing can be encouraged through setting goals that workers can only accomplish together, as a team.

- Do not allow cliques to dominate your teams. Be sure all team members know that you expect everyone to work toward being as cooperative as possible.

- Just because you create a team does not do away with individual roles. With a team you may now have overlapping roles, but you also still have distinct areas of primary responsibility.

- Good teams require their leaders to be cooperative as well. This means you must share information, just as you expect your team members to share.

Alternative #3: Outsourcing

It has become customary for corporations to outsource their computer functions. For example, Solutia Inc., a $3 billion chemical company that was spun off from Monsanto Co. in 1997, decided to have Electronic Data Systems (EDS) take care of its computer systems when Solutia separated from Monsanto, reports *Information Week* (July 27, 1998). The company's computer systems were relocated by Monsanto's data center to an EDS facility. David Matthews, director of IT global operations at Solutia in St. Louis, was quoted in *Information Week*, "We decided that using an outsourcer was the smartest way to go. There was no way to staff up to take on that scale of operations ourselves."

Even computer companies themselves are outsourcing. *Electronic Buyers News* (July 1, 1998) reported that PC giant Compaq Computer Corp. decided to outsource the production of its printed circuit board assemblies for its desktop computers. The company decided to outsource as a result of its restructuring efforts following its acquisition of Digital Equipment Corp. As part of this restructuring, Compaq laid off 5,000 manufacturing workers, including 1,000 at its printed circuit-board assembly plant in Houston.

Employee outsourcing of various kinds can be used by almost every business, from the smallest to the largest. The largest corporations in the country, for example, hire many different kinds of consultants (computer, human resources, marketing, management) on an outsourced arrangement, rather than having them on staff, full time. Most computer "manufacturers" are actually assemblers: They don't make their own monitors, motherboards, disk drives, or RAM chips, but rather outsource that work (sometimes to their own specifications) and then take the finished products and assemble them inhouse into working computers.

The advantages of outsourcing are similar to those of hiring temporary workers: You do not take on additional overhead, and you use the service only when you need it.

If your office seems inundated by work, analyze the situation to see if an outside bookkeeping service, for example, might relieve the workload enough so that you do not have to hire an additional employee.

Alternative #4: Automation

What can and should be automated varies from business to business, even in businesses within the same industry. It depends on the size of your operation, how comfortable you are with technology, what the nature of your business is, and what automation products have been developed for your type of business.

The sales process is a good case in point. There is software designed specifically to automate sales, usually called "salesforce automation software" or "contact management software." This software allows sales people to track their sales calls, take notes on what is said during telephone conversations and person-to-person meetings, analyze success rates for different sales approaches, schedule meetings, have automatic reminders to make calls or send letters, automatically generate thank-you letters and other correspondence, and so on.

David Borys, director of technology at Winningham Becker & Co., a 22-employee CPA firm in Woodland Hills, California, has his accountants use a popular contact-management software package to keep records of contacts with clients. Each user saves one to two hours per day by not having to take files out of file cabinets or hunt for misplaced documents. The software provides an automated way to track contact histories, and all critical information is easily accessible in the computer system.

Donald Kirkendall, vice president of sales and marketing at Jason Data Systems, Altamonte Springs, Florida, used to print and mail an extensive price list to his dealers (numbering about 200) each quarter, which was time-consuming and expensive (about $4 per price list, including postage), and whose delivery took several days via U.S. Mail. Using a contact-management product, he set up his price list and, once done, could quickly change it at will, and e-mail it to his dealers virtually instantly and at no cost.

Software and other automation products make it possible for employers to boost their workers' productivity and avoid having to hire additional employees. (These software products, by the way, are often not expensive; the ones cited above sell for less than $200 apiece off the shelf, although more sophisticated programs can cost considerably more.)

Analyze your operations to see where automation makes sense. If you are not sure, hire a consultant to conduct a study for you.

Hiring your children

If you are a small-business owner, you might consider hiring your children, just as you might consider hiring other family members. There are, however, many legal, ethical, and professional considerations to the hiring of one's own children that are beyond the scope of this book. If you determine that it would be useful and appropriate to hire your children, check with the labor laws in your state for guidelines and requirements.

I am talking here about minor children. Yes, there are child labor laws, but many business owners help cut their labor costs—and provide their children with real-world work experience—by hiring their children. Besides, child labor restrictions may not apply, especially if the job is not hazardous. As with overtime, having your children as your employees has advantages and disadvantages.

The pluses: You know your child, so you are not hiring a stranger. You may be eligible for certain tax breaks (such as not having to pay Social Security). You have the opportunity to teach your child about work, about having a good work ethic, about what the work environment is like. Also, you can teach your child certain skills, depending upon the job, and you provide your child with the opportunity to feel a sense of accomplishment, both from the money he or she earns and from doing a job well done.

The minuses: You continue to treat your child as, well, your child, which means that you may be either overbearing or too lax. This behavior, which

Bright Idea
To find automation experts familiar with your type of business, ask others in your industry who they have used. Contact professional and trade associations in your industry for recommendations. Call up the editors of trade publications and ask if they can recommend consultants and products.

Timesaver
You can quickly find barter exchanges by looking in your local Yellow Pages under "Barter & Trade Exchanges." For further information, two trade associations are available: International Reciprocal Trade Association, 175 West Jackson Blvd., Suite 625, Chicago, IL 60604, (312) 461-0236; National Association of Trade Exchanges, 27801 Euclid Avenue, Suite 610, Euclid, OH 44132, (216) 732-7171.

can be a problem at home, can become magnified in a work setting. Conflict that occurs in the workplace between you and your child can easily be taken home, thus possibly affecting your long-term relationship with your child.

(For reasons of workplace harmony and safety, if you are thinking about this option, it might be a good idea to check with some of your managers to see if they are comfortable with the prospect of having children in the work setting.)

To reiterate, hiring a minor should be handled very carefully. The option is mentioned here for small-business owners as an alternative to hiring a new full-time employee. Be sure to check with the labor laws in your state.

Alternative #5: Manufacturers' representatives

If you need a sales force, you basically have two choices: (1) hire your own direct sales force, which is likely to be an expensive proposition; (2) Sign up independent manufacturers' representatives to sell on your behalf. Saving on overhead costs is the primary benefit of hiring manufacturers' representatives. Reps are independent contractors who sell products for various manufacturers, and they act as a go-between—they sit between you, the manufacturer, and your customers, in effect just as an in-house sales rep does. But, they are not overhead. You pay them only when they perform. They get a commission on each sale brought to you: No sales, no cost to you.

Advantages

- *Low risk.* You usually don't have much up-front investment when hiring a rep, other than supplying some collateral sales material and samples.

- *Low cost.* Because reps are independent contractors, you don't have to pay payroll taxes, fringe benefits, and much of the overhead that comes with full-time employees.

- *Market penetration.* Because of their contacts and knowledge of their markets, reps can penetrate markets that an in-house sales force might have difficulty cracking.

- *Quick introduction.* Reps, because of their long-standing relationships with buyers in their markets, can often develop a market faster than a direct salesperson.

- *Credibility.* Reps have their own reputations, and the reputations of good reps can rub off on the manufacturers they represent. A little-known manufacturer can look highly respectable to a major customer if the rep has the confidence of that customer.

- *Economical small sales.* Reps can make sales calls to small or out-of-the-way customers more economically than an in-house sales person who must cover a very large territory.

Disadvantages

- *Lack of oversight.* Because the rep is independent, you don't have the influence or control over the rep that you would with an employee. It may be hard to tell which ones are working hard for you because they represent many manufacturers. (A direct sales force sells only your goods, so you can tell quicker if a rep is performing well.)

Moneysaver
If you need work done, consider bartering for it rather than hiring an employee. Direct barter is an arrangement between two businesses for an exchange of specific services or goods of equal value without an exchange of money. For example, if you sell office furniture and need a janitorial service, you could arrange to barter some desks and chairs for janitorial services. Barter has its limits, but if you need extra workers and cash is short, it is a useful strategy worth considering.

- *Lack of image control.* Manufacturers' reps are not a uniform representation of your company. You have little control over what they say or over their training.

- *Favoritism.* The rep will favor some product lines over others, usually because they are easier to sell or pay higher commissions.

- *Lack of long-term commitment.* Reps continually look for new lines to augment their current product mix or to find products that sell better.

- *Lack of information.* Reps have a reputation for being less than enthusiastic about supplying their manufacturers with required paperwork and marketing information on a timely basis.

Should you use reps? It depends. Certain industries, such as automotive, leather goods, boating, and paper products, use reps widely, while other businesses do not. If your industry does use reps, then they are certainly worth consideration. If you are in an industry with little experience with sales reps, you are probably better off sticking with an in-house, direct sales force.

Free labor

There *is* such a thing as free labor, if you know where to look. Interns are one source of free labor—well, usually free or nearly free. In chapter 7, "Using Contract Workers," we discuss the use of interns. Generally, interns are students or recent college graduates who lack experience but usually have an abundance of enthusiasm and energy. They are often willing to do grunt work in exchange for learning on the job and getting enough experience to get a paid position either with you or with another company. Your local university is a good place to start when looking for an intern. If you need a computer person, go to the school's computer science department. For marketing help, go to the marketing department.

Volunteers are another source of free labor. Who would do volunteer work for your company? The Service Corps of Retired Executives (SCORE), for one. This is a group of retired executives who, working through the U.S. Small Business Administration, give free advice to small-business owners.

If you want to avoid having to hire additional workers, look first to see how you can change those little things that don't cost much (or anything) but can produce big results. This might mean rethinking processes, eliminating requirements that are no longer necessary or applicable, and being more flexible. Thinking in new ways ("outside the box") can help eliminate your need for more workers and boost your bottom line.

Just the facts

- The advantages of full-time workers include their commitment to their work and focus on their job, availability when you need them, and generally higher skill level when compared with part-timers.

- The primary disadvantage of full-time workers is their cost—you have to pay them whether you use them or not. They also incur other costs, such as for benefits and training.

- Teams can help you circumvent needing more workers, but only if you know how to manage them.

- Manufacturers' reps help you avoid having to hire a direct sales force. However, they represent many manufacturers, and you are in trouble if you are not one of their favorites.

- Consider outsourcing functions. Companies that specialize—such as in computer services, bookkeeping, manufacturing processes—can often do the work for less than you can.

Employee Retention and Problem-Solving

Hiring is time-consuming and expensive, and firing can be costly and risky. There is one sure way to minimize the costs of these efforts and to assure you have the employees you need: If you learn how to keep the employees you have, you limit your need to hire new employees or to fire those who are underperforming. The first part of this chapter will look at approaches to retaining your valuable workers; in the second part, I'll discuss ways to prevent having to fire "problem employees" through identifying and correcting troublesome behaviors.

A 1997 survey by the Society for Human Resource Management and Aon Consulting found that reducing staff turnover is viewed as the greatest employment challenge for management. A survey reported in *Workforce* magazine found that of small-business owners surveyed, 50 percent said the "labor shortage is their biggest business obstacle." At the

time of this writing, the unemployment rate is below
5 percent and the proportion of people with jobs
compared with the total population is at an all-time
high.

When determining whether you need to hire
new employees, consider that the people on your
staff are known to you—they have abilities and experience that prompted you to hire them in the first
place, and you (and their co-workers) understand
their strengths and weaknesses. Such valuable familiarity grows over time, and it's worth noting that
these are things you cannot yet know about newly
hired employees.

Reasons to minimize employee turnover

Reducing the coming-and-going of employees provides a number of benefits to virtually all organizations, including the following:

- *Maintains productivity.* Stability among employees,
  or a low rate of turnover, maintains smooth
  functioning, "institutional memory" (knowledge
  of the company's history, products, customers,
  ways of doing things, etc.), and generally is good
  for staff morale.

- *Minimizes turnover costs.* According to a published report, a major life insurance company
  that carefully tracks its costs of turnover calcu-
  lates these costs to be 93 percent of the outgoing
  person's salary, which includes hiring, training,
  lost productivity, and supervisor's time, to which
  is added the person's annual salary. If an
  employee earns $30,000, then the cost of
  turnover of this one employee would be:

$30,000 × .93 =	$27,900
$27,900 + $30,000 =	$57,900

This means a person who is earning a fairly modest income ($30,000) will cost his employer close to $60,000 if he moves to another company—or if he is fired. A recent article about a specialty chemical company reported that the cost of replacing a sales representative who has been with the firm six months is $50,000, while the cost of replacing a seven-year veteran is around $250,000.

If you have high turnover resulting from failure to retain employees (as distinct from market forces or seasonal layoffs), so that numbers like these are multiplied several times over during the course of a year, you could be wasting tens, even hundreds of thousands of dollars.

It is well known that employers are generally more willing to pay more for a new employee than for the one they are replacing. A factor known as the "across-the-street premium" assumes that employers in the same industry are paying at the market rate; hence, it will cost you salary plus 15 percent to hire away the competition's employees. (The Department of Labor averages the cost at 16 percent.) Keep this turnover cost in mind when adding up the reasons why it's best to not let good employees "slip away."

The costs of turnover

Computerworld magazine recently published a study of staff turnover costs conducted by the Gartner Group (*Computerworld*, January 22, 1998). Gartner estimates the cost of turnover can be 100 percent to 250 percent of the departing person's salary. How many of the following costs might apply to your company?

- Recruiter's fee (20–30% of salary)
- Loss of departing employee's training costs and sign-on bonus
- Cost of temporary worker to fill gap
- Low morale, lost momentum, and other employees picking up workload
- Cost of manager's interviewing time
- Interview expenses (travel, lodging, meals)
- Differential between departing employee's salary and that of new employee (average 15%)
- Sign-on bonus and training cost of new employee
- Learning curve of new employee (50% loss of productivity for three to six months)
- Payback of sign-on bonus and training fees to new employee's previous employer
- Assumption of health-care costs until new employee's benefits kick in
- Temporary housing for new employee
- Travel for new employee's family
- Real-estate fees for buying and selling new employee's home
- Relocation fees for new employee
- Preventing "short-staff" anxieties. Because of today's tight labor market, employee turnover means that good employees are increasingly irreplaceable. Not only the extraordinary but even average workers can cause "pain and loss" if they take another job elsewhere.

Despite all the steps an employer may take to retain employees, however, some will leave. When this happens, try to avoid being reactive. When an employee quits, unless you have been preparing for this possibility ahead of time, chances are good you may begin the hiring mode to replace this employee while in something of a panic. Proceed calmly and methodically, for anxiety increases the chances that you will choose poorly, offer too much money, or go so long without an employee that you hurt your organization's productivity.

Management's actions vs. employees' preferences: often a mismatch

Computerworld magazine surveyed companies and employees about what managers did to reduce employee turnover and what employees wanted, and found a decided mismatch. These results are for information systems employees. Since many of these issues are found in every company—such as compensation, opportunities for advancement, and job security—they likely have relevance for your business.

Top reasons cited by managers for turnover of information systems (IS) employees:

Compensation	70%
Opportunities for advancement	64%
Corporate culture/environment	38%
Future direction of the company	35%
Access to technology	31%
Training opportunities	27%
Job security	17%

Steps managers are taking to retain IS staff:

Better training	39%
Salary increases/reviews	17%
New or improved compensation offerings	17%

No steps are being taken	10%
Access to new technologies	9%
Incentive programs	9%
Career planning/broadening of positions	8%

What IS employees say will increase their job satisfaction:

Higher salaries	57%
Performance bonuses	43%
Use of new technologies	40%
Opportunities to contribute to business goals	37%
Opportunities for advancement	36%
Availability of IS training	36%
Clearly defined decision-making authority	34%

What we see here is a mismatch between what employees want and how management is responding. Among employees, 36 percent said they wanted IS training, and 39 percent of managers said they were offering better training—this is the only area where the two groups basically are in synch with one another.

Where 57 percent of employees want higher salaries and 43 percent want performance bonuses, only 17 percent of employers said they were offering salary increases; an equal number said they were offering new or improved compensation offerings; and 9 percent were offering incentive programs. Thirty-six percent of employees said they wanted opportunities for advancement, while only 8 percent of employers said they were offering career planning/broadening of positions.

If you want to retain your employees, match what you do and what you offer with what employees want. Conduct a survey, ask your employees what they want, try some new approaches, and track closely what works to satisfy your employees and what doesn't. The worst thing you can do is *assume* you know what your employees want and give that to them.

Retaining employees from the start: good hiring practices

You can prevent (or at least reduce) employee turnover through careful hiring practices. Here are some suggestions:

- *Don't over-promise.* If you tell a prospective employee that she will receive a raise or a promotion by a certain date, give it, or don't promise it in the first place. Nothing turns people off faster than broken promises.

- *Prepare the employee for what is to come* (and weed out those who won't like the work). Companies with in-house sales forces will sometimes have a prospective salesperson accompany a salesperson for a half day so they can see at first hand what the job entails.

- *Check references.* If you know whom you are hiring in the first place, you reduce the chances that your choice will come back and bite you later. (A detailed discussion of checking references before hiring appears in Chapter 13.)

Key #1 to reduced employee turnover: know your employees

Holding down employee turnover requires that you know and understand your employees. If you understand what motivates them and what keeps them happy, you'll do a much better job of preventing

Watch Out!
Where's the highest turnover in America's corporations? Historically, it's among the finance, legal, and information systems employees, partly because of these departments' lack of affiliation with their organization's core business, according to Arthur Andersen Business Consulting, as reported in *Computerworld.*

unnecessary turnover. Here are two things you should know about your employees:

- *Understand your employees' emotional needs.* Treat people as people, not as interchangeable parts. Be respectful. This is basic, but many managers and business owners forget or ignore simple courtesies. How do you show respect? One way is to listen to employees when they have ideas for improving a process or function. You can also empower your employees by giving them the ability to make decisions and have some say about aspects of their jobs that they would know better than a supervisor would. Such empowerment requires restraint from "micromanaging."

- *Understand your employees' career needs.* When people feel they are learning, growing, and building up their skills and knowledge, they tend to feel good about their job and are not likely to leave. Recognize that most people have the need to expand their horizons, and they appreciate it when a boss gives them the opportunity to do so. If the training budget allows, you might allocate a certain amount per year per employee for seminars, night classes, and so on, pertaining to their job. Another way to broaden an employee's horizons is to rotate him or her to different jobs. This not only gives the employee the opportunity to learn new skills, but helps you by having a more rounded employee who knows more than just a narrow niche of your business.

"
Stay competitive with salaries. Know what's going on in the market, says Kerriann Vogel, senior research analyst at the META Group Inc., Stamford, Connecticut. Her recommendation to reduce turnover: Don't fall more than 10 percent behind the market rates.
"

Key #2 to reduced employee turnover: recognize and reward

You cannot effectively communicate appreciation to employees without providing some recognition and rewards. Rewards should not be given out haphazardly; decide what you want to accomplish with them. If you want to motivate people, in what way do you want to motivate them? As with bonuses, rewards should be tied to performance.

A top executive at Wells Fargo, one of the country's 10 largest banks, rewards failure—yes, you read that right—because he wants to encourage intelligent risk-taking. He believes that if you fear failing, you limit your ability to improve and grow in the long run. This executive encourages *prepared, thought-out* risk-taking because its benefits, he believes, outweigh its costs. One way he communicates his support of intelligent failure is by having an article published each month in the bank's internal newsletter that highlights—and praises—a noteworthy effort that happened to fail.

Here are a few suggestions on recognition and rewards for employees' good work:

- *Ask for employees' input.* Don't create recognition and reward vehicles in a vacuum. Get input from your employees as to *how* they would like recognition and what kinds of rewards are valued. Recognition and rewards mandated by management tend to lack the full effect of rewards that employees have helped design.

- *Play fair.* For rewards to be fair, the criteria for granting them must be spelled out and applied equally to everyone. Be careful not to choose the same one or two people time after time; this can cause more conflict than it prevents. Rewards based on clear criteria can lessen conflict when given out fairly and objectively.

- *Reward teams as a whole.* When a team works extra hours to complete a project on time, for

> **❝**
> We are not afraid to talk to our people with emotion. We're not afraid to tell them, We love you, because we do.
> —Herb Kelleher, Chairman and CEO of Southwest Airlines, quoted in Stuart Crainer, *The Ultimate Book of Business Quotations*
> **❞**

Bright Idea
Here's a quick test to determine whether an employee can be saved: Describe to the employee the behavior that is troublesome, and how, then describe what would be a more appropriate behavior. Compare the two for the employee, then note his response. If in denial, he is listening and might be able to change. If he is highly responsive and asks for more feedback, prospects for improvement are very good. If the employee is indifferent, chances are this employee cannot be saved.

example, reward everyone and let the entire organization know that this team effort is worthy of recognition.

■ *Reward behavior, not just outcomes.* The banking executive above who rewards employees' failures is certainly not concerned only with results. Rewarding behavior is important because people can control their behavior more than they can control outcomes. Boosting productivity, for example, is not simply a result of working harder, but may depend on a better flow of material or some other factor beyond an individual's control. Also, when behavior is good, eventually outcomes will respond. (It's like a basketball player who keeps getting good shots, but misses most of them; if he keeps trying, eventually the shots will begin to fall into the basket. The law of averages begins to work in your favor.)

■ *Show your gratitude.* Be generous—and sincere— with expressions of gratitude. This is an integral part of good communication—you are showing how much you appreciate someone and what that person has done. For expressions of gratitude to be effective, they must be sincere. Writing in *Workforce* (November 1997), Ann Perle noted: "Gratitude is saying 'thank you,' and meaning it. There's an important difference between simply saying 'thank you' and being grateful to people who contribute above and beyond the call of duty. It's this element of gratitude that has been missing in many of our recognition efforts.... Gratitude is appreciation for benefits received." If you truly appreciate what your employees do for you and let this appreciation show, you can prevent many conflicts that might arise from employee frustration, or feelings that they and their work are not valued.

12 ways to hold on to employees

1. **Good pay.** One often hears that today, people want sources of job satisfaction in addition to money. The *Computerworld* IS survey cited above showed that by far the most important thing to the employees was higher salaries, with performance bonuses in second place. It's a simple fact that underpaid employees are more likely to look elsewhere.

   It is essential to know what companies in your industry are paying. For lower-level employees and lower-skilled jobs, the competition is usually limited to your city or town. For higher-level employees, or those with skills in wide demand, however, you may be competing with companies on a wider terrain. And remember that your competition for workers may come from organizations in other industries that might need people with the same skills you are seeking. Someone with project management skills, for example, can use those skills across a wide range of industries. Your pay must be competitive. As noted near the beginning of this chapter, you may need to pay about 15 percent more than the market. (See chapter 14 for further discussion on finding competitive salary information.)

2. **Communication.** There may be no better way to retain employees than by improving communication. Keep your people in the loop. Some

Moneysaver
Everyone likes
recognition. To
work, the recog-
nition must be
sincere. No-cost
ways of provid-
ing recognition:
An article about
the employee in
the company
newsletter; a
stall in the park-
ing lot with
"Employee of the
Month" and the
person's name on
it; an award cer-
emony at the
monthly
employee meet-
ing; a notice on
the bulletin
board.

entrepreneurs hold regular meetings with employees to discuss not only the business's goals, but its financials; they want their people to know how things are going and feel a part of the company's growth. Keep your people up to date with important events affecting the company—and their employment.

3. **Employee reviews.** Make sure you provide regular employee reviews and that they are done fairly. People want to know how they are doing. Employee reviews are, in part, a means of communication between management and employees. Providing feedback to employees about their performance is a key to holding down employee turnover, and employee reviews are the formal means for providing this feedback. In addition, reviews provide you with the means to legally justify and defend giving—or withholding—promotions, pay raises, and so on.

4. **Training.** One of the best ways to hold on to employees and reduce your turnover rate is to offer training to them. Every employee can benefit from training. Receptionists can upgrade their computer skills or time-management techniques, and sales reps can study listening skills or new sales techniques. Leadership training is valuable to managers, while writing skills "brush-up" courses could benefit lawyers, researchers, and managers—anyone who has to communicate in writing. Consider offering your employees the option of going to trade and professional meetings and conferences, seminars, college courses, and access to tools, computers, and other ways to learn by doing. Look at your projects and needs for the coming year or so,

and see where your company can benefit from training in certain skills. Then try to tie the training to your needs.

5. **Employee assistance.** Good managers appreciate the value of providing support to employees—defined help when they need it. Rand Morimoto, owner and manager of Inacom Oakland, a computer reseller in Oakland, California, worked out a system so that when employees struggle with a project, they have a clear path of "escalation procedures" that tell them to whom they can go for help. If one person cannot help, the employee can move to the next level. "The escalation procedures help retain employees," Morimoto explains, "because they know they can get support. They don't feel they are out there alone, cornered, without options. It's teamwork."

6. **Improved working conditions.** If your office is arranged using cubicles, provide bigger-than-usual cubicles. A few extra feet probably doesn't cost much, but it can help provide a more comfortable work area. Be sure bathrooms and other common areas are well maintained. Provide free coffee, tea, and soft drinks. Little things can really add up to a much more desirable work environment.

7. **Career paths.** This is one of the most important and effective means for reducing employee turnover, though admittedly one of the most difficult to implement. People want to feel that they are progressing, that their career is moving ahead. As an example of an approach to creating career paths, Ray Taggart, co-owner of a

computer reseller business in Salt Lake City, created for his lower-level employees the titles of Level One Technician, Level Two Technician, and Level Three Technician. In order to work at providing meaningful career paths, each title had to come with defined, valued responsibilities. The higher-level technicians not only received more money, but were given lead-technician status on larger projects and could operate with more independence. Likewise, you might review the organization of your company or department to see how you can create discrete stages in the lines of authority that could be translated into career paths for employees. A career path is a series of job positions that provides employees with various gains, be they job titles, new responsibilities, additional power, and/or higher compensation.

8. **Bonuses.** From the employee's perspective, bonuses are a benefit because they help increase income. For employers, bonuses are popular because they are good motivators. Also, bonuses have an advantage over boosting employee salaries to a comparatively high level: It is easier to drop a bonus than it is to cut someone's salary.

9. **"Flextime."** Flextime is an arrangement in which workers' schedules are flexible, or adjustable, provided that they work their full 35 or 40 hours, the work gets done, and any facilities that need to be manned or monitored during certain hours are indeed covered. According to *Government Finance Review* (June 1998), "More than 27 percent of all full-time wage and salary workers in the United States—

about 25 million—had flexible work schedules that allowed them to vary the time they began or ended work. The increase in flexible work schedules was widespread across demographic groups, occupations and industries, reports the Bureau of Labor Statistics of the U.S. Department of Labor."

10. **Relaxation of unnecessary rules.** If you want to drive employees away, a good place to start is by having petty rules. Take a hard look at how many of the forms and reporting requirements are really necessary, and also look at how much time they take. (Some types of reporting are legally mandated, though, and therefore unavoidable.) Keeping office supplies under lock and key is another often unnecessary irritant.

11. **Employee rotation.** Many of us get bored doing the same thing over and over, month after month, year after year. Employee rotation, where an employee rotates to different jobs within a department or a company, could provide a number of benefits. Job rotations could be done for limited periods—say, a few weeks to a few months—then the employee would return to her original job. Or, depending on the position, rotation could be done on a "permanent" basis, with the employee rotated from one job to another. But note that some employees may strongly oppose being shifted around from the job they thought they were hired for. If rotation is part of the business plan, employees should be so advised before being hired. Consider rotation a form of training. Benefits of rotation include the employee's ability to move out of

Watch Out!
Bonuses are a popular way to reduce turnover while rewarding and motivating employees. But to be effective, bonuses must be tied to performance. They lose their ability to motivate if everyone gets a bonus each year regardless of performance.

his usual routine and to learn new skills, and the business can benefit from employees' better morale and more well-rounded view of the company and its operations.

12. **Cross-training.** Long employed by manufacturers, this variation on the rotation technique involves training your employees in various aspects of a business. Employees acquire skills you can draw upon if there's a sudden need for them within the organization. Someone who can work several machines can move from one to another in response to changing demand within the company, or to an employee being out sick.

Dealing with employees' attitude and behavior problems

Watch Out!
According to the American Psychological Association, among the most highly stressed occupations are secretary, waitress, middle manager, police officer, editor, and medical intern. Common complaints are of too much responsibility and too little authority, unfair labor practices, and inadequate job descriptions.

In a perfect world, all employees would be motivated, upbeat, enthusiastic, and lacking in personal problems of any sort. In the real world, however, you hire human beings whose attitudes and behaviors vary from person to person. Personal problems can sometimes affect their performance on the job, and the well-being of your company.

Firing the problem worker might seem the easy way out, but it's often a shortsighted approach; and, in any case, firing is much easier said than done. There are legal issues concerning firing that hamper your ability to fire employees at will. (See chapters 2 and 15.) Firing often sends the message that someone made a mistake in hiring the rejected worker. Plus, firing almost always hurts morale. Even if you could fire difficult employees with impunity, you probably would be better off trying to "save" them. Working with problem employees is generally

the better strategy, not only because it's more considerate, but because it often makes better business
sense.

Common employee behavior problems

Whether through absenteeism, poor attitudes, or
substance abuse, problem employees make work
difficult in a variety of ways. A further cause is lack
of leadership by management, as in a timely intervention with an employee's irritable attitude or
unprofessional behavior. Other factors include
incompatible personalities, pressures within the
organization (such as the desire for a promotion),
external pressures (including financial problems or
strong competition), and just plain old pathological
behavior.

Here are some of the more common ways
employees can cause difficulties, with suggestions
for handling these problems.

Attitude

It is generally agreed that the biggest single factor in
a person's success—or failure—is their attitude.
Some people have positive attitudes, while others
are almost always negative. Many problems on the
job are related to attitude, so trying to work with a
person's "improvable" attitude can be worthwhile
for you and your company.

The place to start is with your own attitude. If for
some reason you are often disagreeable, then don't
expect to see sunshine reflected in your employees'
faces. Recognize your own attitude and how it
affects your employees.

To help improve the attitude of your employees,
you needn't try to be a psychologist, just remember
the golden rule: Try to be appreciative and show

Moneysaver
You can prevent
many costs of
poor performance
by: (1) institut-
ing rigorous hir-
ing practices, so
you screen out
potential prob-
lems beforehand;
(2) having an
effective orienta-
tion program for
the new employ-
ees, which helps
get them accli-
mated to your
company and
fosters good
relationships
between new
employees and
veterans.

your gratitude in little ways. Small signs of appreciation can go a long way toward helping make employee attitudes more positive and productive.

Attendance problems

An employee, no matter how good, does not help you if she does not show up for work. Such behavior is often highly detrimental to the entire organization because everyone else has to cover for the missing employee. This also holds for employees who are chronically late.

What causes absenteeism? A 1997 survey by CCH Inc., Chicago, found that often absenteeism is due not to laziness or poor attitude, but rather to family issues and personal needs, such as a child's illness. These factors accounted for nearly one half of all unscheduled absences. Stress was also a frequent cause.

How do you save an employee who is absent too frequently? First, find out what the problem is. If family obligations are the cause, you may be able to assist by providing flexible scheduling or opportunities to work at home full- or part-time. If stress is the culprit, try to learn the source. If it comes from the workplace—for example, from excessive overtime or a crushing workload—then you can try to minimize the source of stress. But if the pressure comes from the employee's personal life, professional counseling may be in order (you can be supportive, but remember that it is not your job to be a counselor to employees—that is better done by professionals).

If absenteeism is a result of a bad attitude toward the job, set down clear and meaningful consequences. Make a clear statement of policy; be sure the consequences of such infractions are spelled out in the employee policy manual. (For example, if a

Unofficially...
According to a 1997 survey by CCH Inc., Chicago, absenteeism averages 2.3 percent, and the average cost per employee is $572 per year. This does not include such indirect costs as overtime pay for other employees or the cost of temporary workers to cover for the absent employee. These can add another 15 to 25 percent to the direct cost of unscheduled absenteeism.

person is absent without just cause for one day during a specified period, nothing happens; if absent for two days, a certain privilege is revoked; if absent for three days, they lose their job.) These rules must be applied to everyone equally.

Whenever an absence occurs, just as with any other problem, you need to communicate. Conduct a return-to-work interview—it can be just a few minutes—to determine why the person was absent, and to convey the consequences of further absences. Put everything in writing—what you told the employee and what the employee said—in the event that more serious measures, such as termination, later become necessary. Remember, you cannot discriminate. Whatever rules you choose regarding absenteeism, put them in writing, and make sure everyone sees them when they start their employment with you.

Anger

It is only human to get mad occasionally, if warranted by a specific situation—and if the anger is rare. Frequent, habitual anger, however, is a serious problem, and has no place in a work environment.

During an outburst is not the time to try to reason with an angry individual. When someone raises his voice, keep yours even and calm. If the person starts gesturing and flailing his arms and pointing, keep your arms at your sides. Don't make fists, and try to appear as relaxed as possible. You don't want to meet force with force. Your calmness can help dissipate the angry person's energy.

Try to find out the cause of the anger (after the episode has passed). If reasonable, alter the employee's work situation so that such an incident does not happen again. Some people, admittedly,

Moneysaver
The least expensive means for helping to adjust an employee's attitude is also one of the most effective: Just say "thank you." Give praise for a job well done, and *sometimes* give the praise publicly. That helps make everyone feel good—the employee receiving the praise and those who hear it.

Watch Out!
Watch carefully for employees with substance or alcohol abuse problems. Generally, the earlier these problems are addressed, the better the chances the employee can be helped.

have a nasty anger streak that is difficult for them to control. If you have such an employee, try to get him to seek professional help. Do not ignore a flare-up of anger—particularly if it alarms or threatens the other workers. Address the matter, and keep records of what you did to help ameliorate the situation. If things get out of hand, call the police. You cannot make all employees happy, but an employer has an obligation to create a safe work environment. If you have a loose cannon among your workers, you need to get that person reformed or shipped out.

Substance/alcohol abuse

Among the most serious and intractable problems facing management are those related to drugs and alcohol. It has been estimated that 5 percent of all workers have an alcohol problem. Statistically, this means you are likely to have 1 alcoholic on your payroll for every 20 employees. Add in the number of employees with drug problems (a smaller number than alcoholics), and you can see that even small businesses may have one or more employees with substance abuse problems.

And it usually is an intractable problem. An article in the *Journal of the American Medical Association* (April 15, 1998) reported that of those receiving treatment for alcohol or drug addiction, only 20 to 50 percent of patients remain abstinent during the first year after treatment. This means that most people who receive addiction treatment relapse in a relatively short period of time. And remember that drug abuse extends beyond illegal drugs, such as cocaine and heroin. Many people abuse legal, prescription drugs, too.

What do you do about it? First, if you are not a physician, do not try to act like one. A manager or business owner's primary concern has to be how the employee's addiction affects job performance. Of course, you are concerned with the employee's health and well-being, but you must focus on the job the employee is doing. Consider the following:

- How has the addiction affected the person's job performance? Has the person's absenteeism increased? Has quality decreased? Is there friction and conflict between the employee and colleagues, as well as management?

- How has the employee's supervisor dealt with the problem? Sometimes supervisors don't recognize there is a problem, or they choose to ignore it, or they may even try to cover it up. If you detect any of these signs, you may have a problem that goes beyond the individual employee's addiction.

- The Americans with Disabilities Act (ADA) has this to say about drugs and alcohol (according to the Web site of University of Missouri at Kansas City College of Law [law.umkc.edu]): "Congress intended the ADA to be neutral on testing for substance abuse. Persons using drugs or alcohol are specifically exempted from the coverage of the ADA, and tests for substance abuse are not regulated by the ADA. This means that employers can do preemployment drug screening and refuse to hire persons testing positive (as allowed by other laws and union agreements) without violating the ADA. Persons in the workplace may also be screened and disciplined without violating the ADA. . . ."

  "The ADA does apply to a person who has 'successfully completed a supervised drug rehabilitation program and is no longer engaging in the illegal use of drugs, or has otherwise been rehabilitated successfully and is no longer engaging in such use' or 'is participating in a supervised rehabilitation program and is no longer engaging in such use.'"

What does all this mean to a manager or business owner? It means that you do the following:

- First, establish a written policy regarding drug and alcohol problems that explicitly states what you will you do if an employee has such a problem.

- When talking with an employee about his problem, focus on the problems of performance— what has been going wrong, how the employee's performance has deteriorated. Do not try to diagnose the problem. The best you can do is be objective and try to point out how the problem is affecting the employee's performance and the well-being of the company.

- Provide training to your management team and supervisors, addressing how to identify employees with drug and alcohol problems and what to do. Your city or state government probably has printed material addressing this, and perhaps can provide more extensive assistance.

- Provide help to the employee. If the employee admits he has a problem, offer some assistance, such as helping to pay for counseling or rehabilitation program. Even if yours is a small business, you might be able to arrange telephone consultations with a local therapist or counselor for your employees. These consultations would be a first step, before more in-depth counseling done face to face.

■ If you are a small business, you can set up third-party interventions that the employee can choose to go to. The employer should not get in the middle; lawsuits have arisen over smaller matters.

■ As always, document in writing what the situation is, what you have done, and the employee's response.

Communicating with the employee about problem behavior

There is usually an underlying problem that pervades organizations with serious cases of employee conflicts: a lack of communication. Many instances of problem behavior can be prevented by managers who communicate with employees about how employees are doing their job and, when necessary, about problem behaviors that may be counterproductive for the organization. Let your people know how they are doing so that they won't be operating in the dark. Don't leave feedback to an annual review—that's too little, too late. Let your troops know how they are doing on a continuous basis. Tell them in one-on-one meetings. (A word of caution: When communicating with employees, understand that e-mail is regarded as a formal and permanent form of documentation. In a lawsuit against an employer, e-mails can be subpoenaed. A good rule of thumb is to not send by e-mail anything you wouldn't say to someone's face.)

Take notes

Keep a written, dated record of any communications regarding problems—either with the person's job performance or how he is affecting other workers. If you want to prevent legal problems in the event you have to discipline or fire someone, your best protection is keeping a "paper trail" of what and when you told the employee, and what the employee did to change his behavior. If you never give feedback, you cannot suddenly tell him that he hasn't been performing well or that he is disruptive to the office, and therefore must be fired.

But communication is needed for more reasons than simply to avoid potential legal trouble. Feedback helps direct an employee to the path best taken, improves the chances that the employee can be saved, and can save you from having to hire a replacement.

Listen attentively

Likely the most important part of communication, though often ignored, is effective listening. I will discuss listening in more detail in Chapter 12 on how to prepare for an interview, but note here that listening is essential for both communication and conflict resolution. By listening, you may gain a "bigger picture" of the problem situation than you saw at first. Hear what the employee is saying—and what he is not saying. An employee who feels "listened to" will be much more likely to cooperate.

Be prepared

If an employee's behavior is somehow disrupting the workplace, you need to communicate your concerns, but first, prepare for the meeting. Don't start shooting from the hip—talking to the employee without thinking through what you want to say and understand what you want to accomplish. Consider the following steps:

1. When did you first see the employee exhibit the problem? Write down examples.

2. Try to understand what prompted the actions. Put yourself in the employee's shoes.

3. Consider how the employee will react to what you will tell him or her. You can help head off an ugly confrontation by letting the employee know ahead of time what you want to talk about and allowing him or her to prepare a response.

Take action

If any communication concerning a problem behavior is to be effective, action must be taken. If all you do is air your grievance or listen to the other's story and do nothing about it, not much will have been accomplished. (Also, of course, if the employee is later fired, an employer's failure to take corrective action can put the company in a weaker position if the dismissed employee files a lawsuit.)

- Make specific recommendations.

- Involve the employee. Ask her what solution she thinks would be fair. A new method of gauging performance might be called for. In consultation with the employee, you might set up new criteria for productivity or quality. If it's a behavioral problem, a set of parameters within which the employee must operate could be effective.

- You might want to put an action plan in writing and have the employee sign the statement. In any case, after the meeting, be sure to write up notes about what occurred and keep these notes on file.

- Set specific goals and deadlines.

- Finally, for any action to be worthwhile, you need to follow up. This might mean establishing a monitoring procedure, such as a weekly log of an employee's tardiness. Establish what the consequences are if the targets are not met. The best-laid plans of action are useless without stated, specific consequences.

A word about conflict

After discussing problem behaviors in the workplace, perhaps it should be mentioned that conflict is not inherently bad. For one thing, conflict is natural and unavoidable. Disagreements or rival approaches can stimulate new ideas. Also, if conflict is ignored or suppressed, it can fester and grow into something much more damaging than if acknowledged immediately and dealt with.

What's good about conflict?

- People sometimes conflict when they feel strongly about things. That's good. The opposite is apathy. That's bad. You want employees who are passionate about their work.

- It avoids having decisions made in a "rubber-stamp" manner. "Yes men" are not conducive to good decision making. With conflict, assumptions are confronted, decisions questioned, and better choices often result.

- Questioning and "constructive disagreement" often stimulate creativity. Rivalry between individual employees or between groups or teams— if conducted respectfully—also stimulates creativity.

- Finally, working through disputes in respectful, rational ways generates respect and camaraderie among the participants.

What is important to recognize about conflict is that it can be beneficial or destructive, depending on how it is handled.

Formal grievance procedure

Employer-employee conflicts are inevitable—the question is how well you deal with them. If you handle an employee's grievance well, you can often save that employee and keep her as a productive member of your workforce. The key to a grievance procedure is recognizing that employees want and need to be heard.

The benefits of having a formal, well-designed grievance procedure include:

- Having a structured, uniform process that employees can rely on.

- Resolving conflicts quickly, with minimal damage.

- Maintaining the quality of your workforce, because good employees don't feel ignored or look elsewhere for work, and dissatisfied employees get to be heard.

- Often, employees who take the risk of complaining about significant issues and offering solutions are good candidates for management positions. By offering an effective grievance procedure, you may well find some leaders among your workers.

- Employee complaints may be justified, meaning you have problems and the issues that the employees raise should be dealt with. Two results of effectively handling grievances are better productivity and management.

The elements of a grievance procedure include the following:

- An established reporting hierarchy. It needs to be spelled out to whom employees must first bring their grievances, and to whom to go next if they do not get satisfaction from the first-line manager. Typically, this line of reporting starts with the employee's immediate supervisor. You need to also note to whom the employee reports the grievance if the problem is with their immediate supervisor.

- The grievance procedure needs to spell out management's responsibility for investigating a complaint. What will management do? Will the information be made public during or after the procedure? At their most basic, effective grievance procedures are fact-finding missions. You need to answer these questions: who, what, when, where, why, and how.

- As with goals, grievance procedures should be accompanied by time limits. Procedures should enumerate when management needs to take action after a grievance has been filed.

- Make clear whether employees will be paid for time spent on grievance proceedings.

- Put the policy in writing.

Just the facts

- Turnover can be reduced by the employer's careful attention to employees' needs, ideas, and interests.

- Understand what your employees want—ask them, survey them, and follow up.

- A "problem employee" is one who causes problems with your business or other employees, detracts from the performance of your other employees, is less productive than others in similar positions, causes difficulties with customers, or is in some other way a hindrance to the smooth operation of the company.

- It is generally worthwhile to try to keep a good but discontented employee.

- A carefully structured, clearly outlined formal grievance procedure can help save your employees.

Hiring Options

GET THE SCOOP ON...
Why you need a hiring strategy ▪ How to set
your goals ▪ How to explore the labor market of
the 1990s—and beyond ▪ How to calculate your
hiring needs ▪ How your company's maturity
affects your hiring practices

Developing a Hiring Strategy

Chapter 5

I f you don't know where you want to go, chances are good you'll end up somewhere you don't want to be. Hit-or-miss, seat-of-the-pants—these clichés describe strategies that may work in some parts of life but are rarely productive in business, and they certainly should not describe your approach to hiring.

The benefits of a hiring strategy include reducing your costs. You become more efficient and effective in your hiring methods, and therefore waste less time and choose better candidates. In addition, it speeds up your hiring process. In today's market, where there is often considerable competition for desirable candidates, the sooner you can identify the best job applicants and give them an offer, the better your chances of hiring them.

It has been observed that companies will often spend more time analyzing, researching and planning for the purchase of a $40,000 photocopy machine than for hiring a $40,000-a-year employee. That's crazy, but probably true. Your most important competitive advantage comes from your people, not your machinery. And with the current labor shortage in many industries around the country, a hiring strategy is more important than ever to assure you get the people you need.

According to the U.S. Bureau of Labor Statistics, the 10 industries with the fastest employment growth (on a percentage basis) between 1996 and 2006 are projected to be computer and data processing services, health services, management and public relations, miscellaneous transportation services, residential care, personnel supply services, water and sanitation, individual and miscellaneous social services, offices of health practitioners, and amusement and recreation services. If your business is in one of these industries, it seems likely that you will encounter considerable competition for workers because these industries will be growing so fast.

Let one example illustrate the hiring challenges posed by the current tight labor market, and why your business needs a coherent hiring strategy. A recent newspaper article told of a recruiter who went to a local university seeking an accountant from the school's Masters of Accountancy program. Not a single student contacted the recruiter for this accountant's position. The would-be employer: Intel Corp., one of the hottest and most respected companies in the country.

The benefits of having a hiring strategy include:

- *Competitive advantage:* In today's knowledge-based economy, brain power is worth far more than muscle power. With a hiring strategy, you improve considerably your chances of finding

Unofficially...
A widely used survey of recruitment costs conducted by employment expert Gary Cluff for the Society for Human Resource Management uses the following variables when calculating cost-per-hire: internal costs (salaries, benefits), external costs (travel, entertainment), company visit expenses (applicant travel), direct fees (advertising, job fairs, agency fees), and supplemental average annual salary of new hires, relocation costs, and any sign-on bonus.

smart, productive workers who will give you a leg up on your competition.

- *Avoid the costs of poor hiring:* As shown in Chapter 1, hiring mistakes can be very costly. A hiring strategy cannot entirely eliminate such mistakes, but it can help you prevent them.

- *Speed up the hiring process:* If you have a strategy in place, you can get the hiring process into gear faster and more effectively when you need new employees. A strategy gives you a blueprint to work from so you can take advantage of opportunities as they arise.

Matching hiring to your company's development stage

Particularly for smaller companies, hiring the best people is difficult because of the business's limited resources. A high-powered, experienced executive who seems just the right person to move a small company up to the next level of development may be out of reach because the company cannot afford the salary and benefits the executive wants. Or, the company may seem too risky a bet for an executive who is looking for a more established and prestigious corporation. You cannot have an effective hiring strategy unless you know your company's limitations—and strengths.

Start-up company

If your business is a start-up, chances are good that money is short and cash flow tight. The money your company has is probably better off being reinvested in the business rather than paid out in large salaries and hefty benefit packages. In this situation, your strategy for hiring experienced hotshots is to provide long-term incentives.

❝
Goals for hiring must be clear-cut, numeric, accountable, specific, measurable, realistic and time-trackable.
—Paul Lemberg, president of the consulting firm of Lemberg and Company, San Diego
❞

Rather than pay cash now, offer stock or stock options. If you do not plan to go public, you can offer either ownership options exercisable down the road, depending upon certain performance criteria set out at the time of hiring, or a profit-sharing plan, also tied to long-term targets. The idea is to get the desired executive interested in working for you and to have an incentive to see your company do well, because his or her future earnings are tied to your success, while at the same time you want to limit your financial risk up front and minimize the demands on your cash.

Growth company

Your business has passed the start-up stage, which may have lasted from several months to a few years. You are in a strong growth mode with sales increasing as well as your number of employees. Cash is not flowing freely and the business still demands a high degree of reinvestment to keep the growth fueled, but there is more cash and profit than before and salaries and benefits can be increased. Executive salaries can now approach market levels, though you still cannot pay top wages. The bag of goodies you can offer, though, is larger than before. These include 401K plans, better health coverage, and more vacation. You won't have to strain to sell yourself to executive prospects because they can now see that you are succeeding. You have a track record of success that will help you attract top-notch executive, technical, and other talent.

Mature company

You've now hit your stride. Growth is slow but steady, and your reinvestment needs are more limited than before, thus freeing up cash. At the same time, long-term rewards are probably not as appealing as before, especially not stock options. That's because your company's growth potential is limited, which limits the upside potential of your stock's price. As a result, your hiring emphasis shifts from long-term incentives to short-term ones. Cash and performance-based rewards keep executives from seeking greener pastures. However, some types of rewards can be very appealing, such as partnerships, which are offered in such professional organizations as consulting, accounting, and law firms.

Declining company

You are now on the far side of your company's life cycle, with your market share at best steady and maybe declining. Your entire industry could be heading downhill. You now focus on trying to cut costs, find new markets, and develop new products. Enticing those you want is again difficult, as it was when you had a start-up company. But you can't use the same incentives as before. Who wants long-term benefits with a company in decline? Your hiring strategy at this stage in your company's life is to offer immediate cash rewards, namely salary.

Action plan

Tying the life cycle of a company to hiring points out how hiring strategies change given the abilities of the company. When cash is short but the future looks bright, offer prospective employees a piece of the future. When a company is mature and throwing off lots of cash, but the future is unexciting or even dismal, offer cash and downplay the future. You can improve your chances of successfully hiring those people you really want by understanding where your company is in its life cycle.

Bright Idea
To make the most of your goals, write them down, visualize them often, break a large goal into manageable units, and review progress toward your goals on a regular basis. Revise your goals periodically.

Set your goals

Your hiring strategy must have goals. Where do these come from? From your business plan. Tie your hiring goals to your business's overall goals as stated in your business plan. The most commonly used goals for hiring involve quantity: How many people will I need to hire over the next 12 to 24 months? To answer this, consider which of these scenarios best describes your situation:

- Your need for employees will decrease due to contraction of your business, increased efficiencies, or other reasons. In this case, your biggest personnel concern will be how to retain the right employees and decrease your workforce as necessary—efficiently and humanely.

- Your need for employees will likely remain at approximately today's level. Here, your challenge is limited to replacing any workers who happen to leave.

- Your need for employees will likely increase over time, due to the growth of your business. A growing business must not only replace employees due to turnover, but hire to fill newly created positions.

Know your labor market

Effective hiring strategies are only possible when you know your labor market. Let's look at the idea of the labor market within the context of your hiring strategy. The labor market consists of people identified from many sources, including the following:

- Recent college graduates found in on-campus recruiting

- Those currently employed in corporations who respond to newspaper advertisements

- The "wired" or technically savvy who find employment opportunities on the Internet
- Those registered with headhunters
- Those registered with employment agencies

How to get savvy about the marketplace

Smart managers have many good ways of staying informed about trends and opportunities in their line of business, and are always looking for new sources of good workers. Here are some of the best sources:

- Watch the ads placed by your competition. How frequently do they advertise? What salaries do they list? For what positions do they advertise? How many weeks do the ads run? Where do they advertise? What kind of advertising copy do they use? Who are they targeting for each position?

- Subscribe to industry publications and local business journals. See who advertises in them and what positions they are advertising for. Join local business organizations. They often know about the local labor market.

- Ask your state employment department for its view of the types of people in the job market. Is the labor pool filled with inexperienced people? The uneducated? Is there now a pool (or soon to be one) of unemployed workers with certain skills because a large employer or a particular industry has fallen on hard times?

- A certain computer reseller regards vendor reps as one of his best sources for job applicants. Vendor reps are the salespeople who represent

Timesaver
Consider looking for employees as an ongoing business activity. You never stop marketing; likewise, you should never stop looking for good employees. When at business meetings, mention to the other attendees that you are always interested in learning of potential employees. Tell acquaintances that you really do keep resumes on file and use them. These steps can save you a lot of time when a position opens in your company.

manufacturers and service providers. They get around to many companies, and they hear things, such as who is unhappy and might consider jumping jobs. These reps need coaxing, so don't just ask them once if they know of anyone who is qualified and might be looking for work. Gently remind them on an ongoing basis that you are looking for good employees. Also, go to vendor conferences.

- The Internet is an increasingly good source of job applicants, and I will discuss it in detail in Chapter 10. Use the Internet to see who is available, because job seekers often post their resumes online. And use the Internet just as you should the daily newspaper—to see what the competition is doing.

- If you plan on hiring, say, 15 or more employees during the coming year, it might be economically worthwhile to hire a full-time employee to do your recruiting, especially if you are in an industry with a shortage of desirable applicants. And while you are hiring a recruitment specialist, hire those with skills beyond recruiting, such as those who understand compensation and legal matters. A company does not have to be a giant to need its own recruiter. One 15-person firm I know of has a person spending much of her time on recruiting and hiring. At a 50-person company, a recruiter not only finds applicants but runs the interview process and the orientation program all employees go through once hired. Before he came on board, the orientation program was haphazard because no one person was in charge of it. With this full-time recruiter on staff, orientation is now organized and quite effective at smoothing the new hire's transition into the company.

■ Look outside your industry. IBM hired Lou Gerstner, an executive who had never worked in the computer industry, and it worked out well. Consider looking "outside the box" at individuals who work in industries other than yours. This strategy probably works best with companies that are moving into new markets and have rivals or other challenges requiring particular expertise. If you want to start generating sales over the Internet, you may look for an employee whose experience is in computers or in a company with electronic commerce experience, instead of someone who has worked only in your particular industry. A law firm seeking to attract clients through a direct-mail campaign might consider hiring someone who works in an industry with a history of direct-mail experience, such as publishing.

Strategies for today's labor market

Today's labor market requires you to be proactive in your pursuit of top-notch employees. The days when you could sit back and wait for job-seekers to knock on your door are long gone. Here are strategies for today's labor market.

Talent searches

The labor market of the 1990s means that employers have to be more aggressive and more creative than ever before. Hundreds of thousands of jobs are now being listed on the Internet at any given time, and they are attracting talented people who might never know you are looking to hire if you do not post your openings on the Internet. (See discussion of online hiring in Chapter 10.)

Compensation

Be prepared to spend more than ever to attract workers. I'm not just talking about the cost of want ads or your time, but sign-up bonuses, tuition rebates, and other enticements. One gasoline chain hung signs in its stations promising it would pay for students' books if they came to work for the company. A fast-food chain promised to pay for tuition, something unheard-of a few years back for such lower-paying jobs. Your company can be just as imaginative as these.

Lifestyle issues

"Lifestyle" issues are of increasing concern to employees. Traditionally, pay was employees' primary motivation to work for a company. Secondarily, security. Pay is still important and security decidedly less so, but other attractions are motivating workers today, with lifestyle high on the list. This can include flexible hours, child care, telecommuting (where the employee works from home some or all of the time), company-subsidized cafeterias, in-house fitness centers (or paid memberships to health clubs for companies too small to have their own fitness center), and other such goodies. More than ever, the non-work environment—the support you give people outside work for personal affairs—is of interest to potential employees. Perks are typically provided depending on circumstances, which include such things as what you can afford; what companies in your local area (who are competing for the same workers as you) are providing; and what is typical in your industry nationally. Even local situations can affect when and what you offer. For example, workers in Utah, which has the highest birth rate in the country, might value child care more than workers in downtown San Francisco or Manhattan, who are often single or childless and who might place more value on health club memberships.

Training

In the world of high technology, one of the most important perks is training: People want their skills to include the most up-to-date computer programs and languages, and the company that promises to keep them on the leading edge has a decided advantage. A computer reseller, for example, attracts people by promising that they will periodically get to work with the leading-edge technologies, even if the company is not selling them. The company always has in-house at least one latest-and-greatest computer and lots of new software that is not yet on the market. This gives the company the image of being "hot," and since all employees can use these machines, it attracts and helps keep top-notch workers.

Sell yourself

Perhaps one aspect of the current job market that not enough employers consider, but which should be included in your hiring strategy, is the need to "sell" you and your company. That is what this computer reseller is doing with the promise of the latest-and-greatest technology. Another example is a law firm that promised a new attorney she would be able to work in a number of departments and learn about various areas of the law, and then be able to choose which area was of interest to her, rather than being pigeonholed from the beginning. A software company gives all employees, after their first few months on the job, stock in the company. Do not promise what you cannot deliver, but recognize that you need to stand out from the other employers at least as much as job applicants have to stand out from other applicants. In fact, to a degree, you have to cater to them.

Calculating future hiring needs

There are different formulas available to calculate future hiring needs, some more suited to certain businesses than others. A retail company or a mail-order firm might look at transactions per employee, but not a software company or day care center, which have relatively few transactions. A company with many employees for a given amount of revenues and profits, such as child-care centers, could benefit from looking at profits per employee, while a company with relatively few employees but with considerable investment in tangible assets, such as a mining company, would consider the ratio of tangible assets per employee. It all depends on your business and industry, and you probably already have a feel for what's important to your business.

The differences between businesses can be striking. Microsoft, for example, in 1997, had sales of $11,358,000,000 and 22,232 employees, which works out to over a half-million dollars in sales per employee, on average. Open Market Inc., a software company involved with electronic commerce, had 1997 sales of $61,300,000 and 527 employees, which averages out to $116,000 or so in sales per employee, a fraction of Microsoft's. But that's hardly a difference when compared with an industry that's really labor intensive, like child care. The biggest operator of child-care facilities is KinderCare Learning Centers, which had 1997 sales of $563,100,000, about one-twentieth of Microsoft's, but had virtually the same number of employees (22,400). Sales per employee at KinderCare come to about $25,000. Children's Discovery Centers of America, the fourth largest child care company in the country, had 1997 sales of $93,000,000 and 4,700 employees, for an average of sales to employees of just under $20,000.

The point here is that ratios vary enormously from industry to industry, and from company to company, and you have to find the ratios that are most revealing for your company.

Below are four formulas you can choose from in calculating future hiring needs. For the purpose of demonstration, I'll use a single, hypothetical company that is planning to hire additional employees. The four formulas used by this company are (1) measurement by sales per employee; (2) measurement by profit to the average number of employees; (3) measurement by the number of transactions to the average number of employees; and (4) measurement by tangible assets to the average number of employees.

Measuring by sales per employee

Here's a way to measure your future hiring needs, using sales-per-employee, which I will illustrate with an example. This example presumes the following:

- You own a retail store.
- Your business is growing.
- You are now reasonably efficient, and so there is not much room for productivity improvements.
- You currently have five employees (including yourself).
- Two employees left the company during the year and had to be replaced.

- Current annual sales are $1.5 million.

- Your business plan projects sales for next year of $2 million.

The task here is to determine how many employees you should be planning to hire next year. That number will be your hiring goal (the time frame is the next 12 months and the number will come from this calculation, thus meeting the requirements for setting a useful goal).

Calculating your annual sales per employee is one way to determine your hiring goal for the next 12 months. Here's how to calculate it:

$$\frac{\text{Current Sales}}{\text{Number of Employees}} = \text{Sales per Employee}$$

Using our sample scenario, the numbers are as follows:

$$\frac{\$1.5 \text{ million}}{5} = \$300,000$$

With sales next year of $2 million, you need enough new employees to handle $500,000 in additional sales next year. Since each employee can handle about $300,000, based on your current staffing, you can project your need for additional employees at 1 or 2 next year.

Turnover rate

Let's assume that last year you had 3 full-time employees at the beginning of the year and 5 at the end, so you averaged 4 full-timers for the entire year. Divide this by the number of full-time employees who left during the year. That gives you an employee turnover rate of 50 percent (2 divided by 4). Based on this information, you will probably have to replace 2 employees next year due to turnover.

Bright Idea
You should know how many employees you average during the year. Use full-time positions (or full-time equivalents) for this calculation. The simplest way to calculate this average uses the following formula:

[(*Number of employees at beginning of year*) + (*Number of employees at end of year*)] / 2 = *average number of employees for the year*

Note, if you have a highly seasonal business, you must calculate employee needs at different times of the year.

In this example, your goal for the coming year will be to hire a total of 3 to 4 employees: 1 to 2 to cover growth, and 2 to cover employee turnover. You now have an estimate of how many employees you will need to hire during the coming year, roughly one every three to four months.

But your employee needs may not all be for employees in similar positions or functions. You may need to replace a departing sales person and add a new salesperson, add a bookkeeping person and maybe add a delivery person. In this case, you need to refine your goals to the types of employees you are likely to need.

Measuring by profit to average number of employees

This calculation is similar to the sales-to-employee ratio just discussed, but here you'll consider profit. If your net profit was $300,000 last year, each employee, based on having an average number of employees of 4, generated $75,000 in profits. If your business plan projects profits for the coming year of $400,000, or $100,000 more than the previous year, then you need an additional 1 to 2 employees to produce those profits. To this you need to add the number of employees that probably will need to be replaced due to turnover, namely 2, so your hiring needs next year will probably be 3 or 4.

Measuring by number of transactions to average number of employees

If your store averages 200 transactions a week, and you averaged 4 employees during the year, then each employee handled 50 transactions a week, on average. If you expect the number of weekly transactions next year to increase to 250, then you need 1 additional employee next year. Again, add in the turnover, namely 2, so your target number of hires is 3.

Measuring by tangible assets to average number of employees

Let's assume you are in a capital-intensive business, say, the manufacture of wrenches, and this year you had 5 employees and your tangible assets were worth $1 million. In this case, you are supporting each employee with $200,000 worth of tangible assets. If you expect to add $400,000 worth of tangible assets next year, you will need to hire 2 additional employees. This measurement says you will need to hire 4 employees next year, 2 new ones to handle the additional tangible assets, plus 2 to replace those who left.

Linking business and hiring goals

> Workers typically work in teams, and the best teams are well balanced. With a balanced team, the whole is a lot stronger then the sum of its parts.
> —Tom Probert, smelter general manager, Kennecott Utah Copper

Calculating your future hiring needs is vital to the success of your business—and your hiring activities. You are connecting your hiring goals, namely 3 to 4 employees, to your business's goals, such as growing the business by $500,000, increasing profits by $100,000, boosting transactions by 50 a week, and adding $400,000 in tangible assets. When you make the connection between your hiring and business goals, you have moved hiring away from a reactive chore—something you do when a position opens up—to a strategic activity, an intentional action tied to achieving your overall goals.

Mix-and-match hiring

To mix and match is like assembling a suitable outfit to wear in the morning from the broad choice of colors and styles hanging in your closet. You wouldn't really want a closet full of ten sets of the same uniform, would you? Diversity works in hiring as it does in fashion. What I am talking about here is really an attitude toward hiring that requires you to look as objectively as possible at yourself in relation to your business. One of the worst things you can do when hiring is hire everyone in your own image— people who have your personality, your strengths and weaknesses, your attitudes, your take on life and work, your background. Cloning is not a good strategy for hiring. Restricting your hiring to people with the same ideas and abilities, over and over, limits your company's potential to expand and stretch.

Let's assume that there is some truth in the stereotype that those who are people-oriented are outgoing and communicate well, but are not detail-oriented, nuts-and-bolts types of folks. Salespeople, for example, tend to be people-oriented. If you hire only this type of employee for your department or company, you will end up with a labor force that's outgoing, communicative, probably good at selling. But your operations—your ability to deliver—will almost certainly be poor because you lack the people who know how to execute. Create a balanced team of workers with a range of complementary skills so that the limits of each are offset by the abilities of others. Only then can the whole be solid and productive.

Mix-and-match concerns go beyond job descriptions and into personality types. You will already be considering diversity factors such as the fact that you cannot discriminate on the basis of age, religion, sex, or race. But there are other kinds of diversity worthy of consideration, too, when building a team, including:

- *Educational background:* Don't hire a team whose members all went to similar colleges or had similar majors. Liberal arts majors, for example, sometimes prove very effective in a wide variety of unrelated fields, such as computers and management.

▪ *Economic background:* You can probably benefit from hiring those with varying economic backgrounds—lower-income, middle-class, and upper-income. Each will bring different perspectives to the work environment.

▪ *Experience:* Don't limit your search only to those who have worked in your industry. A theater company took a chance on hiring a woman for its marketing and public relations department even though she had no marketing experience and had never taken a business class in her life (she had majored in anthropology). But what she did have was smarts, creativity, and a good work ethic. The match was a winner for both parties.

▪ *Other:* Although you cannot discriminate because of legal concerns, you should want to hire a diverse group of people anyway. Your business's potential is enhanced if your employees represent a variety of ages and ethnic groups.

Diversity of background and experience is good, but there are qualities—particularly values—that should remain consistent and true to your company's purpose and culture. There are certain values you want because they reflect on your company and are necessary for building a team:

▪ Integrity

▪ Work ethic

▪ Consistency in performance

▪ Commitment

▪ Positive attitude

❝
Your first question shouldn't be, 'What kind of person do I want [to hire],' but 'What is my culture?'
—Vince Webb, vice president of marketing, Management Recruiters International Inc., Cleveland
❞

Get input from your employees

Don't go the hiring route alone. No one knows better what is needed than the people who are doing the job. Ask your employees, especially those who will be working with the new hire, what skills, experience, and other attributes they want the applicant to have. Beware though, that employees will tend to emphasize the type of people they like, not the skills that are important to the job. It's okay to address issues of what types of people employees like, since they all have to work together. But be sure you thoroughly cover the *skills* needed.

There was a baker who always had his bakers and retail clerks talk with job applicants so that his employees could have a say in who was hired. He found that his employees, who were sensitive to what type of person they needed and wanted to work with, were adept at separating the good applicants from the poor ones. This baker wanted to create and maintain a collegial, family-like culture in his business, and involving his workers in the hiring process helped achieve this. Your employees can help you in the same way.

Be realistic about your needs

Gopal K. Kapur, president of the Center for Project Management, a San Ramon, California-based consulting and training firm, recommends dividing your hiring needs into three types:

- *Must-haves:* The indispensable skills or experience the job applicant must bring to the job from day one. You should not have to teach the applicant these skills. A pharmaceutical sales rep, for instance, needs to know the vocabulary that comes with the healthcare industry and how to make a presentation to a hospital.

- *Should-haves:* The sets of skills of which the applicant should have one or more. A computer programmer might need to know two out of three programming languages. A pharmaceutical sales rep might need to know about three out of four types of drug delivery systems.

- *Nice-to-haves:* The skills or experience that it would be good for the applicant to have, but which are not necessary or can be developed after hiring. For example, it would be helpful for the pharmaceutical sales rep to have experience as a team leader, but if that role will not open up for another 12 months, it could be well enough if the applicant lacks this experience now because the applicant can be trained in becoming a team leader.

Keep these distinctions in mind when drawing up your hiring strategy and creating job descriptions. They help you focus on what is important and immediate, and what is less important or urgent.

Watch out for hidden issues

When creating a hiring strategy, beware of hidden issues. For example, hiring someone from inside the company may not be the way to attract the best employee but may be desirable because it will boost morale among your workers. You may lose the benefit of new ideas that an outsider could bring, in exchange for having happier workers. In this case, the ostensible reason for hiring the person was that she was the best candidate. But, in fact, the hidden issue was to boost morale. Of course, this kind of trade-off may not be worth it, but be aware that this is a "hidden" issue that should be considered.

Watch for managers who habitually hire in their own image. They may not mean to hire people just like themselves, but they may be doing it just the same. A basketball team with one Michael Jordan can be great; one with five could be a disaster.

Also, beware the insecure manager who can derail your best-laid hiring strategy because he is worried about his turf or potential for advancement. An applicant may seem likely to become the apple in one's supervisor's eye and be rejected for this reason alone because the person doing the hiring is worried the newcomer will leapfrog over him in the corporate hierarchy. A supervisor known to favor men, for example, might discourage a manager from hiring too many men because he thinks they might limit his own career. To help head off this situation before it occurs, put job descriptions and rules in writing—such as reviewing resumes with the names of applicants covered so that their sex is hidden. Have candidates interviewed by more than one person.

In addition, watch out for those who refer family and friends. This may work, but often it has potential for disaster. Family and friends are hired because they are easier to choose than having to go through the whole hiring process. And often there's the rationale of doing someone a favor. The potential for problems here are enormous, including:

- Strained relations because there is much emotional "baggage" that comes to a work relationship when involving family or friends.

- Underqualified workers hired for reasons other than competence.

- Difficulties borne of the fact that the casual, close relationships that characterize relationships between family and friends often lead to detrimental liberties, unprofessional behavior,

"

Most new managers are reluctant to hire people they see as equal or better than themselves, which is what they really need to do. They need to find people who will stretch them and be stretched. That's always life-threatening if you're a new manager. You're looking at the guy that could potentially be your replacement.
—Richard Lennon, vice president and CIO, Brown-Forman Corp.

and ignored shortcomings that would otherwise never be tolerated.

If you hire family or friends, make clear *in writing* how the relationship will be structured, when raises can be expected, when reviews will be conducted, and what standards of performance you expect.

Have an interviewing plan

I will discuss in Chapter 12 how to plan for and conduct a hiring interview, but it is worth noting here that interviewing—including *how* you will do it—is an integral part of your hiring strategy. Recognize that, like public speaking, interviewing is a skill that can be learned. Perhaps the single most important part of interviewing—so simple people ignore it—is to *prepare*. Read the applicant's resume, write down a list of questions, and create a game plan for the interview.

Employers' blunders and lessons learned

Janet Long of Integrity Search Inc. conducted a survey of job applicants and asked what displeased them about prospective employers. Among the mistakes and lessons we can draw from her findings are the following ones:

Mistake: Organizations do not provide applicants with sufficient feedback on the status of their candidacy.

Lesson: Treat job prospects like customers. You wouldn't ignore your customers, so don't ignore people applying to work for you. Tell them what's happening. Keep communication lines open, but don't make any commitments you can't keep. Tell the applicant, "We will look at . . . , we will get back to you by . . ." Let the applicant know he or she is being considered, but don't raise false hopes or promise things you will regret later.

Mistake: Written job descriptions are not available or are inaccurate.

Lesson: The job's functions should be clearly in mind and on paper. (I will discuss the characteristics of well-written job descriptions in Chapter 6.)

Mistake: The process takes too long.

Lesson: Act decisively and quickly, or someone else may grab the people you want and need. The days are gone when job applicants were so desperate for work they would wait weeks or months for you to come to a decision.

Mistake: Applicants are frustrated by interviewers' lack of preparation and focus.

Lesson: Do your homework. Do your part to prepare for an applicant's interview; otherwise, the applicant will notice your lack of preparation and will not be impressed. (Interview preparations are discussed in Chapters 11 and 12.)

Mistake: Prospective employers do not appreciate the time and energy applicants put into the job search.

Lesson: Respect the applicant's time. A company that needs good workers takes interviewing—and the applicants—seriously.

All of these negatives that applicants sometimes experience in the job search can be prevented if you engage in good communications:

- Be honest with applicants (but remain objective, and avoid going into detail).

- Be prepared so you know what you need to say.

- Know what you want, and convey this to the applicant.

■ Keep applicants apprised of how the job search is going and when you expect to make a decision. Don't leave the applicant hanging.

Just the facts

■ Develop a well-considered hiring strategy based on your business's short-term and long-term goals.

■ Know the difference between: "must-haves," "should-haves," and "nice-to-haves."

■ Employee turnover can be a bigger force behind your hiring needs than the creation of new positions.

■ In today's job marketplace, pay and security, while still important, are losing ground to lifestyle compensations.

■ Don't just react: Prepare for your future needs so that when the unexpected occurs, you won't panic or be pressed for time.

Creating a Job Description

Chapter 6

A s you found in the previous chapter, if you do not have a plan for where you want to go, it's easy to get lost. In the same way, if you do not fully understand the position you are hiring for, then how can you hope to hire the best person for the job? A lack of specificity is really symptomatic of something much more critical: namely, the absence of having thought through your needs. In the hiring process, one of the places where fuzzy thinking is most common and most harmful is in job descriptions. This chapter will give you the tools for creating effective, winning job descriptions—your road map to intelligent hiring.

My first job out of graduate school was with a public relations firm. I was hired as a copywriter, which is a common position in many public relations agencies, but was a first for this one. The owner thought it was a good idea to have a copywriter on staff, but what became readily clear was

Watch Out!
If you cannot succinctly describe to the job candidate what the job entails, go back and do some more homework. You are not ready to hire until you have fully thought out what you want the person to do.

that no one had thought about what the copywriter was supposed to do.

I was assigned to a man whose responsibilities included writing and producing publicity for various major museum exhibitions. Some of this publicity was quite elaborate, including fancy brochures and study guides for schools to use in conjunction with class trips to the exhibits. Several weeks passed, but I was never asked to assist in these projects. Finally, I asked when I might help, and my supervisor told me he wrote the material with his girlfriend (not a company employee) during several all-nighters, so he didn't need me. As a result, I walked around the company's offices like a beggar looking for work, asking people if they needed something written. After two months, it became clear that the company had no particular use for me, so, with two weeks' severance pay, I left.

I don't think my experience was unusual. Many times we think we need someone, hire them, and only then think through what we want that person to do. If you've ever left a job interview having a hazy notion of what the job entailed, then chances are you just experienced talking to a manager who had little idea what he was hiring for.

Without detailed, well-thought-out job descriptions, you reduce the hiring process to a hit-or-miss exercise. You might get lucky, but chances are much better you will hire someone who cannot do what you need. Even if the new hire is quite capable, you can't take full advantage of her skills until you have decided what you want her to do.

Why you need job descriptions

It is said that most employees have never seen a written description of their job, while those who have often find them incomplete or out of date. Job descriptions are often lacking in one way or another, and even companies with detailed job descriptions usually do not write them for all of their positions.

Perhaps well-conceived and detailed job descriptions are rare because the effort is time-consuming. The task also requires a considerable amount of thought to do well because it requires that the owner, manager, or human resources person think through the needs of the department or company, consider how individuals interact within the organization, plan and organize the department or company, and commit to giving certain individuals specific responsibilities. There's potential here for conflict and turf battles. Some managers prefer to avoid strife by not spelling out specific responsibilities.

The lack of job descriptions is not always due to laziness or fear of conflict. Sometimes companies grow so rapidly that their managers don't have time (or at least think they don't have time) to sit down and think through their personnel needs. Many companies react to situations, rather than plan their futures. One reason we spent the last chapter discussing how to create a hiring strategy was to avoid feeling so pressed for time and reactive that you cannot do what is needed for good hiring. Job descriptions, after all, are integral to a sound hiring strategy.

Companies with high employee turnover also frequently lack job descriptions—a double problem. No one seems to know precisely what the previous worker's job was, or the person before that. There's no "institutional memory," so as time goes on it becomes harder and harder to define existing

Unofficially...
Defining a job's parameters is not easy—witness the number of major corporations that have hired expensive talent, only to discover they made a mistake. Two recent examples are the (former) CEOs of Apple Computer and AT&T, who lasted only a short time before being canned. It's not just the small and inexperienced businesses that don't know what they want.

jobs, and less likely that any descriptions will be written.

Benefits of well-designed job descriptions

Taking the time to create well-defined job descriptions will be well worth the effort because they:

- Provide the criteria you need to define what skills, education, and experience a good candidate should have.

- Identify the type of worker you need, such as temporary, full-time, or independent contractor.

- Help you decide where to look for candidates and where to advertise the job.

- Create the most effective marketing strategy for finding the candidates who best fit your needs.

- Provide critical information for marketing material, such as want ads for the job.

- Give you a feel for how hard it will be to find a suitable candidate, based on the job's responsibilities and demands.

- Help you identify the best job candidates, and weed out unsuitable applicants.

- Explain the job to applicants so they know what to expect when they are hired, and understand the job better and quicker once they begin work.

- Minimize employee turnover because the job candidate knows up front what is expected.

- Clarify interrelationships between a company's positions and functions (possibly supplemented with an organizational chart), thus minimizing likelihood of turf battles.

- Define reporting relationships and establish lines of communication and promotions.

- Anticipate training needs, as when there is a gap between an employee's training or experience and the requisite skills defined in the job description.

- Provide a basis of comparison for positions at other companies, which helps you set reasonable and effective salary ranges.

- Provide a means for measuring performance: A definite standard by which the employee's work can be evaluated makes evaluation simpler and more accurate.

- Minimize potential for litigation. Clearly defined duties reduce the likelihood of legal conflict over discrimination claims or wrongful discharge, and they protect your company by serving as objective evidence that the employee has been deficient on the job.

These are among the primary benefits of having clearly defined job descriptions, particularly as they pertain to individual employees. In addition, job descriptions can be used to benefit the business itself in structural, organizational ways, such as:

- *Revise the organization's structure when needed:* Job descriptions can be tools to analyze an organizational chart and reveal weaknesses, such as functions for which few or none have responsibility, while other operational areas are divided among too many people.

- *Review current practices:* Because job descriptions are detailed statements about what goes on in a company, they are an effective means for reviewing how work flows from one department to another and how rational the company's lines of communication are.

- *Planning:* By periodically reviewing job descriptions, management can monitor changes in the responsibilities of employees and make changes when needed, such as upgrading compensation or adding new positions when responsibilities increase significantly.

- *Help the organization change as its environment changes:* For example, if the company wants to explore electronic commerce before making a major commitment, the job description can be used to start the e-commerce ball rolling within the information technology department and then, if the project works out, a new job description can direct the project to another department, such as marketing.

Preparing to create job descriptions

While almost everyone thinks that some written job descriptions are necessary, some believe that too much detail is detrimental because spelling out every little activity restricts options for meeting changing company needs. This is a reasonable concern.

Suppose, for instance, that your marketing manager's duties are spelled out in great detail: responsible for developing, writing, and placing all print, radio, and television advertisements. But what if the job description was written before the Internet became popular? If your marketing person thinks that the Internet is not her responsibility because it is more technical than promotional—and it's not spelled out in her job description—then your business could suffer until the situation is resolved.

The job description must match the actual job—one of the reasons why a definition requires careful consideration. Some descriptions should be confining, while others may need to be flexible, or even liberating. Supervisors, for example, need flexibility because they manage people, and people are unpredictable and often must be accommodated individually. Someone who runs a piece of machinery, on the other hand, will likely benefit from a job description that is fairly limited.

When to write job descriptions

Don't limit new job descriptions only to new job positions. When someone leaves a position, take the opportunity to rethink and possibly redefine the position. And sometimes a position should be restructured while the employee is still in it. I knew someone who was in a marketing and public-relations position for several years. When she took that job, its responsibilities included writing press releases and placing ads. About a year after she started, she was sent to a training course on telemarketing, and over the next several years she developed the telemarketing function until it became a major marketing medium for the organization. As the telemarketing function grew, her original responsibilities continued, and the demands of her job became increasingly unmanageable. Some responsibilities were shifted around, but not in a well-thought-out way. When she left her job, the department decided it was a good time to redesign her position and others in the department. Her replacement had the telemarketing responsibilities but fewer of the other responsibilities, which were spread among other employees in a well-designed, rational way.

Companies are not static organisms. They evolve in response to internal changes (such as growth, revolving personnel, new priorities) and external factors (including competition, technological innovations, and changes in the economy). Likewise, as job responsibilities and needs evolve, so too should job descriptions adjust accordingly.

When big changes are in motion, do not make the common mistake of waiting until an employee leaves before reviewing the job description. The marketing department mentioned above would have done better by reviewing its job descriptions once telemarketing became a major responsibility. Some feathers may be ruffled among the well-entrenched when you start redefining jobs, but the benefits of writing job descriptions can easily outweigh the costs.

Defining the parameters

Job descriptions are to be used as a well-defined tool for establishing responsibilities, but they should also set boundaries. People who are new at writing job descriptions have a tendency to make them into "wish lists" or "kitchen sinks," where all manner of potential or desirable tasks and duties are thrown in along with the job's essential functions. I'll explain how you can keep the description focused, and I'll give warnings about temptations to watch out for, such as "job-description creep."

Job descriptions should be focused and realistic

Sometimes job descriptions look more like wish lists than serious business objectives. The *San Francisco Examiner* printed a winery's ad seeking a point-of-sale assistant who could process POS orders:

> Maintain departmental standards and procedures . . . work flexible shifts . . . have at least one year of office/shipping and receiving experience . . . able to sit/stand for a minimum of 7–8 hours per day, able to lift and carry 50 pounds . . . able to read, understand and follow written and verbal instructions in English . . . able to be trained in forklift operations, and must be proficient in mainframe and PC computer systems.

Be proficient in mainframe and PC computer systems, operate a forklift, follow instructions in English, do heavy lifting . . . maybe this winery found its ideal employee, but it's hard to imagine there is even one worker who has all of these attributes simultaneously, especially the computer expertise.

Here's an ad from the *New York Times* for a marketing coordinator at a software company:

> Responsibilities include sending out press releases and fostering relationships with key media, monitoring PR opportunities within North and South America, organizing conferences, trade shows and customer events, producing and coordinating translations of sales collateral for use in Latin America. The ideal candidate should have 1–3 years of experience in marketing communications . . . superior proficiency with computers . . . be experienced in creation of Web pages utilizing HTML . . . have a strong desire to succeed. Experience in the market research industry, or Spanish/Portugese fluency a plus.

This business wants someone who is everything from multilingual to a trade-show coordinator to a webmaster, with some market research, press relations, and writing ability thrown in. Again, such a person might exist, but it seems the company hasn't set priorities. Instead, it has defined its job opening as a wish list of everything it could ever hope the person can do. It is difficult to distinguish here between the "must-haves" and "nice-to-haves." A potential job candidate would not be able to tell from the ad what really counts, and whoever is hired will probably have trouble figuring out where the emphasis lies. Any business so all-demanding in a help-wanted ad would have difficulty attracting applicants who would otherwise be successful in the role, but are intimidated or put off by the "wish list."

By being realistic up front, you can create a job description (and subsequent want ads) that are attainable, focused, and designed to maximize the benefits to your company.

Here are two reality checks you might run against your job descriptions:

- Would someone reading the job description know which responsibilities and tasks are most important, which are less important, and which are merely wishful thinking? If there's any ambiguity about the job's main focus, then you need to sharpen the description.

- Write out each task you include in the job description (these are always included in the job description but not as frequently in want ads). Next to each task, write how long it takes to accomplish. If your employees typically work 40 hours a week, recognize that meetings and other activities take up time, so the actual productive hours usually do not add up to a full 40 hours. If the total is far from 40 hours, you know the job as designed is not going to work out (unless you expect the person to put in considerable overtime, in which case the employee should be informed during the hiring process— and you should budget for it).

Be careful not to break any Equal Employment Opportunity Commission regulations. This means you should not ask about religion or ethnic background, gender, age, marital status, criminal past. (See Chapter 2.)

Beware of "job-description creep"

Another aspect to consider is what I call job-description creep. Responsibilities, areas of influence, objectives, skill requirements, duties, working conditions, relationships between workers, lines of communication—all can evolve over time in unintended ways and without any thought or plan. What made sense when the job description was written may not make much sense today.

A talented teacher I knew was hired to teach the academic side of theater—literature, criticism, and theater history—but what he really wanted was to direct. He started directing shows here and there in the community. The theater department let him direct one of its productions, and he kept pressing to direct more. Then he went into a nearby city and began finding directing work there among small professional theaters. He was still teaching, but it was obvious that his interests were elsewhere.

When he came up for tenure, he was turned down. The department had hired an academic, not a director, so it used the tenure process to force him out. Interestingly, he was able to quickly get another teaching position—as the head of the directing program at a major university. He had successfully transformed himself from an academic to a working director, which helped him in the open market, but was not of much value to his original employer.

Job-description creep is often driven by personal interests, as with the teacher-turned-director. It is common for job duties and responsibilities to change over time simply because the person in the job has certain likes and dislikes, strengths and weaknesses, and chooses to redefine the job accordingly. It does not happen all at once, nor does it necessarily occur according to any plan. And, as we saw in the previous chapter, when things happen without a plan, the likelihood of undesirable results increases. The employee is enjoying his newly defined responsibilities and duties to his employer's disadvantage.

Planning the job description

Who is responsible for writing your job descriptions? If your company is large enough to have a human resources department, then this task naturally falls to someone there, sometimes called a job analyst, with input from departmental managers and the person in the position itself.

There are two ways to deal with writing job descriptions: Assign the task to the individual responsible for personnel administration in your company, or outsource the job to someone outside the organization.

In-house or outsource?

Smaller businesses would generally do well to keep the responsibility for creating job descriptions in-house. Typically, in a small business, lines of communication and responsibility, the interaction of employees, the job responsibilities, and the needs of the business are fairly obvious. An experienced executive who is willing to think through the needs of the organization should be able to do a quick, effective job. When things are complex, as in a large organization with myriad lines of communication, then it may be worthwhile to hire a professional consultant.

But there are a few possible drawbacks to consider. Objectivity may be lacking, there may not be time for an employee to write a job description properly, or the employee may not know how to evaluate a position and write a description.

Pros and cons of in-house writing

There are certain benefits to assigning a staff member to create job descriptions. An insider can pick up the nuances of the job, is familiar with the lines of communication in the company, understands the organization's values and culture, knows the history of the job firsthand, and knows the shortcomings in previous job descriptions (or, if there was no description, what is needed). No additional expenses are incurred when the description is written by someone already on the payroll.

Pros and cons of outsourcing

The advantages of hiring a professional consultant include experience and a more objective point of view. A professional employment consultant will know what questions to ask, what to look for, the legal pitfalls, and how to structure the description so that it addresses your needs and concerns. This arrangement also frees your employees to concentrate on their jobs.

Outside consultants, however, can be quite expensive. Depending on the complexity of the task, an outside expert may charge hundreds or even thousands of dollars. Also, outsiders do not know your business as well as you and your employees do. It will take them a while to see the big picture and the details, and even then they may miss

Watch Out!
Do not delegate responsibility for writing job descriptions to a clerical or junior employee. They may give input, naturally, but this is too important a task to leave to the lower-level employees. The business owner, senior executive, or department head should have primary responsibility for the final shape of job descriptions.

important nuances. Further, your employees may feel that they have lost some control because something that affects them is now being driven by an outsider.

Researching the job description

How do you know what to include in a job description? You must do your homework. The two most useful researching techniques are:

- *Conducting interviews:* Whether the job currently exists or is to be newly created, interviews are probably the best way to learn about a job. Talk to the person currently in the job. If it's a new position, talk to those who will be affected by the new employee, and ask what responsibilities and tasks they want the new position to include. Always interview colleagues, direct supervisors, subordinates, and even customers.

- *Observing performance:* For a position that already exists, watch what the employee does and find out how much time the major tasks require. Pay particular attention to any responsibilities that may have crept into the job since you last gave it a close look. You may be surprised at the number of tasks and the time involved that you were unaware of, or rarely thought about. These kinds of activities—which can include meetings, tasks not anticipated when the job was first created, and duties moved to one position from another—can be important and time-consuming, and they must be taken into account in the job description.

Other techniques for researching a position include asking the current jobholder to keep a log of all of her activities, how long these activities take, and whom she frequently communicates and interacts with. You might even use a questionnaire to learn more about a job.

Determining salary

It is while researching the job description, while scouting what comparable companies expect of similar positions, that you can explore the range of pay the position brings. You may be quite certain of the salary you intend to offer, but you're in a better position all around if you know what the competition is paying. This information will be valuable later on when you are advertising to fill an opening, interviewing, and making an offer. You don't operate in a vacuum for customers, and the same holds true for employees. Especially in today's market, you are likely to be competing with other employers for a good candidate's services. How do you find out what others are paying?

There are several ways to learn what the market rate is. One way is by checking the classifieds. Not all list salaries, though many list pay ranges. If you find an ad for a position similar to one you want to fill, call the employer and see if you can get an idea of what the job pays. Another good source is your professional or trade association; it probably does surveys and can tell you what various jobs are paying in different parts of the country.

Planning for a new position

If you are going to be hiring for a newly created position, think through exactly what the job will entail. Consider the purpose of the new position. This is more difficult than with an existing job, where you can see what the job entails and make

Bright Idea
Some companies are now using the technique called benchmarking when creating job descriptions. They look at the skills, attitudes, traits, and other attributes of those who are the top performers currently in the job and then use these as the criteria for hiring new employees. The idea is to have your new employees emulate the winners currently on your staff. Criteria should be consistent and applied fairly.

adjustments from that foundation. Creating a new position requires forethought.

The first thing to do is consider what you hope to achieve by creating this position. Businesses generally hire for the following reasons:

- Growth of the company and the consequent need to keep up with the increased work load

- Need for new skills, due to changes in the marketplace or technology, or the desire to move into new markets

- Replacement of employees who quit

- Replacement of employees who are fired

- Replacement of employees who move to another position within the company

If someone is already performing tasks the new employee will perform, consider how to divide and delegate the tasks. If new tasks and responsibilities will come with the new position, will the new employee get all of them, or will some be done by current employees?

Think about whether you really need a full-time, permanent employee. I will discuss alternatives to full-time employees in Chapter 7, but keep in mind that when planning for a new position, your options include part-time workers, temporary employees, independent contractors, and paid and nonpaid interns.

What will be the goals of this position, and what is your time frame for achieving them? For instance, if you are opening a new geographic market and hiring a sales rep to service this new territory, how will you measure success? You may require the new employee to generate a certain number of sales dollars or open a specified number of new accounts, all within a certain time. You need to know goals such as these before you begin your hiring process, and the job prospect needs to know them during the process, too.

The job description

Here is a sample outline you can use for drafting a job description. The rest of this section describes the various sections and what type of information to include.

JOB DESCRIPTION OUTLINE

Overview: The Basics

Title

Department

Date job description written

Title of supervisor

Status of job (full-time, part-time, etc.)

Job Description

Goals of the job

General description

Principal duties

Minor duties

When, where, and how often job duties are performed

Other (less obvious, occasional, and hazardous aspects of the job, etc.)

Hiring Criteria and Skill Requirements

Skills, education, training, etc.

Credentials, licenses

Overview: the basics

First, give the job a title. "Sales representative for the New York City region," "service manager," "mortgage processor," "machine cleaner," "Lotus Notes administrator," "grants coordinator," and "copywriter" are some examples. A title helps keep functions distinct, positions the job in the corporate

Bright Idea
If you have a small business and need to hire just one employee, keep your job-description process simple. List all the tasks and responsibilities the job entails. Rank them. Follow this with the skills and experience the job applicant needs to complete these tasks. Focus on the top five or so most important skills. Finally, trust your common sense as to what you really need.

Timesaver
Job descriptions can change for unforeseeable reasons, but sometimes they change because they were unfocused in the first place. Keep a copy of each job description and each revision in a computer file or a loose-leaf notebook. Over time, this will enable you to quickly analyze how good your job descriptions have been.

hierarchy, and clarifies for job candidates and employees what the job entails.

Write the date you created the job description. Every time you revise the description, give it a date. Dating the description can help you keep straight what is the most recent job description and how long it has been since the description was last revised.

If your company is large enough that it is divided into departments, include in the description which department the job is in. Also include the title of the position that supervises the job. Note whether the job is full-time, temporary, part-time or has another classification.

The description

Give a general description of the job. As an example, the following might describe a position of credit checker for a factor, bank, or other credit-oriented business:

> This job's purpose is to check the creditworthiness of individuals or institutions seeking credit with our firm. Responsibilities include: conducting background checks of the company applying for credit that include, but are not limited to, banks, suppliers, customers, accountants, and other credit-granting organizations. The applicant's financial statements must be obtained and subjected to various financial analyses, as specified by the employee's supervisor. The employee is responsible for thoroughly checking the credit history and worthiness of the applicant in a timely manner so that the supervisor has enough accurate information to determine whether to grant credit. The employee will conduct at least 10 background credit checks per work week. The work week runs Monday through Friday, 9:00 a.m. to 5:00 p.m., with an hour for lunch.

Include in your job description a list of duties the employee must perform. In the above credit-checker position, for example, this might include doing the following for each credit applicant:

- Calling the applicant's bank and asking for a credit reference

- Calling the applicant's accountant and asking for financial statements and a credit reference

- Calling others who have granted the applicant credit and getting credit references

- Calling suppliers of the applicant and getting credit references

- Calculating various ratios and other financial calculations

- Writing up a report that summarizes the findings of this credit background check

If the company is large enough, this job might deal exclusively with a particular industry, such as garments or furniture. You might want to include a further responsibility, such as helping credit checkers in other departments when they have more work than they can handle. The job description should rank the duties in order of importance. The six listed above might have about equal importance, while the one just mentioned, helping other checkers, would have less importance and should be noted as such.

Hiring criteria and skill requirements

List all hiring criteria you will use to evaluate candidates, such as experience, skills, and knowledge. And include all requirements the person must have, such as licenses or certifications.

Include any physical, educational, experience, technical skills that are required. In the want ad for a point-of-sale assistant above, it was mentioned that the person would have to stand/sit for a minimum

Bright Idea
When writing a job description, have an audience unfamiliar with the job review your draft, even if it describes an existing job. If you can adequately explain the job to the uninitiated, chances are you have done a good job of thinking through the position's functions. After writing the description or specification, have someone read it to check your thinking and spot any errors or omissions—including misspellings!

of seven to eight hours a day. This type of specification needs to be in the job description. Knowledge of specific programming languages, such as HTML, should be one of the technical skills included in this job's description.

Define clearly the employee's lines of communication, reporting channels, and expected contacts with others, both inside and outside the organization. This is, in effect, defining the position within the company's organizational chart.

The goals of the job should be spelled out. This may be more difficult than you think. For example, you may want a sales manager who will open a new territory by creating a new sales department to serve that territory. Typically, sales goals are set in terms of dollars of sales, quantity of items sold, market penetration, etc. But a manager really has a different set of goals. You may want a manager's main goals to be creating and nurturing a dynamic department that serves the company's strategy of growth through market expansion. Such a person would likely have very different skills from a person whose goals are defined in terms of sales dollars or volume of product sold.

What not to put in the job description

While comprehensiveness is generally desirable, some things do not belong in a job description: anything that violates (or might violate) employment laws, such as references to age, sex, marital status, and race; religious affiliation; or sexual orientation, unless it is somehow a bona fide occupational qualification.

Also, don't include every single task or responsibility you can think of. That just deflects and

Moneysaver
A comprehensive source of information about job titles and job descriptions is the *Dictionary of Occupational Titles,* published by the Employment and Training Administration of the U.S. Department of Labor. The ETA is establishing a Web site, called O*Net, that includes the information in the *Dictionary* and more. Its address is: www.doleta.gov/ programs/onet.

obscures what is really important. If a task or responsibility is likely to consume less than 5 percent or so of a person's time, leave it unsaid.

Do not include duties or responsibilities that are the preferences or strengths of the current job holder or a potential candidate, unless they are justified by the job. If you include extraneous duties and responsibilities, regardless of relevance, you may be serving an employee's whims at the expense of your business—and possibly eliminating potential future replacements. You run the risk of an employee focusing energies in an extraneous direction, and, if you have approved the change in direction in the job description, you might have trouble if you fire him.

Just the facts

- The clearer your job descriptions, the stronger your competitiveness and bottom line.

- Use job descriptions to define what you really want and need—they can enhance not only your hiring but your entire business.

- Research before writing—job descriptions are too important to guess at.

- Don't make your job descriptions a wish list—be realistic.

- Job descriptions—and employees—need goals and priorities, not just lists of tasks.

Using Contract Workers

Chapter 7

The answer to your staffing needs may be the use of contract workers—including temporary and leased employees, and intern and co-op students—instead of hiring someone full-time. "Contract workers" is the generic term most often used in this chapter, but occasionally I'll use the synonyms "temporary," "temp," or "contractors" for variety. Don't let the terms confuse you—they all refer to workers who are either outsourced workers or self-employed independent contractors. This chapter explores some of the ways for you to use workable but less expensive alternatives to full-time workers, and I discuss the advantages and disadvantages of these workers and how best to manage them.

Contract employees

You may have heard of "The Kelly Girl," an advertising moniker created years ago by a temporary employment agency named Kelly Services. This image exemplifies for many business executives and

> **"**
> It is estimated that the temporary services business has grown more than 360 percent since 1982, and that 90 percent of employers currently employ temporary workers.
> —Courtney von Hippel, et al., "Temporary employment: can organizations and employees both win?" in *The Academy of Management Executive* (February 1997)
> **"**

owners what they think of contract employees: typically clerical or blue-collar workers with few skills, who for some reason may have difficulty retaining permanent employment.

In fact, contract employees come in all varieties and styles, from low-skilled folks hoping to eventually land a full-time job, to highly skilled workers who for a variety of personal reasons prefer to work on a temporary basis.

Recent Bureau of Labor Statistics data, according to *HR* magazine (February 1997), report that nearly 1 in 10 U.S. employees is employed in an alternative working arrangement. "In a typical corporation, conventional employees may make up about 60 percent of the workforce, with the remaining 40 percent divided among various types of alternative staffing."

The use of temporary workers has grown rapidly in the 1990s. Bruce Steinberg, spokesperson for the National Association of Temporary and Staffing Services, Alexandria, Virginia, says the number of professional temporaries supplied by staffing companies has quadrupled since 1991. As reported in an *HR* magazine excerpt of Phaedra Brotherton's book *The Contingent Workforce,* "In 1994, staffing companies paid out $1.2 billion in payroll to professional temporaries as compared to $335 million in 1991. Professional temporaries include accountants, auditors and chief financial officers as well as legal, sales and marketing, and middle and senior management professionals."

To give you an idea of how sophisticated the contract employment market has become, the healthcare industry has its own temporary agency industry called *Locum tenens* (Latin, "place holding"). Locum tenens agencies are temporary staffing agencies that provide nurses, physical and occupational thera-pists, and other healthcare workers, including physi-cians, to hospitals, clinics, and other healthcare providers on a temporary or contract basis. According to the head of a locum tenens firm, physicians want temporary work for a variety of rea-sons, especially when:

- They have just finished their residencies and are interested in temporary employment because it allows them to try different job situa-tions and geographic locations before deciding where to settle down permanently.

- They are in a period of transition. They want a change, and they need a job until they line up something permanent.

- They want to "semi-retire." These physicians are at a point in their lives where they want to cut back their workload while not giving up their profession entirely. Also, temp work provides these physicians with the stimulation of work-ing in new locations and in different clinical settings.

While your business may not need to hire physi-cians, this example shows that contract workers are not at all limited to clerical or blue-collar positions. Business executives, too, are finding temporary situ-ations desirable. A recent article in a computer mag-azine noted that temp firms were now supplying corporate America with chief information officers on a temporary basis, particularly surprising in that the CIO is among today's most demanding corpo-rate positions because of technology's costs, com-plexity, and rapid change. A business magazine has reported that some companies are even hiring tem-porary CEOs.

It is important to realize that temporary workers can be highly skilled and motivated, and not simply a last resort to use when you either cannot find someone better or lack the time to do a proper job of hiring. If, instead of thinking of temporary workers as people who "can't hold a steady job," you regard them as able workers who can help you out "in a pinch," you'll make much more successful use of them. Recognize that not only can temps be very talented, but (as you'll see in some anecdotes below), they are often excellent prospects for productive full-time work.

I know of a woman who, after receiving a master's degree in acting, followed her dream to New York, did some performing, and paid the rent by taking temporary jobs. She was bright, capable, energetic, and an excellent worker. At one job, a major advertising agency, she was asked to stay on full-time. She had not been looking for full-time work, but she surprised herself by finding that she liked the world of advertising, so when the job offer was made, she took it and hasn't looked back since. Her career has included highly responsible positions at several of the world's leading advertising agencies. Today she works in a management position involved in Citibank's Internet marketing efforts.

Stories like this abound. As reported in *U.S. News & World Report* (October 27, 1997), American Precision Plastics in Colorado, which produces plastic dishes and flatware for hospitals, used temps for only 10 percent of its factory labor in 1994. Today 90 percent of its 180 plant workers are temporary, hired from a staffing service. I'll talk later about where to find employees, but it is worth keeping in mind here that temp workers can be an excellent source of labor, both temporary and permanent.

When contract workers make sense

Not every company or situation is conducive to using contract workers, but some situations in which contract workers can be useful include the following:

- Seasonal businesses whose labor demands vary considerably during the course of the year.

- Companies that have received a large contract that will last a limited amount of time. This is not permanent, just temporary business.

- Companies whose industry is cyclical, such as construction.

- Companies that face a shortage of labor because a large contingent of workers will be out as a result of vacations.

- Businesses undergoing considerable growth which management is not yet certain will be sustainable and therefore does not want to commit to hiring full-time workers.

- When a company has purchased an expensive piece of equipment and wants to make the most of it in the short term.

- Businesses with customers who frequently but unpredictably request rush jobs.

- When the company is starting a major initiative, such as the introduction of a new product or other marketing campaign, and needs additional staff to get the initiative up and running.

- When there's a natural ebb and flow to a business, such as the periodic mailing of catalogs, which generate a short-term surge in business.

Unofficially...
Although temporary staffing agencies have been around for decades, at no time have businesses used temporary and contract workers more than today. As a result, being a temporary worker is more socially acceptable than ever, which has helped attract those with better skills and training to temporary work.

- When a company has a special project that needs staffing, such as a trade show or a one-time maintenance project.

- When permanent workers are having to perform a lot of overtime work, which is billed at time-and-a-half or more; temporary workers can be less expensive than full-timers in this situation.

- When an organization has budget constraints in place for permanent hires. Often, a department may have discretionary funds it can use to hire workers on a temporary basis but needs difficult-to-get authorization when adding a permanent employee.

The advantages and disadvantages of using contract workers

There are some advantages and disadvantages to using contract workers that you should consider as you determine whether or not they are suitable for your situation.

Advantages

Temporary workers can bring a number of benefits to your company, including:

- *Extra hands, quickly:* You need not spend a great deal of time, money, or effort to find extra help if you are willing to use the services of a temporary agency. (Finding highly skilled workers, however, may take longer.)

- *Flexibility:* Of all the reasons for using temporary employees, flexibility is among the most important. By relying on temps, you can adjust your labor force to meet changing needs.

- *Less Costly:* Temporary workers are costly on a per-hour or per-day basis because you must cover both their salary and the agency's costs and profits. Yet, temporary workers can still save you money because you don't pay them benefits; you pay for these employees only when you need them; and they may not earn as much per hour as do permanent workers. Further, they may be already trained, which cuts your education and training expenses.

- *Lower legal risks:* Documentation of compliance with labor protection laws may become the responsibility of the agency from which you get the temporary workers. And the likelihood of being subject to wrongful termination suits when dismissing temporary employees is lessened compared with permanent workers.

- *Reduced administrative demands and costs:* Your paperwork, for example, will probably be less.

- *Reduced recruitment costs:* You don't have to pay for advertisements and your own recruiters.

- *Expertise:* A highly skilled temporary worker can bring needed skills and expertise to your organization. For example, if you are setting up a direct-mail division, you might want to beef up your internal expertise by hiring someone experienced in direct mail to instruct your staff.

- *Wage level vis-à-vis permanent workers:* If your company pays above-market wages, temp workers may be available at lower wages, thus saving you money while allowing you to sustain your image as a high-paying employer. Conversely, if you have a function that requires high wages, hiring a permanent worker at the high wage level might increase pressure to boost the wages of your other full-time workers. You can pay temporary workers a higher wage without having

> **❝**
> The most frequently cited reason for using temporary employees is to reduce wage and benefit costs.
> —Courtney von Hippel, et al., "Temporary employment: can organizations and employees both win?" in *The Academy of Management Executive* (Feb. 1997)
> **❞**

your permanent workers complain because temporary help can be thought of as having special skills as well as being employed for only a limited time.

- *Avoid layoffs and firings:* By using temps, you avoid the costs, time, and morale-busting that comes with laying off employees.

Disadvantages

It has been estimated that the employer pays the employment agency 30 to 60 percent over what the worker earns. That covers the agency's recruitment costs, administrative expenses, and profits, as well as the worker's payroll taxes, unemployment insurance, and even vacation; so it's not that the agency is ripping you off when it charges what seems a high per-hour or per-day rate. But you should recognize that you may be paying more for a temp than if you had directly contracted with the temp yourself.

Companies with high employee turnover, or ones that tend not to make long-term commitments to permanent employees, will not benefit from contract workers because they tend to cost more per hour than permanent employees, especially if an agency is involved and must be paid a fee. Fast-food restaurants, for example, have very high turnover rates, and it probably would not make sense to hire temporary workers via an agency unless the restaurant has an unexpected, temporary surge in business.

Among the disadvantages of using contract workers to consider are these:

- *Hurt morale:* Contract workers may hurt the morale of your permanent workforce. This is especially likely if the temps reduce the amount of overtime work available to your permanent workers.

- *Disruptive:* The use of temporary workers can sometimes be disruptive to the maintenance of a smoothly operating team. When workers need to function as closely meshed teams, new players moving in and out for short periods can hurt productivity and efficiency.

- *Unfamiliarity with corporate culture:* Temporary workers often don't know an organization's business, people, or culture, nor how it functions. This can make a difference if the job is complex and requires considerable interaction with others in the organization. Good management of contract workers can help shorten the learning curve—a subject I will discuss later in this chapter.

- *Less control:* Employer has less control over temps than permanents. They generally do not expect to be with you for long, and therefore may not be as responsive as you might want.

- *Quality:* The quality of temporary workers may be lower than that of permanent ones.

Are contract workers right for your business?

When determining whether to use contract workers, there are many variables to consider, mostly particular to your business and situation. One important question is how long "permanent" hires tend to stay in a given job. If their "staying time" is three to six months, it may be time to consider hiring permanent ones. These and other questions you will have to discern for yourself.

Timesaver
You can save time by first checking with the U.S. Department of Labor regarding labor regulations and other legal and governmental issues affecting workers. Go to the Department's Web site for the fastest service: www.dol.gov.

The following questions address some of the more common variables to consider:

- *Is my need for more workers temporary or permanent?* If temporary, then contract workers make sense. If permanent, consider hiring full-time, permanent workers.

- *Can my need for more workers be satisfied in some way other than by hiring contract or permanent workers?* If you can satisfy your need for more workers through means other than hiring new employees, it is generally best to add temporary workers or ask your existing workforce to work overtime.

- *Is it important to me and my employees to have a stable workforce?* Not every business situation requires a stable workforce where employees get to know how to work with one another and develop a camaraderie, but sometimes these qualities are vital. If they are important, contract workers may do more harm than good.

- *Is employee turnover acceptable?* If your permanent workforce tends to turn over frequently, say every few months on average, then it probably does not make sense to hire contract workers, unless you get into a real pinch, as when several workers are on vacation at the same time.

- *Do I need expertise for only a limited time?* Expertise is often expensive. If you need it and cannot afford to hire it permanently, or only need it for a limited time, contract workers can prove highly cost-effective.

- *Is my demand for workers stable or variable?* If you have a seasonal business, you probably already have an equivalent of a contingent workforce. If you cannot predict the amount of business you are likely to have because demand is volatile, go with contract workers, and take on permanent workers only when you are reasonably certain you will need them permanently.

Planning for the use of contract workers

In Chapter 5 I discuss the uses of a hiring plan as it relates to permanent employees. But planning is no less important for contract workers. If you try getting contract workers without planning, you may well end up with workers who are unsuitable, unmotivated, expensive—or none at all.

What are the job requirements?

Consider the requirements and the purpose of the job. The job description must make clear why the position is a temporary job. You need to know what skills and experience the contract worker will need and what will be the responsibilities of that person. Look at the type of work you need done, the volume, production schedule demands, and any special skills. This knowledge will help you anticipate your temporary staffing needs.

Having the contract worker's job well defined helps the employment agency find the right person. It also is critical when dealing with contract workers because what you pay for them is usually tied directly to their qualifications and experience— perhaps even more so than with permanent workers. (Employment agencies tend to set up a pay scale based on the employee's skills, education, and background in a more formalized way than one finds in the general workplace.)

You might be tempted to lower the qualifications of the position in order to save money. Generally,

Bright Idea
You generally want to match your borrowing needs to the type of debt you use. Likewise, if you have a long-term need for workers, you generally want permanent employees, whereas temporary needs are better met by short-term, contract workers.

this is short-sighted. Bringing someone on board who cannot do the job well can cost you far more in poor productivity than what you save in wages.

How long will the job last?

Determine how long you will want the employee. Think through exactly what the employee will be used for and what the project or job requires today and in the future. If you do not know approximately how long you will need the employee, you may find the employee gone before the work is finished, and then you'll have to start over. Plan your needs to avoid being left shorthanded at a critical time.

Who will supervise and train the employee?

Before a contract worker is taken on, be certain you have set up a reporting structure and have determined who is responsible for supervision, who will train the newcomer, and what kind of orientation program will be provided. Just because someone is a temp doesn't mean they don't need to know about your company, especially if they will be employed for a period of weeks or months. Have a short orientation program set up so that all employees receive some orientation training.

The temp agency

Your source for temporary employees starts with a temporary agency. Every city has them and, in fact, some of the larger ones, such as Manpower, claim to be among the largest employers in the nation. Look under "Employment Agencies" in your local Yellow Pages.

Think of a temporary agency much as you would your lawyer or accountant. You work best with these professionals when you develop a personal relationship with them. They get to know your needs, and

Moneysaver
Unless you know your temporary agency well and trust its judgment, do not leave the hiring decision entirely to the agency. You can get a big payoff on the time you spend interviewing prospective temps, especially for those hired for longer-term projects.

you get to know them and what they can do for you. A good temporary agency may even be able to anticipate your needs and plan to meet them.

Generally, you will work with one person at the agency with whom you can develop a professional relationship. The Nordstrom department store chain has built a thriving business, in part, because it understands customer service. The salespeople get to know their better customers and call or send postcards when a suitable article of clothing or other item comes into the store, and customers appreciate this.

You want an agency that handles your needs in the same way (this applies to agencies you use for both temporary and permanent workers). If it learns of a person who is ideal for you, your rep should call and let you know this person is available. If the agency believes there will soon be a shortage of the type of workers you need, it should notify you. This level of customer service is not always available, but if you work closely with a competent agency, you should be able to get very good customer service.

Selecting a temporary employment agency

Here's how to choose a temporary agency:

- Ask the agency for customer references, and check them carefully. Try to get references from companies in your industry. (If you own a retail store, you're probably better off not signing with an agency whose strength is with high-tech temps.)

- Meet in person with an executive of the firm. Explain your needs and goals. If you will be working on a regular basis with a lower-level employee, be sure to speak with that person, too. You want to build a personal rapport with

Moneysaver
Don't rely on lots of employment agencies, whether temporary or permanent. Have two—one primary and one as a backup. With a primary agency, you can get to know its strengths and weaknesses, while the agency gets to know your needs and preferences. If you give them a lot of business, you may be able to negotiate a better rate. You need a backup in case your primary agency can't get you the people you require.

Moneysaver
You can hold
down costs of
contract workers
by proper plan-
ning, including
using the same
budgeting and
tracking
processes you
use for other
expenses. By
having a budget
for these
employees, you
reduce the risk
that their costs
can run out of
control.

the agency, and for this you need to meet the people at the agency face to face.

■ Check out with your local chamber of commerce the reputation of the agency. Ask professionals you know, such as lawyers and accountants, if they know anything about the agency. Ask if they can recommend an agency to you.

■ How interested is the agency in learning your needs? If the agency shows little interest in learning about you and your company, it is probably not worth your while.

■ Ask how the agency recruits workers. Does it seek out college students? Does it use your state's unemployment department's database? Does it advertise in local newspapers? Which ones? Does it use the Internet?

■ Does the agency carry workers' compensation insurance for the temps it sends out? What are its limits?

■ Does the agency have experience with your type of business and your needs?

■ What kinds of benefits, if any, does the agency extend its contract workers?

■ Does the agency have performance criteria for certain skills and standards? What are these? How do they match up with your needs?

■ Does the agency make an effort to keep its work-ers coming back, or does the roster of temps turn over a great deal? It helps if workers stick with an agency, since this makes it easier for the agency to quickly get workers it knows are good. Plus, you may find temporary workers you want to hire back at later times, so you want them to stay with the agency.

- Does the agency make any attempt to train its temps and keep them up to date? This is especially important in types of business characterized by rapid change. For instance, when a new version of a major spreadsheet or word processing program comes out, does the agency upgrade its workers? Has the agency familiarized its workers with e-mail and the Internet?

- What kinds of screenings and tests does it do? If the agency claims that certain prospects are knowledgeable in various spreadsheet programs, how do they know? What kinds of tests do they put prospects through?

- What kind of guarantee does the agency provide? (A guarantee might be that the employee stays with your company a minimum of three months or part or all of the fee is refunded.) Does the agency have a guarantee or refund policy concerning workers who do not work out? If so, what are the terms?

- You want an agency that is financially stable. Check the financial viability of the agency. Ask for a financial statement. If it's a public company, read its annual report.

After hiring the agency, track how quickly the agency responds to your needs. What is its turn-around time on a search?

Leasing employees

Staff leasing companies, now often called professional employer organizations, take on the human resources management responsibilities for you. You can transfer your full-time employees to the leasing company which, in turn, leases these employees back to you. Everything essentially remains the same

Watch Out!
Use of contract workers is unlikely to be successful if you hire them under pressure. If you find yourself weeks behind schedule on a project, throwing people at the problem may do more harm than good—especially considering the time that may be required to brief and train them on the work needed. Plan ahead to make the most of contract workers.

except that the leasing company handles all the paperwork, pays the salaries and benefits, files the taxes due and otherwise handles all the bookkeeping and human resource management issues that you now handle.

Leasing workers is not for everyone, so you should carefully consider the following advantages and disadvantages. For example, the initial hassles and the loss of control may make it not worthwhile, and the promised benefits may not materialize. However, if you find you have trouble competently staffing your human resources function, having professionals take over these duties is well worth your consideration.

Advantages

Here are three advantages that leasing workers can offer to your company.

- *Saves money.* By taking on your employees as theirs and by combining these employees with those of other employers, staff leasing companies can, at least in theory, save money on health and other insurance, workers' compensation, and other expenses because their pool of employees is larger. They can negotiate better terms than a single, relatively small employer—at least that's their claim. Because of these savings, leasing companies should be able to pass some of these lower costs to you, for your benefit. Check it out and compare what the leasing company offers you compared to your current costs.

- *Convenience.* By taking human-resource administration off your hands, you can concentrate on what you do best and that which is most important to you—running your business—

and leave the demands of personnel issues to others.

■ *A source of expertise.* The leasing company can help with personnel issues, such as assuring you are doing what is needed to protect yourself before you fire someone. Other legal and compliance concerns can be run by the leasing company. In effect, you are getting a consultant.

Disadvantages

Here are two disadvantages of leasing workers.

■ *Loss of control.* Perhaps the most significant disadvantage is the loss of some control. You are relying on the expertise and competency of others, rather than having these skills in-house.

■ *Layoffs.* You may have to lay off people, such as those in your human resources department and, since your workers are no longer your employees, they may be more tempted to look for new jobs than if they had remained under your employ. Layoffs—or the threat of layoffs—may also affect employee morale.

Interns and co-op students

Younger workers can be quite productive. Interns and co-op students can be good sources of these workers.

Interns

One way to hold down your labor costs is by using free labor. Who will work for free? Interns will. These are students or recent college graduates who are willing to work as interns for a variety of reasons, including:

■ They have not found a paid, full-time job, at least in the field they are interested in or with

> "
> From a student's point of view, if [an internship is] set up properly, it's not only a way to get an overview of the activity in a particular department or the company overall, but there's also an opportunity to do substantive work across a range of groups.
> —Mark Flanagan, executive vice president, Kurzweil Applied Intelligence Inc.
> "

the type of company or organization they want to work for.

- They need experience in the field of their choice, but they can't get a job without experience and can't get experience without a job.
- They have their eye on a particular position or company and want to use an internship as a way to get a foot in the door.
- They seek experience during the summer in a field of interest.

In recent years, internships have become quite widespread and accepted. There is, admittedly, a degree of desperateness to those willing to be interns, especially if they have already graduated from college. But they are willing to work for nothing—or below market wages—because of the benefits listed above.

Kurzweil Applied Intelligence, a software company in Waltham, Massachusetts, uses internships to fill various needs and find potential full-time positions. Mark Flanagan, executive vice president, did an internship himself when he was in college, which led to his being hired by the company. He's a firm believer in internships, now that he's a manager. One college intern who worked for Flanagan during the student's last two summers in college did market research, tested competitors' products, and investigated what Kurzweil might want to include on its Web page. These were all valuable projects for the company. And, at the end of the day, Flanagan offered the student a job. Flanagan had seen the student in action and had helped train the student, so his risks in hiring this student were considerably less than if he hired someone he didn't know.

Contact the placement centers and alumni associations of colleges and universities in your area and let them know you are looking for interns. Be specific in what you want, such as the coursework you expect an intern to have had, as well as other training and any job experience. Let the college and university (and the intern) know exactly what type of work is available, what the intern will be doing, what he might learn, what responsibilities he will have and, if you know, what prospects there are for the intern to eventually be hired full-time.

Co-op students

Co-op or cooperative students are always paid, and sometimes get paid as much as regular employees, so do not confuse them with interns. Also, they are available through formal programs, which are operated by the colleges and universities which they attend.

Co-op education is a formal program set up by a college or university that combines work and education and is designed to give students both classroom and real-world, professional experience. Engineering, which is where co-op began, probably remains the academic field where the practice is most widely used. Over the years, though, it has become very broadly used in many academic departments.

Co-operative programs vary from school to school. For example, here is the calendar of a co-op education program which is fairly widely used: The student is in a bachelor's degree program that traditionally runs four years. With a co-op program, the student goes to school the first three quarters of her freshman year, just like a traditional student. Then the student gets a job in her major with a

Unofficially...
Co-op education got its start in 1906 at the College of Engineering at the University of Cincinnati, which continues the program to this day. Northeastern University in Boston was quick to take up co-op education, and all of its students now co-op. Today, hundreds of colleges and universities offer their students co-op educational opportunities; there are said to be as many as 250,000 co-op students.

company, government agency, or other employer registered with the student's college's co-op program. From then on, she alternates between work and school, quarter by quarter, for the remainder of her undergraduate education. Because of the time spent at a job, a traditional four-year program takes five years.

Bright Idea
Internships and co-op programs can improve your employee selection process by allowing you to use actual on-the-job performance as a basis for deciding whom to hire permanently.

Employers of co-op students are frequently small firms, but many major corporations and public agencies also participate, including Eastman Kodak, Digital Equipment Corporation, General Motors, IBM, and Toys'Я'Us.

Why would a student spend an extra year in school? Here are some of the reasons.

- It's a great way to finance college. The money earned during the periods of work can pay for part, even all, of one's college education.

- The combination of academics and the working world enhances the student's experience in each realm.

- The experience gained is usually excellent because the college checks out the appropriateness of the job and tries to assure that the work will actually add to the student's understanding of the subject he is studying.

- At the time of graduation, the student not only has a four-year degree, but two full years of applicable experience, giving her a big jump on other newly minted college graduates. (According to the National Commission for Co-Operative Education, 80 percent of co-op students get an offer for full-time employment from their co-operative employer.)

- Students are semitrained in the field.

- Co-op employment is a way to have temporary employees throughout the year.

- Co-op employment can be a marketing tool for your campus program.

Employers hire co-op students for four basic reasons:

- Co-op programs provide a ready, enthusiastic pool of employees.

- It is a relatively low-cost way to find potential permanent employees and try them out before hiring them.

- Use of co-ops can improve access to minority students.

- It is a relatively low-cost recruitment tool.

Managing contract workers

Managing people is tough in the best of circumstances, but it has challenges all its own concerning contract workers. In fact, many managers and business owners seem to think that it's not worth the effort to "manage" contract workers because these people are only on the premises for a limited time, so why take the trouble to manage them? Managing is trying, time-consuming, and often difficult. But, after all, contract workers are costing you money, and may be costing you more per day than your permanent workers. Not only that, they are there to do a valuable, needed job.

Preparing for the temp's arrival

To manage contract workers, first put their responsibilities in writing. Know what you want from the employee, just as you would define a permanent worker's responsibilities. Then notify your permanent workers that you are hiring a temp, and why.

Moneysaver
Co-op students can save you money because they are educated in your field and can sometimes be hired for less money than permanent workers. Also, there's little out-of-pocket expense in recruiting these students. For more information, contact: The National Commission for Co-Operative Education, 360 Huntington Avenue, Boston, MA 02115; (617) 373-3778.

Bright Idea
Temporary workers can boost the morale of permanent workers when they are viewed as extra help by the permanent staff and not as competition.

Explain the person's responsibilities and how she will interact with the permanent workers. To prevent fear and any spread of rumors, such as that temps are coming in to replace "old-timers," let your permanent workers know what is going on.

As already advised, prior to hiring you should have in place someone who will supervise the new worker. Also, be sure you have the temp's workplace set up before he arrives. It often happens that a temporary worker comes into a workplace and no one has even thought about where he should sit. If the employee is to do typing or set up spreadsheets, be sure you have a computer available with the needed software already loaded on. Don't expect a permanent worker, who operates his own equipment, to now start sharing, unless you have made arrangements beforehand.

Have a plan for the worker to follow, including detailed instructions, and, if applicable, a schedule of "mile markers" or project completion dates. Be realistic about what the new worker can accomplish. When appropriate, have instructions in writing, but also have the supervisor or another employee provide verbal instructions. And be sure there is someone designated to answer questions from the worker. The "guide" has to know about personal things, such as the location of the bathroom, lunch hours, available times for coffee breaks, and telephone privileges, as well as business issues, such as how a machine works, where needed information or files are located, and what exactly is wanted.

Learn as much as you can about the temp's background, experience, training, expertise. He might have abilities and experience you do not know about but which could be very valuable to you.

Working with the temp

It is very important to treat temporary or contract workers as a person, not an appendage: Treat them just as you would a full-time employee by making them feel welcome and wanted. Introduce them to the people they will be working with and working near. Explain what is expected of them and how their work fits into the department's or company's overall workload so they understand how their efforts fit into the company's operations. People appreciate it when others show an interest in them and do not treat them as mere ancillary assets.

Give the contract worker feedback, and praise when earned. Ask if he has any recommendations of ways to improve his job. Some temps have worked in a great number of different companies and have learned what ways work better than others. Because they have no connection to you or your business, they can also bring a degree of objectivity and perspective that your permanent workers may lack. And don't just give temps the worst jobs in the place, as that will discourage them from doing their best. The bottom line: Treat the temp as you would like to be treated.

Allow contract workers some of the same privileges as your permanent workers, if appropriate. If you offer your regular workforce flextime, offer it to your temps. This is especially true if the contingent worker will be with you for some time.

And don't mislead temps about such matters as how long they will be needed, or the prospects of their being hired permanently. That would not be fair, and it would get back to the temp agency that you are less than straightforward.

Moneysaver
Whenever you have a contract worker on staff, consider whether that person might make a good permanent employee. You can cut some of your recruitment costs and time by using temporary workers as a pool for finding permanent employees. Consider asking the temp agency what their arrangements are in case you should want to hire one of their employees full-time.

Evaluating the temp's performance

Another difference between permanent and temporary workers is that, with permanent workers, since their responsibilities are generally quite broad, it is difficult to immediately judge how well the person is doing and how well they fit the job. That's why it is common to have 90-day probationary periods. With temporary workers, however, their job is usually very focused and well defined, so you can often judge their suitability for the job quickly.

Without "hovering" or "micromanaging," keep close supervision of the person's work early in her stay with you. Set up "deliverables"—specific tasks that you can review to evaluate the worker's performance. With temporary and contract workers who are not up to snuff, you have the option of calling the agency and telling them this person is not right for the job. Often, the agency will call you to check on how things are going, and if you haven't reviewed the employee's work, you can't give an accurate answer. You may even jeopardize your chances for a refund or other consideration if you say everything is working out, only to report later that you were mistaken.

As soon as the worker's contract is up, evaluate how things went. Do not simply wait until the next time you need temporary help to try to remember the details, or you may miss something important that will help you in your next situation of need. Here are some questions to consider:

- How good was the temporary worker's performance? Was the worker productive?

- Was the worker worth the wages and agency fees?

- Was the worker worth the "soft costs," such as the time spent on supervision, the cost of the worker's telephone calls, disruption of the work of your permanent workforce, the expense of providing a work area for the worker?

- How well did the temporary worker interact with your permanent employees?

- What was the full-timers' response to the temp?

- What were the disadvantages to having the temporary worker?

- Ask your employees what they thought of: (1) The temporary worker as a person; (2) Using temps in the way you did; and (3) The use of temps in general.

Just the facts

- Think of a temporary staffing agency much as you would your lawyer or accountant. You work best with these professionals—and agencies—when you develop a personal relationship with them.

- By relying on contract workers, you can adjust your labor force to meet your changing business, market, and economic needs.

- Don't view temporary or contract workers as being not important enough to manage. They should be supervised and given goals because they are providing you with services your business needs—and you're paying for them.

- There are many good reasons to hire temps, but recognize that in some situations you may be paying more for a temp than if you had directly hired the person yourself.

Watch Out!
If you will be using a staffing leasing company (also called a professional employer organization), be sure to check its credit record, reputation, and other aspects of its business. It will become the employer of your employees, and you want it honest and financially sound.

- Co-op education is a formal program set up by a university that combines work and education. It benefits employers by providing a trained, enthusiastic pool of potential employees and gives students both classroom and real-world, professional experience.

Outsourcing Your Hiring

Chapter 8

Outsourcing is when an organization hires others to provide goods or services it could otherwise do itself. Today, there are companies that have outsourced their entire information technology (IT) departments, hiring a company such as IBM or Electronic Data Systems (EDS) to take over all aspects of a company's computers. But it's not just giants that have decided to outsource. Companies of every size have long outsourced certain functions, such as advertising and accounting. And, as you'll see in this chapter, relying on employment agencies or search firms rather than conducting the entire hiring process internally is a form of outsourcing. This chapter is about using professionals to perform tasks that, at least in theory, a company could do for itself. I'll focus on executive search firms, employment agencies, and consultants.

Advantages and disadvantages of employment agencies and search firms

The appeal of outsourcing in general, and in regard to hiring in particular, is varied and compelling.

When using an outside professional, define your hiring need, define the position, and let the professional know as explicitly as possible what you want. The better you communicate your needs, the less time is wasted.

Before choosing it for your business, you should consider its advantages and disadvantages.

Advantages

Using professionals provides a number of potential benefits, including:

- *More time to concentrate:* For one thing, outsourcing frees up time for other things, such as marketing, management, finance, and research and development. Placing want ads, sorting through resumes, conducting interviews, checking references, and doing all the other things involved with hiring new employees is time-consuming. Employment professionals cannot do everything pertaining to hiring (I will discuss below what they cannot do), but they can take much of the burden off your shoulders.

- *Expertise and efficiency:* If you have ever bought a car, you know you need a lot of negotiating experience in order to be on an equal footing with a practiced car salesman. Likewise with hiring. You may have hired a number of people during your career, but it is unlikely that you have been involved with the hiring process as intensively as an experienced executive recruiter. After all, a recruiter's entire professional life revolves around the hiring function. Any good recruiter will be more efficient at using advertising, at interviewing, and at checking candidates' backgrounds than you are. In addition, a recruiter should be able to "cast a wider net" into the labor pool.

- *Widespread contacts:* Very likely, your best employees have come to you through recommendations, contacts, people you have met at professional settings, or those you have dealt with in the course of your business. The more attention you pay to identifying and staying in touch with promising prospects, the greater your likelihood of finding good employees. The employment professional can—and should—spend much of her time looking for those who would make excellent employees. And from this, the employment professional builds her business—and helps your business in the process.

Laurie Levenson, president of Direct Access, a technology staffing firm in San Diego, says, "I help people get great positions, and they in turn help me find great employees." When she helps someone get a great job, he lets his friends know how Levenson's agency helped; often, when these people want to make a career move, they come to her. An employer is unlikely to create a network of skilled, desirable employees the way a recruiter can. Creating such networks is her business, and that is why professional recruiters, headhunters, and employment agencies are able to find potential employees whom the employer might never otherwise meet.

■ *Reputation:* Unless your company is fairly large, you are unlikely to attract great numbers of job applicants until you advertise or otherwise spread the word that you are hiring. Among the best-known employment firms are Korn/Ferry, Manpower, Kelly Services, Olsten Staffing Services, Snelling Personnel Services, and SOS Staffing Services. Many others, from the national level to the local, are well established.

Moneysaver
To save money on employment agencies, register with your state and local governments. Your local government unemployment office probably offers placement services. Get to know the person who will be sending you applicants because a personal relationship usually improves the quality of candidates you receive. But don't expect to get management-level employees here; these services are for lower-skilled job openings.

Because job seekers come to these well-known firms, the agencies have access to a large pool of potential applicants.

Watch Out!
Beware the professional recruiter who inundates you with resumes, particularly if few are pertinent. If you have to spend a lot of time sorting through resumes, you're better off doing the search yourself—or finding another recruiter. Again, be sure you have given the recruiter a precise definition of the position you want to fill.

- *Anonymity and confidentiality:* By using an executive recruiter, you put the search for applicants at arm's length. There's a degree of anonymity and confidentiality (or a "formal distance") that is often not possible if you are conducting the search yourself. This is especially important in delicate situations where you want to shield your hiring activities from your competitors, or there is someone now in the job whom you're seeking to replace. And, by recruiting at arm's length, you lessen your exposure to legal difficulties, such as charges of discrimination, because another firm is doing the screening.

Disadvantages

Not everything about outsourcing is positive. There are a couple of disadvantages to the use of professionals particularly worth noting.

- *Lack of familiarity:* Outside professionals can never know your business as well as you do. You can explain the position and how it fits into the larger scheme of your organization, but, at the end of the day, there are nuances and aspects to your business that an outsider will have trouble learning—and may never learn. You have to match the employee to the organization. A mismatch, no matter how competent the employee, is likely never to work out satisfactorily.

  As an owner or manager, you have a better feel for the type of "good fit" your organization needs than an outside professional could have. You might immediately reject an applicant, while a recruiter would look at his resume and believe he is perfect for the job. By relying on outsiders to help with your hiring, you may end up with employees you do not really want, or miss out on some you would dearly love to have.

- *Loss of control:* When you use an employment agency or executive search firm to find employees for you, you are relying on someone over whom you have little direct control. It is hard for you to know how hard your agency worker or headhunter is working for you or how wide a net the recruiter is casting for job candidates.

Employment agencies

Employment agencies tend to deal with positions below the executive level, primarily in clerical, support staff, and entry-level jobs. Often the job seeker, not the employer, pays the agency's fee.

Employment agencies typically function within a local market. These firms will advertise your opening, and they have a database of potential candidates from which they draw when trying to fill your job slots.

Often, the employment-agency industry is somewhat rough-and-tumble. If you have an opening, they'll send over some applicants who may not have been screened carefully, and they'll send the same applicants to other employers as well. When you find someone you like, act quickly. There's usually nothing exclusive about the relationship between the employment agency and the employer.

The applicants sent by employment agencies are not commodity products; people are individuals, with some being better at certain jobs than others. It is beneficial for you to try to create a strong,

Watch Out!
Be sure to have a written contract whether you work with an executive search firm, an employment agency, or a consultant. If you pay an agency its fee for finding you an employee and a few weeks later that employee leaves because he has found a better job, can you be reimbursed? Not likely, unless (1) you have a written contract that specifies when and if you are entitled to a rebate, or (2) you can show that the agency and the employee were in cahoots to defraud you.

Watch Out!
Unscrupulous
recruiters have
been known to
locate a good
candidate and
then, six months
later, steal that
candidate from
you by offering
him or her to
another com-
pany. You can
help avoid this
by confirming
the recruiter's
good reputation
and by establish-
ing a long-term
relationship of
earned trust with
the recruiter.

long-term relationship with an employment agency just as you would with a search firm. Not only will the agency better understand your needs if it works with you often, but when a particularly good applicant comes in, you may get the "first pick."

Employment agency fees vary considerably, but they frequently run 20 to 25 percent of an employee's first-year salary.

The executive search firm

Call them headhunters, executive recruiters, or executive search firms—these are the Rolls-Royces of professional employee recruitment. They generally deal with the highest levels of the organizational chart, are the most sophisticated in terms of how they operate, and, of course, they are expensive.

Executive search firms are a branch of management consulting that help companies find, evaluate, and select management-level employees, or higher. Headhunters are for senior-level managers and professionals, such as chief executive officers (CEOs), chief financial officers (CFOs), and chief operating officers (COOs).

Some characteristics of executive search firms are as follows:

- They work for you, the client, not for the prospective employee. Think of these companies as you would a real estate agent. The real estate agent helps the prospective home buyer understand the type of home that's appropriate and then finds a home that fits the buyer's needs, but the agent is not paid by the buyer. Instead, the agent is paid by the seller, and therefore, ultimately, the real estate agent works for the seller. Likewise with executive search firms. They will usually work with those who need a job or want to change jobs, but they work ultimately for the employer because the employer pays their fees.

■ They deal with upper-level managers, executives, and professionals. Though the lowest salary they deal with varies from firm to firm, as a ballpark figure, these firms find employees only for jobs paying $50,000 to $75,000 a year and up.

Search firms basically come in two varieties, retainer and contingency. According to the *1998 Directory of Executive Recruiters* (published by Kennedy Information, Fitzwilliam, New Hampshire), the characteristics of each are:

■ **Retainer firms:**

— Typically used to fill positions paying $70,000 and above.

— Usually hired for 90 to 120 days and are paid whether the search is successful or not. They may also be kept on retainer by clients to fill whatever assignments they have.

— Only one retainer firm is used for each job opening.

■ **Contingency firms:**

— Used for junior and mid-level executives with salaries below $70,000.

— Are paid only if they are successful, meaning that the client hires a candidate the contingency firm referred.

— Typically do not work exclusively to fill a client's position; they compete against other recruiters to fill any particular position. Because of this, they will often work faster than recruiters who are on retainers and submit more candidates, because the more candidates they submit, the better the chances that one of their candidates will be chosen.

Contingency firms usually also are paid 25 percent of the salary that the position pays, whereas retainer firms are paid 33 percent or more. The payment schedule for retainer firms usually is: one third on signing, one third a month later, and the final third upon selection. With a retainer firm, the employer is paying for the firm's expertise in a particular field and its focused search.

Contingency versus retainer executive search firms

Contingency and retainer executive search firms share a number of characteristics: They both work to find employees that fit your predefined needs. As a general rule, contingency search firms focus more on the lower levels of management, say from middle to upper management, while retainer search firms deal almost exclusively with upper management up to the very top of the corporate pyramid. Retainer firms will look for executives who will be paid in the hundreds of thousands of dollars a year.

Another important distinction is that job positions handled by contingency search firms are usually being serviced by two or more search firms. These firms do not have an exclusive on the job. The client company typically contacts several search firms and asks each of them to fill a job slot. The search firm that brings in the candidate who gets the job is the firm that gets paid; the others get nothing. Retainer search firms typically are hired on an exclusive basis. They alone are looking for someone to fill the designated slot.

Contingency recruiters are used for positions paying around $50,000 to $75,000 and under, and for full-time and permanent positions but almost never for the executive level. Ninety-nine percent of the time, contingency firms are paid 25 percent of the salary.

Recruiters on retainer, however, are paid about 33 percent (or more) of the salary for positions around $50,000 and upward—mostly upward. A retainer firm generally receives one third on signing, one third a month later, and the final third upon selection.

Note that a retainer firm is highly focused, usually smaller than a contingency firm, often staffed by people from the fields that the firm specializes in, and generally would not be interested in recruiting for any position being sought by a contingency firm (which is lower level and less focused). With a retainer firm, the employer is paying for the firm's expertise and its focused search.

Fees are based on the employee's first-year salary and any additional bonuses, such as a sign-up bonus. If a position pays $100,000 a year and has a $20,000 sign-up bonus, and if the search firm's fee is 30 percent, then the firm will get 30 percent of $120,000 ($100,000 plus $20,000), or $36,000. The firm that works on a contingency basis gets this fee only if it is the one that finds the person who is hired. The firm that works on retainer gets the fee whether or not the search is successful. (Of course, a retainer firm would quickly lose its reputation and ability to attract business if it consistently failed to find acceptable candidates.)

Timesaver
Professional recruiters can save you money. An article in *Public Management* (July 1995) reported that a search by a university for a dean without the use of a search firm took 15 months; a search involving an external recruiter took six months.

Because contingency firms get paid only if their search is successful, they tend to send many applicants to the client. The more they send, the better their chances are of placing the one who gets hired.

Retainer search firms are more selective in their screening and send generally three to five candidates. They can afford to be more selective, to screen many applicants with an eye toward identifying the very few who are top-notch, because their searches are not at-risk (they're getting paid, either way). The contingency firms assume the risks (time as well as financial) of the search because if they fail, they get nothing. Retainer firms get paid whether you hire one of their "findings" or not, so they can afford to spend more time searching and weeding out undesirable candidates.

Because these two types of firms search for different levels of professionals, they have different ways of operating. For example, a contingency firm may advertise your job opening, while a retainer firm rarely does. Often a retainer firm is looking for an executive officer and must maintain complete discretion and privacy.

Working with executive search firms

To use executive search firms effectively, you need to establish a relationship and pay attention to the process. Among the things to do when working with a search firm are the following:

- *Manage the process:* Just because you decided to use a search firm (whether contingency or retainer) does not mean you can leave the entire hiring process to the outsider. Stay involved and manage the relationship by communicating regularly, inquiring how the search is going, asking for reports about how many

Bright Idea
When working with a recruiter, manage your relationship much as you manage an employee: Stay involved, but not so involved that you hamper the person's ability to do the job.

people were contacted, who was contacted and what were their qualifications, any marketing or advertising that was done, and so on. When an applicant is presented to you, immediately give the recruiter feedback: Was the candidate good? If not, why not?

If you have had a problem with recruiting, don't view search firms as a means for you to hand off the problem onto someone else. The search firm will help, but it cannot do everything. Strike a balance between making sure the search stays on track and being removed from the search.

- *Have the recruiter visit your premises:* Invite the head of the search firm, or the manager of the local office, to visit your premises, see your operation, and meet some of your people. If this person will not be working directly on your account, then also invite the person who will be doing the actual work for you.

- *Be considerate—and accurate:* If you want a good working relationship with your recruiter, be considerate. Be clear and accurate about your hiring needs—and be certain that your company has actually allocated the money to hire someone for the position. (Search firms are sometimes disappointed by clients that admit, after a long search, that they don't have the funds, after all.) After you interview a candidate, get back to the recruiter immediately as to whether you will be hiring the person and, if not, why not. Do not keep people waiting.

- *Create a long-term relationship:* Ideally, you want a long-term relationship with the search firm and your recruiter in particular. Do not view using

Unofficially...
Sometimes the "real" work in a search firm is done by researchers, who do the grunt work of finding good candidates. You would do well to meet (if possible) the researchers working on your account, and get to know them.

the search firm as a one-time activity, any more than you would view using your accountant for a one-time tax statement.

Executive search firm case study: Kaufman Hunt Inc.

Adam Kaufman is a partner in the executive recruiting firm of Kaufman Hunt Inc., in Woodland Hills, California. The firm specializes in accounting, finance, and information-systems personnel. Kaufman, who is a specialist in accounting and finance, is also a CPA and was a practicing accountant before becoming an executive recruiter.

He says good headhunters are sincere, honest, passionate about their work, and know their market. Headhunters deal with mid- to upper-level managers who are themselves successful people. Kaufman says the worst headhunter is one who has to close your deal in order for him or her to survive. This is someone who may well compromise his or her ethics to make a buck.

Why hire an executive recruiting firm? "A headhunter can ask questions the employer can't," Kaufman explains. "I can ask the candidate what's not perfect about their current job and what they don't like about the job opening they are applying for. I'll ask things like, 'What's really important? If I can get you that, will you work there? Does your spouse not like the job? Do you not like working for a woman (or a man)?' These are things you as an employer really cannot ask. The headhunter therefore can learn things about the job applicant that the employer can't."

Searches typically take one week to one month from the time the employer calls the headhunter to when it makes an offer to the candidate, though sometimes the search can stretch to two or three months. In 90 percent of the searches, Kaufman negotiates with the candidate. Typically, Kaufman sends the client three to five candidates, so the client doesn't have to spend a lot of time screening them, though Kaufman has worked with companies that have asked for as many as 10 or 15 candidates.

In 90 percent of the searches Kaufman does, clients are working with other headhunters, usually a total of three to five. He will drop his fee 5 percentage points if the client agrees to give him an exclusive on the job opening.

Kaufman charges 20 to 30 percent of a candidate's first-year base salary, with 25 percent being the average. His fee is due within 30 days of the candidate accepting the offer. He often provides a guarantee: If the person doesn't work out within three months, the client gets his or her money back.

"My best clients," he says, "are those that let me do my job. They accept my advice and don't think I'm just trying to make a buck. Also, they have to be motivated and prepared to move quickly."

Employment consultants

Although this chapter is about outsourcing your hiring—through employment agencies or executive recruiters—you may want to outsource the analysis of your current staff and staffing needs. Perhaps hiring might not be necessary after all. Among the other things they do, employment consultants can be brought in to examine the psychological mix of a department; analyze its functioning and interrelationships with other departments in a company; and determine whether, for example, some employees would actually be better employed in a different function or department. If indeed hiring

Watch Out!
No matter which type of professional you use—executive search firm, employment agency, or consultant—be realistic. If you enter the hiring process with unrealistic expectations, such as getting a perfect employee for below-market wages within three days, you are bound to be disappointed, and you may well hamper the effectiveness of the professional recruiter you are working with.

is necessary, an employment consultant's perspective can be helpful in determining the most suitable types or qualifications of applicants.

Employment consultants are probably the least known and least understood among the kinds of professionals you can use to outsource your hiring. Stephen J. Chen, Ph.D., president of Assessment Resources in Salt Lake City, describes what a consultant can do.

The first thing a consultant does for an employer is a needs analysis, in which he looks at the business's personnel concerns. This often includes analyzing problems with selecting and hiring productive employees, difficulty in retaining employees, difficulty in getting rid of unproductive employees, and any situations involving employee conflict.

In a department having particular problems, a consultant might run psychological assessment tests on individual employees to evaluate their abilities and interests, understand their strengths and weaknesses, and match the person to his or her job to see how well they fit. Chen says that mismatches are usually not the result of incompetence. "In my experience," he says, "a large number of people are not appropriately working in the area that they are best suited for."

The employment consultant will then analyze a department or management team. He evaluates teams by six criteria:

- How clear is the team or department on its purpose?
- How well does the team or department plan and prevent problems?
- How well are they able to accomplish tasks that are critical for the department's performance?

- How well do they communicate and provide feedback to each other and to other departments or teams?

- How much control do team members feel they have?

- What are the individuals' perceptions of their relationship to other team members?

With this, a consultant is able to get an idea of where the team thinks it is compared with an ideal, and where it thinks it should be. "That helps me understand, overall, the team's perspective of its strengths and weaknesses," Chen says.

A consultant presents to the owner or manager an analysis of how well individual employees fit their particular positions, along with ways to deal with incompatibilities. For example, Chen may suggest ways of redesigning a job to better fit the employee or recommend that the employee move to another position within the company, or he may suggest ways for management to work differently with its employees or ways to redesign the team. When there's conflict, he will recommend conflict-resolution intervention, including coaching. Sometimes the consultant recommends firing an employee, but usually he designs a program to work with the employees already on hand. When new employees are needed, a consultant will work on the advertisements to attract candidates, screen prospects, and help select the best person for the job.

According to Chen, there are three ways consultants charge for their services:

- By an hourly rate

- By a daily rate

- By a per-project rate

Unofficially...
According to *Workforce* magazine (August 1997), 5 or 10 years ago, search firms successfully completed about 90 percent of their searches. Today, the completion rate is maybe 80 percent, even less. Let the buyer beware.

The average ranges from about $250 an hour to $800 an hour. That may sound expensive, but considering the cost of searching for and hiring an employee only to find a few months later that the employee isn't right, such fees can be worthwhile.

Advantages

There are several advantages to using an employment consultant:

- They are unbiased.

- They work for you, so they should have your best interests in mind.

- A consultant can deliver messages to your employees that you may have trouble saying because he or she is an outsider, a professional, and involved with your company on a temporary basis.

- Likewise, a consultant can convey from employees to management certain messages that would be difficult, or risky, to deliver themselves.

Disadvantages

Here are some disadvantages to using an employment consultant:

- No tests, licenses, or certificates are required to be a consultant. (Ask for references.)

- They may lack experience in your industry and therefore be ineffective.

- They can be very expensive.

Just the facts

- Outsourcing the hiring function can save a business time and money; on the other hand, such services can be expensive.

- Employment agencies deal primarily with clerical, support staff, and entry-level positions.

- Contingency firms work with lower-level positions, give their clients lots of candidates, and get paid only if one of their candidates is hired.

- Retainer firms conduct searches for upper-level executives, may take longer (than contingency firms) to conduct their searches, provide a short list of candidates to their clients, and are paid whether or not their search results in a hire.

- View your search firm as a partner, just as you do others who provide you services, such as accountants and bookkeeping services; and develop a good, long-term relationship. Don't view a search firm as a tool you will use only once.

Marketing Your Job Openings

GET THE SCOOP ON...
When to advertise ▪ How to write help-wanted
ads ▪ How to attract job seekers ▪ Where are
the best places for your ads ▪ The difference
between in-column and display ads

PART III

Using Paid Advertising

A study done by the Newspaper Association of America a few years back, as reported in *Editor & Publisher*, found that, "despite a growing usage of online job hunting, newspaper classifieds remain the most popular way to look for a job." You'll learn ways to attract employees through the Internet in the next chapter, but in this chapter I will focus on paid advertising—specifically the classified, help-wanted ads that are most commonly found in newspapers, and less frequently in magazines. Of all the ways to advertise for employees, help-wanted ads are the most commonly used and the most widely read.

Help-wanted ads are found in the classified advertising section of virtually every newspaper, whether daily or weekly. Many people turn to them first, especially on Sundays, before reading any other section of the newspaper—even if they are not "really" looking for work. They want to know what's going on in the job market, who is looking for employees, what the pay is for positions comparable to theirs, and how many openings there are.

The constant monitoring of help-wanted advertisements is akin to keeping one's resume constantly updated: You never know when lightning will strike and an opportunity may become available. Because help-wanted ads are so popular and read so widely, they are a vital medium to any company that is looking for workers.

Which media should you use?

Should you advertise in the major daily newspaper in your city? A suburban daily? A small weekly? A trade publication? The following considerations should be based on such primary factors as the position to be advertised, the pay, advertising budget, and where your business is located.

Major daily newspapers are good in that they blanket a market, but because they blanket a market, you have to pay for that extensive coverage. As a rule, the large daily newspapers are the most expensive media for help-wanted advertisements. Dailies are effective if you operate throughout a metropolitan area or if you are trying to attract applicants from a wide geographical area. If you are a small high-tech firm, you know it's difficult to find experienced, knowledgeable programmers and systems engineers. So, even though you are small, you may well have to advertise throughout a market in order to attract enough qualified applicants. If you have a chain of retail stores that operate widely, and you have openings in several geographically scattered stores, then you will need to blanket the market with your ad and are likely to find that the major daily newspaper your most cost-effective advertising medium.

But if you have more localized needs, advertising in an expensive major daily can prove unnecessarily expensive. A small retail store or neighborhood restaurant on Long Island would waste money advertising for a sales clerk in the *New York Times* because readers who want those jobs are unlikely to commute from the city or from Westchester County. (Some newspapers print separate editions based on geography, however, and if available, these can make the major daily a worthwhile media outlet.)

In fact, this is true for almost any type of advertising. If you have a small clothing store that sells items found in many other stores, you probably want to advertise your lines of clothing in a local "penny saver" or other weekly that targets a concentrated market. Customers are unlikely to travel long distances to buy products they can find closer to home. The same is true of advertising for potential employees in a large metropolitan area. Workers for lower-level or less-specialized positions—receptionists, secretaries, clerks, waitstaff, manual labor—can usually be found throughout a city, and thus are better sought through more geographically localized (and less expensive) publications such as penny savers.

If there is something unique about your business and the job opportunity you offer, however, or if you find it very difficult to attract qualified applicants from your local labor pool, it may be worthwhile to use the major daily newspaper in town. If you have a hard-to-fill position, even if you are small, you should advertise throughout your metropolitan area. A computer programmer, a physical therapist, an experienced writer or graphic artist—for positions like these you may need to spread your net far and wide. Be prepared to compete on a regional or even national basis, otherwise you may not land the people you need. This means you must provide benefits, training, pay, career advancement, and any other perks offered by your competitors.

When should you advertise?

Help-wanted advertisements run seven days a week in daily newspapers, yet Sunday is typically the most important. Prospects can reply that day or the next, and the job search gets off to a quick start at the beginning of the week. If you are not sure which day is the big one in a particular market, simply ask the clerk at the newspaper's classified section which is the most popular day. Another way is to look at each day's edition and see which has the most advertisements.

Ira Gordon, director of affiliate sales and training for Careerpath.com and former vice president of recruitment advertising for the Newspaper Association of America, says: "If your daily newspaper offers a Sunday edition with a strong, effective employment market base with several pages of employment ads, including display advertising, then you've got to be in there. Sunday's the first recruiting day of the week, and that's when people tend to concentrate their readership for this type of advertising. They know that's when the bulk of the job ads are being featured in the newspaper."

Of course, if you want to advertise in a weekly, then you have to go with whatever day that newspaper comes out. If you are using a paper that comes out twice a week, again, check to see which edition carries the most want ads.

What type of ad is best?

Help-wanted classifieds are published in two formats:

Unofficially...
Advertising for jobs on a regular basis provides you with a presence in the marketplace—a practice known as "branding." If you can afford it and have an ongoing need for new employees, you should advertise routinely. Doing so builds your credibility among those who read the want ads regularly—when they want or need to make a job change, they will be more favorably disposed to your company.

- *In-column ads* are the classifieds that fit within the confines of a column of newspaper (or magazine). Their length varies—they can be as short as two lines, or as long as 100 or more lines.

- *Display ads* are often larger and more graphically distinctive than in-column ads. They are sometimes illustrated, stand-alone ads located at the bottom of the page below the in-column ads. In addition to their size and graphic look, they typically differ from in-column ads in that they are for higher-level, higher-paying positions. An exception to this is when a company has a number of job positions to fill, and it may use a display ad for several positions, some or all of which may be lower- or mid-level positions.

Moneysaver
If you decide to advertise on weekdays, skip Monday. Since most job seekers respond to the ads on Sunday—and spend Sunday and often Monday doing so—they don't have the time or the interest to pay much attention to ads in the Monday newspaper.

In-column ads

In-column ads are the most common form of help-wanted ads, and are usually used to advertise lower- to mid-level job openings. (Upper-level positions are often advertised through display ads.)

You probably will use in-column ads most often because they work for all types of positions, with the exception of upper-level ones. They can be effective but must be planned carefully in order to distinguish your listing from those of your competitors, and to keep yours from being "lost in the shuffle" among many other advertisements.

Display ads

A display want-ad is very much like any display ad, such as the department store and furniture store ads you see in your newspaper. It usually has a headline, and will often contain a copy of the company's logo to give it a graphic "look" consistent with the company's image or identity. Their costs generally are commensurate with the space they take up. If you run a display ad that is 10 times the size of one of your typical in-column ads, expect to pay about 10 times as much.

According to Ira Gordon of Careerpath.com, "Display ads do out-perform in-column ads. Ads that are larger than the in-column ads, with fancy borders and artwork and logos—those get more attention and more response. In certain categories, display advertising can get anywhere from 20% to 100% more response than in-column ads."

While display ads generally out-perform in-column ads in industries across the board, Gordon says they are especially effective in such industries as retail, manufacturing, health care, high technology, engineering, science, business, management, and professional positions.

A low-rent ad will have trouble attracting a high-pay employee—in fact, it may not even be noticed. An important point to keep in mind is that display ads often attract a different type of job applicant from an in-column ad. "There are some people who are so self-confident about their ability to find new jobs," says Gordon, "that they only read the display ads. They believe that the companies that would want to hire them are those willing to spend more to get their attention, and hence would likely pay a higher salary. Display advertising sends the message, 'Yes, we are willing to pay you what YOU think you are worth.'"

(This concern with "image projection" is similar to what law firms, major corporations, and other firms do when they invest considerable money in decorating their offices. They use wood paneling and fancy carpets because they want to be seen as successful and also suitable to service other success-ful people and companies.)

Trade publications

Trade publications are different enough from news-papers that they need to be considered separately. The actual ad copy is basically the same, but your audience in a trade journal is more focused than in a general daily paper. For example, *Computerworld* runs ads for computer-industry executives, *Internet World* advertises for technicians and webmasters, and *Editor & Publisher* has an extensive help-wanted section geared toward the publishing industry. You are probably already familiar with the major trade publications in your industry; depending on the level of positions you are seeking to fill, they can be well worth considering as an advertising venue.

A trade publication makes sense for specialized or uncommon positions. For example, a 1998 issue of *Editor & Publisher* lists ads for sports editors, busi-ness editors, entertainment reporters, circulation managers, and display advertising managers. These positions are specialized enough that it makes sense for newspapers and magazines, even smaller ones, to advertise in a national trade publication because job applicants are often willing to move long dis-tances for such jobs. Trades are also used for hard-to-fill spots, managerial positions, or above, and ongoing needs.

Trade publications differ from general-audience newspapers in several ways, including:

- *Wider distribution:* Trade publications tend to be national. Some industries, such as theater and film in New York and Los Angeles, and comput-ing in most sizable metropolitan areas, have local trade publications. As a rule, however, trade magazines are distributed nationally. You have to decide if what you have to offer is strong enough to attract someone to move to your city from another part of the country. Note, however, that many trade publications sell ads geographically, so you might want to ask the classified advertising department if regional advertising is available.

- *Issues are less frequent:* They tend to come out monthly or weekly. Although there are trade publications that come out daily (*Variety* for the entertainment industry) and weekly (*Advertising Age* for advertising and *Computerworld* for information technology), most trade publications are monthly. The problem with such infrequent publication is that the jobs listed may no longer be open by the time the readers see them. Advertisers usually have to get their ad copy into the publication two to four weeks before the magazine goes to press. By the time the magazine reaches its readers, the job is often filled, and job seekers know this.

- *Highly defined, focused markets:* In general, trade journals are best used for particular, high-skilled positions. You wouldn't advertise for a dishwasher in a restaurant trade publication, but you might for a gourmet chef.

How much do ads cost?

The costs of help-wanted ads can vary considerably, depending on the size of the ad and the publication. Jerry Bellune, editor of the weekly *Lexington County Chronicle* in Lexington, South Carolina, sells a 20-word ad for as little as $5 in his weekly newspaper, which has a circulation of 6,000. For example, *The*

Chicago Tribune charges $28.50 per line for a Sunday job classified advertisement (there are about seven lines per column inch). If you run the ad the next Sunday, you get the second ad at half price. A package deal of four days is available—Sunday-Monday-Wednesday-Sunday, run consecutively—at a cost of $46.75, total, for the four days. The cost per line for days other than Sunday is $18.00. For display advertising rates, call your newspaper's advertising department. Display ads are usually priced according to column width (horizontal) and inches in height (vertical). Ask about any quantity discounts that may be available for running more than a single ad. To give an idea of ad rates in trade journals, *Editor & Publisher* charges, per line: $11.15 for one time; $9.85, two times; $8.60, three times; $7.45, four times.

For both in-column and display ads, the factors that determine the cost of a help-wanted advertisement include:

- *Size:* As a rule, the larger the ad, the more you will pay for it. You will have to balance cost against size when choosing the ad you want to run.

- *Circulation:* Generally, the larger the circulation of the publication, the more you will pay. If you have two newspapers in town, and one has a circulation of 50,000 and the other 100,000, you will pay more for an ad in the second newspaper than the first.

- *Audience:* While it is generally true that the larger the circulation the more you pay, it is also true that a publication with a specialized audience, such as a trade journal, can command advertising rates above what you might expect

Bright Idea
There's no hard-and-fast rule as to what size ad to run. If you are not sure, look at the ads of your competitors. You will probably want to have an ad at least as large as your competitors' ads. To run a small ad against larger, flashier ones, puts you at a competitive disadvantage.

for its circulation. However, a more expensive medium might, in the long run, prove less expensive than publications that charge less for ads. If you pay $100 for an ad in one publication and get no response, but pay $250 in another and get three well-qualified applicants, which is the more expensive ad? The $100 ad was a total waste of money, while the $250 ad was quite productive. The difference is the audience the publication targets. ("I'll discuss shortly some of the factors to consider when choosing where to advertise.)

■ *Discounts:* If you advertise one time, you will pay the full cost listed on the publication's rate card (a listing of the publication's costs for various types of advertising). A small advertiser tends not to have much leverage, so if you advertise infrequently, don't expect any discounts. The prices on the rate card are generally not negotiable to the small or one-time advertiser.

If you advertise more frequently, however, you might be able to negotiate favorable terms. If you agree to advertise 10 times, you'll probably get a better per-ad or per-line rate than if you advertise two or three times. Ira Gordon says that he knows of major daily newspapers in which, if one advertises for eight straight days, including two Sundays, the advertiser can get the second Sunday for 50 percent to 75 percent less than what the first Sunday's ad cost. As another example, he says that if you agree to advertise on one Sunday plus several weekdays, too, you can get 20 percent to 30 percent off the rate-card price. If you will be advertising frequently, don't hesitate to inquire about discounts.

Where in the publication should you advertise?

One of the hardest things to choose in Yellow Pages advertising is under which heading to place your ad. This holds true for help-wanted ads, as well. There are two primary ways newspapers organize their want ads:

- *Alphabetical order, or "alpha-sorted":* In this type of organization, which is probably the most common, ads are placed in alphabetical order based on the first word or the headline of your ad. "Project Manager" would be placed under "P," "Receptionist" under "R," and so on.

- *Occupational categories:* The second type of organization is by broad occupational categories, with ads sorted alphabetically under each category. Common categories are accounting, agents and sales, clerical/secretarial, education, engineering, health care, mechanical, medical, professional/technical, trades/skilled, and general (which might include anything). Newspapers' occupational categories tend to differ from city to city, so read your paper closely to see which category is most fitting for your open position.

As for these two types of organization, you will have to go with whatever format your newspaper uses. With the strictly alphabetical format, you simply choose which word you want to be listed by, whereas with the broad occupational category format, you not only have to choose what word you want your ad listed under alphabetically, but also what category you want to be included in.

In deciding which word or category to use, the best approach is the simplest: Look at what your

Unofficially...
Headlines in help-wanted ads have three basic functions: (1) To tell about a unique *feature* of the job; (2) to tell about a unique *requirement* of the job; and (3) to tell about a unique *benefit* of the job.

Moneysaver
Be prepared to handle the responses to your ad. Designate someone in the office to answer the phone, open the mail, handle the inquiries, hand out applications, and generally deal with the logistics of people responding to your ad. If your telephone lines are always busy because you don't have enough bandwidth to handle the response, then you've turned off potential job applicants and wasted your money.

competition is doing, and where they are advertising for workers like those you want to attract. Chances are that those seeking jobs in this field are looking at the same listings because that's where most of the jobs of that type are found. Going off on your own with an unusual listing (in hopes of beating the competition) usually doesn't work. Help-wanted ads can be creative, but playing with category headings is not the place to show your inventiveness. If you are not sure how to classify or describe your position, the U.S. Department of Labor can provide listings of job titles and classifications.

What should your ad say?

As with all kinds of writing, help-wanted ads have their own style.

Determine your target audience

In Chapter 6 I discuss the importance of developing clear, functional job specifications. A good job specification forces you to define precisely what you are looking for. And with this knowledge, you can target your help-wanted advertisements for maximum effect.

You attract those who are looking for better opportunities by emphasizing benefits in your advertising copy; you can address your ad particularly to those whom you want to attract. In fact, you might *not* be looking for those who are currently employed and seeking better opportunities, as these are folks with some ambition and drive and may be more expensive to hire. As such, you may gear your advertising copy to reflect this, such as not mentioning career-ladder possibilities or areas of responsibilities if your main concern is to fill a certain position without regard to the worker's ambition. But you can only orient your ad toward certain types of job seekers when you know the kind of worker you want. For this reason, before you do any advertising, consider the *type* of person you are looking for, and not just their qualifications.

Include basic details

The first rule in writing help-wanted ad copy is to be specific. Think about what you are saying and how readers will interpret it. Specificity goes beyond just being accurate in your headline. You need to be clear about what you are looking for and what you are offering. Here is a list of items to include and to state clearly:

- Company name
- Contact information, including fax number and Web site address
- Job title and level
- Clear, concise description of the job and its duties
- Salary (or salary range)
- Date to start
- Experience required—number of years needed, familiarity with certain operations or regulations (software, equipment, government regulations, types of markets, etc.)
- Travel required
- Intangibles—great team to work with, exposure to interesting people/technology/experiences
- Perks, such as medical insurance, dental plans, vacation, bonuses, retirement plans, day care, and so on.
- Legal language (if applicable): "Company X is an equal opportunity employer"

> 66
> Compelling ads . . . are written from the perspective of the person reading the ad. A good ad provides the answer inevitably asked by the reader receiving your offer of employment: 'What's in it for me?'
> —From "Solid Suggestions for Preparing Effective Help Wanted Advertising" (MacDonald Classified Service, Lafayette, Indiana)
> 99

Moneysaver
You can make your ad dollars work more effectively if you use the second person ("you") in your copy. Say, "You can become part of a wonderful team," instead of the more impersonal, "The successful job applicant will become part of a wonderful team." (Save that for the formal job description.) Job listings are people-to-people situations, and your advertising copy should reflect this.

Include benefits information

Whatever the job you are advertising for, be sure to include benefits to answer the reader's natural question, "What's in it for me?" Benefits include:

- Pay/bonuses
- Perks
- Responsibilities
- Career growth potential
- Flex-time, telecommuting, and other special arrangements
- Travel opportunities

To improve your advertisement copywriting:

- Place yourself in the applicant's shoes. What does your position offer that will excite the applicant?
- Read and re-read the job description you wrote. Look at it with an eye toward the benefits it provides the employee.
- Study the ads placed by the competition. What benefits are they offering?

Of course, you don't want to promise more than you can deliver. If there really is no job advancement potential, don't say that there is. Likewise, do not advertise pay "in the high 40s" unless you are willing to go that high. (You can make up for a lower salary by offering other benefits, such as job skills training, enhanced responsibilities, or travel opportunities.)

Promote your company

Finally, cover all the details. Tell about your company. Consider mentioning a salary or a salary range. Generally, the more specific you can be, the better. But watch for what the competition is offering. You don't want to appear to be paying significantly below market wages. If you don't want to state a salary or salary range, you can say "salary is negotiable"—but be willing to negotiate.

Write dynamic copy

If the primary rule in writing help-wanted ad copy is to be specific, it follows that what you don't want is to be vague, general, or incomplete. Jerry Bellune of the *Lexington County Chronicle* found the following example of how not to write an ad in his own paper:

> **Receptionist**
> Position available immediately
> Mid-sized downtown law firm needs recep-
> tionist. Please call [name and telephone
> number]

To begin with, the headline, "Receptionist," is boring, uninformative, and does nothing to get a job applicant excited and eager to call you. "Position available immediately" isn't necessary to say at all because readers will assume the job advertised is available immediately unless the ad specifies otherwise. "Mid-sized downtown law firm needs receptionist" gives you an idea of location (which is good), but it says nothing informative or exciting about the job or the employer. The best thing about this ad is that it gives a name and number to call.

How could this vague, lackluster ad be improved? Here's a possibility:

> **Dynamic Law Firm Needs Friendly**
> **Receptionist**
> Meet interesting people. Learn to operate
> the latest telecommunications equipment. Be
> part of an innovative legal team that prides
> itself on treating clients—and employees—
> right. Full benefits and competitive salary to
> the right person. Please call...

Watch Out!
Make it easy for applicants to reply to the ad by providing your mailing address, a telephone number, a fax number, and an e-mail address. If you do not want telephone calls, "drop-by" visits, or any other particular response, say so clearly in your ad. For example, "No phone calls, please. Send cover letter and resume to [address]."

Watch Out!
It is fine to put *minimum* requirements in a help-wanted ad, but, advises Ira Gordon, "Never state it in terms of *maximums*, because you may be discriminating" against older workers. You can say, "This job requires a minimum of X years' experience," but not, "This job has a maximum experience requirement of five years."

Why is this ad better than the one that originally appeared? First, the headline, "Dynamic Law Firm," projects a brighter image of the firm. This positive image is reinforced with the term "innovative" and the statement that the firm treats its clients and employees "right." Saying "friendly receptionist" also gives an impression that the firm does right by its people and its clients. Being part of a team conveys the image that you will not be a receptionist sitting by yourself at the entrance to the office, and taking all the flack. "Full benefits" tells the prospect that among the job's benefits is a full complement of perks. "Competitive salary" says this firm is willing to pay for quality. Asking for the "right person" says the firm is careful and will not hire just anyone; if you are chosen, that will reflect well on you.

Qualifications and requirements: choose your words carefully

Watch out for legal limitations, such as saying you don't want anyone over a certain age, because age discrimination is against the law. Also, beware of qualifiers that really are not necessary or that you don't really want. If you say, "Five years' experience required," think about whether you really need someone in this position who has five years worth of experience. If you really need someone with only a year's worth of experience, by stipulating five years, you would turn away applicants who might be well qualified for the job, and you attract people more experienced than you need. (Remember, in general the more experience a person has, the more money she commands. The more qualifications you include, the more the hire will cost you.)

Always give a telephone number and mailing address. If you wish to discourage a flood of phone calls or "drop-in" visits, say so in a diplomatic way. (Bluntly saying "Don't call" or "Don't visit" is very unfriendly.) But if interested people want to call and ask a specific question or two about the position, they should not be discouraged. It is perfectly legitimate to have questions about a job.

Titles and headlines

Under which word(s) should you list your position? Choices include:

- *A prominent job title:* If you own a magazine and are looking to fill several positions, you might list each separately under: "Sports editor," "Managing editor," "Cultural reporter," "Science writer."

- *Functional headline:* Here, you might have one headline—"Editorial/Writing," for example— and then list each of the above positions under this functional headline category.

- *Don't "reinvent the wheel".* There is a third alternative, which is to imitate what the competition is using.

The advantage of using a functional title—one that describes the function of the job, e.g., "accounts receivable clerk"—is that because you are combining more than one job into a single ad, you can probably afford to pay for a larger, more eye-catching headline. On the other hand, functional titles are, *by definition,* not very specific because they have to cover more than one job. Because of this, you run the risk that the job seeker may miss your individual positions. The only way to know which works best for you is to test. Try them both on consecutive weeks—preferably when you're not in a

Moneysaver
Although newspapers' classifieds staff will sometimes offer to write ad copy for an advertiser at no additional cost, it is generally simplest to write the copy yourself. You (or a good writer on your staff) will know your business and the position's responsibilities better than an outsider. (A more expensive alternative is to hire an ad agency or specialist to write the copy for you. Unless you are advertising in an expensive display ad campaign, however, it's probably not worth the expense.)

critical "time crunch"—and see which brings in the largest number of qualified applicants.

Just the facts

- When writing an ad, emphasize the benefits to the reader. As with any ad, you are trying to sell the reader—on the job and your company.

- The help-wanted ad represents your company to the public. Making it well written, accurate, and friendly in tone reflects well on your company.

- Be creative where you place your ads—there's more than just the daily newspaper. Consider penny savers or trade publications, for example.

- You can enjoy sizable price discounts if you agree to run a series of ads.

- Use "you" in your ad copy. You want the ad to speak directly to the reader.

GET THE SCOOP ON...
The importance of continuous recruiting ▪
Finding employees through your professional
and personal networks ▪ How to set up an
effective employee referral program ▪ How to
choose a job fair

Finding Workers in Unconventional Places

Chapter 10

The notion of thinking "outside the box," which means thinking creatively, outside conventional limits, is increasingly a good idea for managers and business owners. The labor market is too tight, the competition is too sophisticated, and the labor force too demanding for an employer to think that going solely with traditional approaches will provide the quantity and quality of employees needed to make a business prosper. This chapter covers some of the less conventional sources and ways of finding workers.

Take what is given here as a jumping-off point. If you are to do well in the marketplace for labor, you will have to start thinking out of the box. Be creative when on the lookout for workers, and you will find them in places you never expected. The most traditional ways of finding workers are to advertise in newspapers or other periodicals, and to use outside specialists, such as employment agencies and headhunters. These have been discussed in previous chapters. But there are plenty of other ways to find good—even extraordinary—workers, of all types.

Recruit "inclusively"

Here's an example from one of the most highly respected cultural institutions in the world: New York's Metropolitan Opera. Among the world's opera companies, the Met is Numero Uno; it has the largest budget of any performing arts organization in the country, probably the planet. Tickets to a Met performance can easily run $75, $100, even more. So it's not surprising that the people who run the Met and institutions like it tend to be well educated, articulate, and extraordinarily talented.

Except for Joseph Volpe, the Metropolitan Opera's general manager since 1990 and the man *Forbes* magazine has called "the most important man in opera." Volpe didn't start his opera career at a prestigious college music program or by having a stellar career in opera or by growing up among the opera world's elite. This son of a Brooklyn clothier got his start in opera as a carpenter whose primary qualification when first hired at the Met was his skill with a hammer and saw. His first big move in opera was not into a management or performance position, but to become master carpenter. From there, he showed his smarts, and he moved up to various management positions over the years. Then, in a moment of supreme inspiration, the Met asked Volpe to be its general manager. Neither the Met nor opera in general has been the same since.

The lesson here is that an employer should not be too restrictive about hiring practices. You may have a Volpe on staff whom you are overlooking while when you think you need a woodworker with

Picasso-like abilities. A worker who recently came to you from a temp agency may be able to make a real contribution to your business—if you give her a chance.

Recruit continuously

Effective recruiting is not a stop-and-go endeavor—not if your need for employees is more than a one-time need. If, over time, you will need to hire a series of employees, either to replace existing employees or to add employees because of growth, you must approach recruiting as an ongoing need. Barry Shamis of Selecting Winners, Inc., of Seattle, says, "Companies have to approach recruiting today the same way they approach sales. Just as you need a continuous sales pipeline, you need a steady flow of potential recruits. You have to recruit every single day."

In the following sections you will learn about some good sources of job candidates—sources "outside the box" that you might not have thought of.

People around you

The people you know—and those who your acquaintances know—are often the best (and least expensive) source of good new workers. As they say about physicians and attorneys, the good ones tend to travel in packs. So, check with your acquaintances and colleagues whose judgment you trust, and you may be pleasantly surprised at what you find.

Professional network

Every manager or business owner has a network of peers and acquaintances who can provide numerous leads, if the manager lets people know she is hiring. Networks of professional acquaintances are

Moneysaver
You can encourage your employees to provide referrals and hold down the costs of rewarding those who make the referrals by offering non-cash bonuses. These could include time off, tickets to a sports event (if your company has season tickets to a local team, use these as bonuses), or public recognition, such as a mention in the company newsletter or a special listing on a widely seen bulletin board in the office.

among the most productive sources of job candidates you can have. It's not uncommon for a person you thought was content with his job to ask about an opening when you mention you are looking to hire. Or they may know someone to refer to you. Michael Dewey of Virtual Networks Ikon in Irvine, California, says that more than 90 percent of his employees come through referrals. "I ask literally every person I talk to every day if they know of anyone for me to hire," says Dewey.

Personal network

Your personal network is the group of friends and acquaintances you and your family have. Recently, a woman at a Big Six accounting firm in San Francisco was looking for a copywriter. She found the ideal candidate in a place she would never actively look for an employee: at her three-year-old daughter's day-care school. The mother of her daughter's best friend turned out to be just the copywriter she was looking for. As the saying goes, "You make your own luck." If you are open to unexpected possibilities, you may be surprised at how many opportunities present themselves.

Employee referrals

A company's existing employees are an excellent and often overlooked source of employee referrals. For one thing, your employees know your needs and what skills and abilities your job openings require, so they are in a good position to match your needs to a job prospect's skills. Also, because existing employees will have to work with the new recruits— and since the quality of their recommendations will reflect on themselves—they are likely to choose potential colleagues they think can do the job and they would like to work with.

Here are a few tips to make your employee referral program effective:

- *Make it formal.* Put it in writing. Place notices on a bulletin board by the coffee machine and on your employee Web site. Let your employees know you value their opinions about whom to hire. Another reason to make a formal policy is so that the company can have guidelines by level of position hired—guidelines establishing, for example, that payments are made (no sooner than) 30 days after the new hire starts.

- *Ask immediately.* On the first day a person is on the job (or soon thereafter), ask them to provide the names of anyone they know who might work well at your company. Contact these people immediately.

- *Pay a bounty.* Companies that pay their employees for referrals who are eventually hired find that their employee-referral program works better than those that do not pay. How much to pay is difficult to say. Payment can range from as little as $50 to $100 for lower-level employees, to $4,000 to $5,000 for higher-level executives or hard-to-fill positions. If you are in an industry with low unemployment and strong demand, or in a city with few unemployed, you will have to pay more than if the labor market is looser. Barry Shamis frequently sees payments for referrals ranging from $500 to $5,000, with payments of $1,000 to $1,500 being the most common. (That might sound like a lot of money, but compare that to the cost of a headhunter or employment agency. You may pay a professional 20 to 30 percent of the employee's first year's salary. If the position pays, say, $40,000, that could entail a fee of $8,000 to $12,000, which makes the employee-referral program a real bargain in comparison.) Shamis also finds that employers tend to get better employees from referral programs; furthermore, these employees tend to have a higher retention level.

Vendors

Salespeople, too, can be a great source of potential employees. "We put the word out to our vendors that we're looking for job applicants because they get around and might hear of someone making a move or who is unhappy," says Ray Taggart, vice president of Ikon Office Solutions Technology Services in Salt Lake City. Salespeople go from office to office, get to know many people in your industry (or one similar) and get to hear an enormous amount of chitchat. If someone is unhappy with their job or is considering a move for some other reason, the salesperson will probably hear about it.

Other employees of your vendors, such as support staff, may also hear of workers eager for a change. Let the word out that you are looking to hire. But don't just mention this once; gently remind them on an ongoing basis that you are in the market to hire. Vendors can certainly tell you about job candidates you would otherwise never hear about.

Reaching out

In addition to your personal and professional networks, of course, there are the media, the Internet, job fairs, and associations through which you can find good workers. Here are some good approaches to finding workers out there in the bigger world.

The media

News reports can be another excellent source of potential recruits. Read your local newspaper, watch the television news, and pay particular attention to reports about companies that are laying off workers, going out of business, or otherwise creating unemployed workers. Even in today's robust economy, you still find major corporations laying off workers. At the time of this writing, Intel and what was McDonnell Douglas (now owned by Boeing) recently announced layoffs. Every city, no matter how strong its economy, has local employers that are letting people go or are going out of business. This is a source of employees that requires prompt action because these employees will not remain unemployed for long given the tight job market.

The Internet

Looking for job applicants online—and having them find you, online—is arguably the most significant change in the field of hiring in a generation, since a series of laws were passed beginning in the 1960s relating to discrimination. These laws influence to this day how businesses advertise for and hire workers. And the Internet may well do the same in the coming years. Online recruiting is a boat many have recently jumped into but is still so new that many recruiters have yet to have a good day fishing. But the promise of this technology is such that you can't afford to ignore it.

Who's doing it?

According to *Workforce* (August 1998), over 2,500 Web sites now have job postings. A recent survey by the American Management Association (AMA), as reported in *Computerworld* (May 4, 1998), found that

59 percent of the human resources managers who responded to the survey said their companies now use the Internet to find people, and another 13 percent said they plan to. How effective is the Internet as a recruiting tool? Thus far, it seems, not very. The AMA survey found that on a scale of 1 to 5, with 5 being the highest rating, non–human-resources managers rated online recruiting at 3.3. However, among human-resources managers, online recruiting rated only 2.66 for most positions, and 2.68 for hard-to-fill jobs. The study did not compare these rating to other recruiting media.

Conventional recruiting focuses on the employer going into the marketplace primarily via advertising and getting the word out that it has jobs it is trying to fill. It hopes that qualified applicants will learn about the openings and apply. Online recruiting is this and more. True, employers use the Internet to get the word out via sites that list job openings (see Appendix B, "Resource Guide"), as well as the employer's own Internet site which can list jobs. But Internet recruiting, unlike the traditional approach, allows for a more proactive strategy on the part of employers. Rather than sitting back and waiting for applicants to apply, the Internet enables the employer to actively search and contact applicants. That's because the Web is a very active place for job seekers to post their resumes. The *Workforce* article cited above says there are more than 1.5 million resumes online today. This is new. While trade and other publications have long had "job seekers" sections, there's never been an efficient means for hundreds of thousands of job seekers to let employers know they are looking, nor has there been a way for employers to find such people—until now.

Choosing a site is much like choosing a place for a help-wanted ad, only you generally have more choices. The only way to know which sites work and don't work is to test. Run a sample ad and see what the response is. Be sure to carefully track responses from each online ad so you know which are working and which are not. When searching resumes, do the same. See which sites have applicants most qualified for your job openings, and focus your search efforts on these.

Spreading the word

To get the word out, use keywords in your online posting. The search engines used to find sites and information on the Internet typically rely on finding keywords. A *keyword* is a word that job seekers are likely to type into the search engine when searching for job openings. If you are in the oil industry and want an engineer, you might list "petroleum engineer." If you think a chemist might fit the bill, you would have "chemist" in your listing. To figure out which keywords will result in appropriate responses, put yourself in the shoes of applicants and think about what words or job titles they are likely to search for, and use those in your ad. In the above example, you would put "petroleum engineer" and "chemist" if you think applicants might search under these job titles. If you think some qualified applicants might look under "oil" rather than "petroleum," you'd have both "petroleum engineer" and "oil engineer" for keywords.

As with conventional advertising, use qualifiers to weed out applicants you don't want to waste time with. By listing specific qualifications and specific years of required experience, you send out a message of who should or should not apply. Because there's usually little or no penalty for length (unlike traditional advertising, which charges per line), you can use longer advertising copy on the Net than you would in print. Of course, nobody wants to read long-winded job descriptions, but you can explain the job and job benefits, as well as details about your company, in more detail online than in print, so take advantage of that.

Wherever you list your job openings, try to arrange a link to your home page. This lets applicants "visit" your company and learn more about you. Of course, also include your e-mail address so that applicants can submit their resumes to you electronically. To segregate resumes from the other e-mail your company receives, consider setting up a special, dedicated e-mail address, such as jobs@verygoodcompany.com.

Include a closing date with all your online job listings. Resumes and other information can sit on the Internet forever, like signs for long-past garage sales still tacked to telephone poles.

There are many places where you can read posted resumes, such as MonsterBoard and CareerTrack. As mentioned above, you can find these listed in Appendix B, "Resource Guide." If you belong to a trade association, there's a good chance it lists jobs for its members. Listing jobs usually costs money (job seekers are typically not charged). MonsterBoard charges $150 per job listing, and $4,900 a year to search resumes. There is one site that doesn't charge you to search through resumes, but its resumes lack identification; if you find applicants you want to contact, you have to pay $20 per resume. Because online recruiting is still a new and fluid medium, fees can change rapidly, so these prices may have changed by the time you read this. Check around as to what sites are charging now.

Also, if your company has a Web site, post job openings there. To do so is free, of course. Be sure you make it easy for visitors to find your job openings. You might have a button labeled "employment" or "job openings" on your home page. If you are actively recruiting, make it easy for potential applicants to learn of your needs.

Sophisticated sites contain filtering mechanisms. For example, Texas Instruments, Inc., in Dallas, has a 32-question online form (www.ti.com/recruit/docs/fitcheck.htm) that asks for responses ranging from "strongly agree" to "strongly disagree." The questions are varied, including "I prefer a company with a strong global internal and external communications and information network" to "I prefer a smoke-free environment." At the end of the questionnaire, you can see how you did (before you submit the form) and read an explanation of what TI considers the best answers and why.

Online recruiting has great potential, but it's still a bit too early to rely heavily on it. Until the Internet is better established, it is probably best to view online recruiting as one among several means of finding applicants. Use it as an adjunct to your traditional recruiting efforts.

Job fairs

Job fairs, often used to attract recent college graduates, can be effective sources of workers. Highly skilled workers can be found at these fairs, too, depending on the nature of the fair. Often run as money-making ventures by fair-management companies, job fairs may also be organized by a local

Unofficially...
According to the
*Philadelphia
Business Journal,*
the nation's old-
est and largest
job fair is
Operation Native
Talent in
Philadelphia,
which began in
1965 and
attracts about
5,000 job seek-
ers, 80 percent
of whom are
recent college
graduates.
Booths at the
fair cost about
$500 to $1,000,
though discounts
are given to
companies that
register early and
to members of
the Greater
Philadelphia
Chamber of
Commerce.

chamber of commerce, government agency, or other nonprofit organization, such as an industry trade group.

These fairs, which usually last a day or two, have spotty success. Much depends on your particular needs, how well the fair is promoted, and to whom it is promoted. If you need a number of employees with fairly generalized skills, such as secretarial or a recent college graduate with no professional work experience, these fairs might work well. If your need is highly specialized, however, such as for someone with experience in a technical field or a salesperson familiar with a specialized market, then what would serve you better is a specialized job fair, such as one organized by your industry's local trade association. If you are looking for a computer programmer who knows COBOL, a job fair sponsored by your state division of unemployment will probably not be productive, but one put together by your local information-technology association could provide just what you're looking for.

Some fairs charge employers little or nothing, especially if sponsored by a nonprofit organization. Others might charge from a few hundred to a few thousand dollars. Here is what to look for when deciding whether or not to use a job fair:

- Who is its audience, and how well does that audience match your needs?

- How extensively will the organizer promote the fair?

- Will the organizer agree to let an exhibitor include his own promotional piece with its direct-mail campaign? (Direct mail is one of pri-mary ways these fairs are promoted.)

- What other companies will be there? If your competitors will be there, that suggests the fair might be productive for you. Ask the organizer which companies exhibiting this year have exhibited previously. Chances are good that repeat exhibitors found their previous experience with the fair worthwhile.

Be warned that just about every job fair is chancy for the employer. If it rains or snows on the day of the fair, attendance is likely to suffer. Sometimes an organizer's mailing goes out late or is delayed in the mail, and again, attendance suffers.

Be prepared to put your best foot forward. How you present yourself reflects on how job applicants view your company. If the fair has booths, like a trade show, be sure yours is attractive. Provide well-designed and informative promotional material about your company. The people staffing your booth should be articulate and knowledgeable—don't leave the job of attracting applicants to lower-level employees unfamiliar with your company's history, aims, market, and so on. Your company should have a vision that appeals to potential recruits, so make sure those staffing your booth can articulate that vision. Prepare your staff on what types of questions they're likely to get and how to reply.

After the job fair, follow up on leads as quickly as possible. You have to recruit actively, which means you must quickly contact the applicants who are of interest.

Job fairs are worth testing to see if one or two in particular work well for you. But they should be used in addition to your other recruiting efforts, such as networking and advertising, not as a substitute for them.

Government agencies

State employment agencies (please see Appendix B, "Resource Guide," for a listing) can be useful for filling some types of jobs. They tend to have rosters of lower-skilled job seekers, but sometimes they can surprise you. When an employee loses her job, for whatever reason and whatever her position, if she applies to collect unemployment insurance, the state will probably require that she register with a state unemployment agency or job service. As a result, you may find middle managers and even higher-level executives in the pool of prospects at a state agency. Also, you'll be happy to note, these agencies do not charge for their services.

Commonly overlooked sources

Employers often tend to overlook some of the very best workers available—workers with disabilities, for example. The sections below will alert you to some rich sources of talent.

Workers with disabilities

Employers often overlook the pool of talented, motivated people who have some type of disability. These workers are a wonderful source of talent and have a well-earned reputation for being a bit more loyal and motivated than many workers who don't have disabilities. This may be because they often have trouble finding work—sometimes a result of prejudices or employer discomfort—and so they are appreciative when an employer recognizes their knowledge and talents. Your city or state probably has an office for people with disabilities that can help you find workers who fit your needs. Another way to find workers is to contact organizations in your area that represent the disabled and tell them you welcome them to apply for your job openings.

With today's technology, even workers with severe disabilities can be productive. One middle manager at a major oil corporation in Chicago is quite productive, despite his being a quadriplegic. He is able to function by having a modified personal computer controlled by using voice-recognition software, which is now quite inexpensive (less than $100) and more accurate than ever. In fact, the major software suites, Corel's WordPerfect, Lotus's SmartSuite, and Microsoft Office now come with voice-recognition software built in. The accommodations that you may have to make for workers with disabilities may be less troublesome than you might imagine.

A key to attracting workers with disabilities is to project the message that they are welcome. Letting organizations representing these workers know about your interest is one way. Including photos of your company's workers with disabilities in your annual report and other printed material is another way of sending "welcome" signals.

Hiring former employees

When someone leaves your employ for better opportunities elsewhere, are you personally affronted? Do you now dislike this person, even if you liked him the whole time he worked for you? Do you take the departure as an act of disloyalty that can never be forgiven? Think again. Your former employees could be a great source of "new" hires.

If another company offers your employee a significantly better-paying job, for example, why be angry when she leaves? Don't hold it against her.

Watch Out!
When bringing back a former employee, make him feel welcome, and make sure the other workers understand that you are pleased that he has come back and that you don't hold grudges. Also, try not to make money the main motivator for his return, as that could degenerate into a bidding war between you and his current employer. Instead, focus on other things to attract the ex—security, new opportunities, exciting things the company is doing or will soon be doing.

Before a valued employees leaves, let her know that you have appreciated her efforts, are happy for her new opportunity and, if the new job does not work out, you might be able to find her a position back home in your shop, depending on the circumstances of your business at that time. Ask her why she is leaving. Then keep in touch. Former employees become a pool of talent that you might be able to tap in to at a later date.

The advantages of going back to former employees include the following:

- You know their strengths and weaknesses.

- They know you and your business, and, if they are willing to return, you must be offering something important that they find really attractive.

- Your recruitment costs are minimal—you don't have to advertise or hire headhunters or offer bonuses for employee referrals.

- The employee, during the time since he left your company, has probably gained some valuable knowledge and has seen how others operate, which could be very helpful to you.

Displaced homemakers

"Displaced homemakers" (an unfortunate term, perhaps, but it has gained currency in the press) are people who were formerly married or were dependent on the income of someone else for at least two years. They may be female or male, attorneys or secretaries. The "displacement" refers to the income formerly provided by someone else—often a former spouse. These willing workers are often highly skilled—many were on fast-track career paths before leaving the workplace—and employers would do well to take them every bit as seriously as other applicants, even though theirs may not be the most up-to-date resumes in your stack. (It should be noted that some of these "returning workers" may need some upgrading on certain technical innovations, such as recent releases of software, that may not have been in use when they last worked.)

A woman who was an engineer quit work to be with her son, then aged five. Four years later, she decided to reenter the workforce. She did it not by going back to engineering, but by becoming a salesperson who sold engineering supplies to companies, including her old employer. She had no trouble finding a job.

Your local YWCA or other women's organizations might be able to introduce you to displaced homemakers looking for work. Check out classes at local community colleges that are frequently taken by those looking to refresh their business skills (secretarial and computer classes are examples). Advertise in local women's and employment publications.

Unofficially...
For information concerning displaced homemakers, contact YWCA Career Services, 1517 Ritchie Highway, Arnold, Maryland, 21021, (410) 757-5400.

Hiring "retired" workers

Go into a fast-food restaurant that as recently as five or ten years ago was staffed almost exclusively by teenagers, and today you may find a number of "retired" workers on the front line. Millions of Americans are now seniors, and their number will grow dramatically during the next two or three decades. Seniors, in fact, are the fastest-growing segment of the population. A survey by the American Association of Retired Persons (AARP) found that among those retired, 48 percent said they would go back to work if the right situation presented itself.

Consider offering seniors the right situation. Seniors generally have good work skills, a friendly attitude, know their way around an office, restaurant, or other business, are eager to remain active, appreciate being treated well, and don't assume the world owes them a job. They usually don't demand more money than others, but they may have other needs, such as flexible hours so they can take care of grandchildren, accommodations on the job for physical limitations (such as getting tired if made to stand for long periods), and are often in need of certain benefits, especially health insurance. Seniors are probably quicker to learn new skills than you might think. For example, the personal computer was not part of any senior's childhood or probably even their career, yet many have taken to the PC, using e-mail and surfing the Internet in ways that would impress a teenager. (There's even an online chat group for seniors called SeniorNet.) Also—and this is no small consideration—by setting a good example, seniors can teach good work habits to younger workers.

How do you find seniors? Let the word out to various organizations that cater to seniors that you welcome older workers. Include pictures of seniors in your annual report and other printed material. Be accommodating to their needs. Contact charity, community, or religious groups about what you have to offer. Many communities now have one or more publications (often free) that are targeted to seniors, and you might advertise in these, and have them place a notice or article about the fact that you are looking for seniors.

Get the word out

Let the community know you are hiring. Place notices on bulletin boards found at many supermarkets. Join the chamber of commerce and other organizations. Most entrepreneurs join these groups to drum up business, but they can also be good sources of employees. Let it be known what job openings you have available.

Use unconventional advertising media. For example, if you want teenagers or workers in their 20s, consider advertising your job openings on radio stations whose audiences fit the demographics you are targeting. Let counselors at high schools and job-placement offices at colleges know that you are in the market for workers. Visit vocational schools—such as secretarial and technical schools—and let them know who you are and who you want to hire.

Your recruiting will yield better results—better workers, that is—if you scout proactively and with imagination. Don't simply rely on the tried and true, such as newspaper help-wanted ads. Aggressively look for employees and do so continuously. If your business is successful, you probably already know that you'll continue to need workers on an ongoing and perhaps increasing basis.

Bright Idea
Make yourself visible. Give talks at high schools and colleges, and tell your audience you are hiring. In fact, you might offer to give free talks on how to find a job, which means that your audience is in the job market.

Just the facts

- Creative thinking can lead you to sources of workers other employers tend to overlook.

- By using your professional and personal networks—and by telling everyone that you're always accepting resumes—you can find good people you might not find through the classfieds.

- Don't let your ego or social awkwardness get in the way of recognizing that you have a large pool of potentially dynamite workers and referral sources: your former employees.

- Companies that pay their employees for referrals who are eventually hired find that their employee referral programs work better than those that do not pay.
- Consider hiring seniors, workers with disabilities, and "displaced homemakers"—and people from other areas of the labor pool you might formerly have overlooked.

Hiring: Screening and Selection

Screening Applicants

Chapter 11

Because hiring interviews can take a lot of time and energy, a manager should start to work on improving screening techniques well before the interviews begin. This chapter is about how to improve your hiring efficiency through effective screening. Screening is the art—and it is an art—of taking information about applicants, such as resumes and references, and filtering out what you don't need, and identifying what will help you target the best job applicants. In particular, we will look at how to screen resumes and how to screen applicants by using the telephone interview. There are several common factors that can make interviews unproductive—and that illustrate the need for careful screening—including:

▪ *Many interviews:* Managers and business owners who have one position to fill will often interview 10, 15, or even more applicants (larger companies have human resources departments that screen for the company's managers). That's too many. If you consider that a typical initial interview can easily take 30 minutes or more, and then add 15 to 20 minutes of preparation and the follow-up work of writing notes to yourself about the interview and your analysis of the applicant's qualifications, you can see that it's easy to spend 45 minutes to an hour per interview.

Assuming the interview takes an hour, if you do a dozen interviews in a week, that's 12 hours. The time and energy required by interviewing can detract significantly from your productivity. If you consider the time it takes to set up, interview, take careful notes, and then shift gears to resume what you were doing before the interview, you quickly see how the process can be quite a drain on productivity.

- *Too many choices:* Sometimes an abundance of choices leads to bad decisions. The more interviews you do, the more difficulty you'll have in choosing the right candidate. What you want are a few good candidates. A clear idea of the job's requirements and a careful winnowing down of applicants to the most promising ones will help you focus on the best matches for your job opening.

Screening with resumes

Of all the available ways to screen, the tool most widely used is the resume. This piece of paper gives employers a fairly standardized format in which to view an applicant's work experience. But because resumes have become ubiquitous—often required of would-be engineers and cappuccino counter staff alike—some people have become adept at tilting and skewing them at certain angles that can make it difficult for an employer to know what is real. To get

Watch Out!
Beware the resume that contains long descriptions of educational achievements, but little or nothing about degrees or recognized professional certificates earned. The applicant may be trying to deflect your attention from the fact that he or she has not earned a degree or professional certificate.

through the clutter, misinformation, missing information, and the big, bold lies, you need to have a plan for dealing with the resumes you will receive when you advertise for a job.

Dealing with that stack of resumes

Suppose you advertise an open position in the Sunday paper. Job seekers spend Sunday and Monday sending you their resumes. You walk into your office on Tuesday and find a pile of resumes that would stack up well against a Dostoevsky manuscript. How do you get through that pile efficiently and effectively?

Know your essential requirements. Have a checklist of what you're looking for in your applicants. This is a checklist of "must haves," those things the applicant must have at a basic minimum. Some common requirements:

- Education—to what level, of what type, grade point average, honors attained, and so on

- Skills, such as ability to write promotional copy, competency with certain machines, familiarity with types of software, typing speed, and so on

- Experience of a more general nature, such as supervisory experience, dealing with customers, working in a particular industry, managing projects

How do you know what your "must haves" are? When you wrote the job description for this position (as discussed in Chapter 6), you specified the particular needs and responsibilities. These criteria will form the basis of a good checklist. With a checklist, you delegate the initial screening to someone under you, but make sure this person has a good idea of what you're looking for because there will be

Timesaver
What an employer looks for in a resume are detailed, specific descriptions of responsibilities and duties. Look closely at the detail and pertinence of the applicant's work experience. If the descriptions are vague or sprinkled with minutiae, the person may be hiding something or may not understand what's important. But don't be too quick to reject; if the applicant looks eligible in other respects, ask about the parts the resume doesn't make clear.

Watch Out!
"Never write any notes or comments on an applicant's resume or job application," warns Sara Brown, a human resources consultant in Hamden, Connecticut. You may write something that is later thought to be discriminatory, or notes that you would not want the applicant or someone else to see at a later date. Keep the notes you take when you review a resume and job application, as well as those taken during an interview, on separate pieces of paper.

"shades of gray" with some resumes as to whether they are worth further inquiry.

Use a process of elimination. When you start to sift through a stack of resumes, make three piles. Pile A for the most promising; Pile B for promising but questionable candidates; Pile C for the definite rejects. The C's you can definitely discard. And if you have plenty of A's, you can probably quickly rid yourself of all or most B's. That will leave you with the most promising, the A's.

Here are some strategies for dealing with a stack of resumes, including some recommendations from professional employment consultants.

Start your resume screening with your want ad, recommends James Essey, president of TemPositions in New York City. "I try to put something in the ad that's going to help me deal with the resumes when they come in. I will typically ask the applicants to write a cover letter that answers, 'What in your background would make you the perfect candidate for this job?' I require a letter for two reasons: One, it synthesizes for me the key things that they think would make them appropriate for the job. And, equally important, it gives me a chance to see their writing style and their attention to detail."

Nothing disqualifies an applicant like a cover letter riddled with errors. "If I see a cover letter with more than one typo," says Essey, "it's gone. I don't even look any further at it. Same thing with the resumes. If I see a resume that is poorly reproduced or crooked on the page, or one that comes without a cover letter or with a clearly mass-produced cover letter, I'm probably not going to give it a lot of consideration."

After you sort through resumes and cover letters based on their appearance, focus on the qualifications and experience you want the applicant to have. This is the stage where you look carefully at objective criteria.

Pay attention to objective criteria

Among the objective criteria to consider when winnowing through a stack of resumes are:

- *Dates:* Are there periods of time unaccounted for? If a resume that is otherwise appealing includes a number of gaps in employment amounting to substantial "time off," an interviewer should ask about the time between the jobs listed.

- *Job-hopping:* Not so long ago, someone with an employment history that included a number of different jobs was viewed as less than desirable—unreliable or lacking in loyalty. Much of the stigma of job-hopping has dissipated, but not all of it. If someone in his 30s or older cannot seem to stay at a job longer than a year or two, you might have doubts. The acceptable amount of "mobility" can depend on the profession, the field, the industry. If you decide to interview the person, be sure to ask why he changed jobs as often as he did. Sometimes, people lose their jobs for reasons that do not reflect poorly on them. If there is a pattern of job loss or job-hopping, then watch out. If the applicant tells you that he wants to leave his current position because he is not earning enough—and his salary is fairly competitive—then he might quickly leave your employ, too, at the slightest promise of a few more dollars. At the same time, you must be realistic. When we're young, we want an ideal partner, and anyone less than ideal we won't marry. Eventually, reality sets in,

Watch Out!
According to the *Liar's Index*, a study by Jude Werra & Associates, Brookfield, Wisconsin, as reported in *Sales & Marketing Management* (March 1998), 17.9 percent of sales and marketing candidates in 1997 misrepresented their academic backgrounds on their resumes, as did 14.4 percent of candidates in all fields.

Watch Out!
Don't waste time with inappropriate, off-target responses to your ads. You'll be surprised how many such applicants you'll get. Rick Pescovitz, president of Professional Image Apparel, Inc., in Cincinnati, tells of a man with 19 years' experience driving a forklift who applied for a sales position because he wanted a change of career. Concentrate on applicants whose experience truly suits them for the position.

and we realize that our ideal is usually unattainable (and even undesirable). The same holds when looking for employees. Recognize that you'll likely have to make compromises and that the person you hire will not be perfect.

To some degree you can gauge the "quality of the person"—her values, her character—through her resume. Here are a few indicators to look for:

- *Staying power:* The longer someone stays with an organization, the more likely it is that she has proven herself as an individual and as a team worker.

- *Promotions:* Does the applicant have a history of receiving regular promotions? During his career, has he gotten increasing levels of responsibility—and corresponding titles? Higher salary? Other indicators that he was valued by the organization? (To be fair, however, we should note that the frequency and quantity of promotions in some professions or positions may not be as significant as in others.)

- *Performance:* Look at signs of the applicant's track record of project completion. Does the resume show signs that she finishes assignments on time and moves on to equally challenging or more demanding projects?

When you review resumes, have a clear idea of the type of person you want. For example, if your company operates in a competitive industry of fighters, you'll want people with drive. On the other hand, you may have a position that offers limited upward career potential, that has been done successfully in the past by those content with staying in one place; for this type of position, you might look favorably on someone whose resume indicates he can perform well at a given level for a long time. But to understand which candidate you want requires that you think ahead of time of the best type of person for your job opening—characteristics that should spring naturally to mind when observing previous employees and when writing the job description.

Mistakes to avoid

When reviewing resumes, reviewers often make assumptions or perceive "facts" and "situations" that aren't really there. They can make some serious mistakes and hire the wrong person or skip over the best candidate.

One common mistake is to think less favorably about someone who has graduated from a "second-string" college or university rather than a name-brand institution like one of the Ivy League or Big Ten universities. Or the bias may be against an "ordinary" college as distinct from the big state university or a prestigious private university. Many very bright, capable students go to secondary schools, especially public ones; most secondary universities have certain departments that are first-rate by any standard.

Another common error—more positive, perhaps, but a prejudice, nonetheless—is to ascribe certain virtues to employees of well-known organizations simply because of their employer's reputation: quality by association. Certainly, Microsoft has a great reputation as a software company, but does that mean everyone who works there is a wizard at programming or management? Employers can be blinded by reflected glory. You may think, "I know they do a good training job at XYZ Company, so this person must be well trained and know her stuff," but the real world doesn't work that way. Just because someone is employed by General Electric or Disney or some other highly regarded company doesn't mean she will be able to meet your needs. Judge each person individually, rather than by the company she worked for.

Automated resume screening

In a world where apparently every other function is automated, it should come as no surprise that there is software available to screen resumes automatically. According to the *National Business Employment Weekly* (November 30, 1997), "Nearly half of all mid-sized companies and almost all Fortune 1000 companies use computerized resume-scanning and tracking systems. Meanwhile, smaller companies often hire resume-service bureaus and recruiters who use their own scanning systems." And there is software you can buy to track resumes yourself. These software programs create databases of the information of resumes you scan into your computer, let you search for words in the resumes (and even notes you might add yourself), and have the software search for skills you want among the resumes in your database. There are many software packages available. These include: RecruitPRO, by Digital Concepts Inc. (800 529-6200; www.dci-usa.com); Resume Assistant (fax: 905 773-0294; www.resumeassistant.com); and Forage Resume by Advanced Information Management Inc. (972 618-4743; www.forage.net).

Employment applications

Besides the resume, the most common written screening tool is the employment application, which is typically filled out when a job applicant comes to a business to apply for a job. You can make up your own employment application or buy standard forms in office supply stores. Unless you have special requirements, buy ready-made forms. There are perfectly good reasons for going with the tried and true:

1. They are economical. You can usually buy them for 5 or 10 cents apiece.

2. They generally cover all the bases you would want to cover if you created a customized form yourself, such as education, special skills, activities, outside work, employment history, and references, and they usually include a statement to be signed that the applicant has been truthful and complete in the information supplied.

3. They avoid legal traps. An application form may contain the statement, "This form has been designed to strictly comply with State and Federal fair employment practice laws prohibiting employment discrimination." Using commercially prepared forms should help you steer clear of legal problems. For example, you can't ask a person's age because that could lead to age discrimination charges, but a form can ask, "Are you 18 years or older? Yes or No." The answer lets you know for sure whether the applicant is a legal adult. These are subtleties you might miss if you made up your own application form.

However, it may make sense to produce your own form under certain circumstances:

■ Yours is a larger company with its own legal counsel, so it is relatively easy for you to create a company form that fits within the law.

- If you have special needs that generic forms don't address, such as specific skill requirements or experience of a certain type—the kinds of things about which you want in-depth information.

If your company does have special needs, contact your industry's trade association. It may have employment applications designed specifically for your industry, or it can tell you where you can find such forms.

Telephone interviews

Bringing applicants into your office for an interview takes time. If the person isn't well qualified, a face-to-face interview is a waste of time. More efficient is the device of using a telephone interview to sort the promising from the unpromising applicants in the A and B stacks recommended above. Telephone interviews, in fact, can be much more efficient than face-to-face ones.

Advantages of using telephone interviews for screening

- *Efficiency:* You can speak to someone on the telephone and do a limited screening quickly and at little cost, and thereby trim the number of applicants you need to see face to face.

- *Shorter time:* Telephone conversations tend to be completed in less time than face-to-face interviews because there isn't as much small talk, and the dynamics and interactions of the conversation are more limited.

- *Delegate the screening:* If the job position is fairly straightforward, the telephone screening interview might be done by a trained employee on a lower level than manager or owner.

- *Distractions minimized:* Distractions are usually at a minimum during a telephone conversation, so the interviewer can often focus on the issues at hand more effectively than in a face-to-face meeting.

- *Time limits:* You can easily (though politely) bring the interview to a close if it becomes obvious that the applicant is not right for the job. You might say something like, "We had a big response to our ad and have already found many qualified applicants who fit our needs. We encourage you to keep watching our ads and to apply again for another position that might be a better fit with your experience and qualifications."

Disadvantages of using telephone interviews for screening

- Doing a telephone interview "cold," without knowing anything about the person, is difficult and, at best, cursory. Telephone interviews tend to be most effective after an applicant's resume or job application has been received and reviewed.

- Important and revealing communication is invisible over the telephone—particularly the body language and nonverbal cues you would be able to see in person. Even some verbal cues can be missed. That's why, even if you engage in a lengthy telephone interview, you'll still want to interview face to face; nothing can substitute for seeing an applicant in person.

- Some people do not communicate well by telephone, so they are at a disadvantage to those who do well over the telephone. (The opposite can apply, as well; some people don't perform well in face-to-face interviews.)

- If some applicants are being seen in person and others interviewed over the telephone (because, for example, some applicants are out of town), the interviewer may have a subtle bias against one group or the other. For example, although you try to be objective, because you pick up much more information when seeing a person, you may think your judgment about those you see face to face is more accurate than about those you talk to on the phone, and you may well be right.

Prepare a script

A script or a list of questions will help you stay on track in a telephone interview. Your script might include points that were not clear on the resume, requests for further detail, or questions about apparent discrepancies. Shape your inquiries toward what more you need to know so you can decide if this person is worth calling in for a face-to-face interview.

Some employers don't mind being queried by phone, while others prefer mailed responses. If you're screening people who are calling in cold from a want ad but who haven't yet sent in a resume or filled out an application, you'll want to prepare a list of questions to quickly screen out those who really are of no interest to you. This type of telephone interview will largely focus on the "must haves," those things the candidate must have for them to be of interest to you.

No matter what type of telephone interview you conduct, keep in mind that you still need to project a positive, informative picture of your company. The interviewee will want assurance that your company is worth joining.

This could be done quite simply in your opening statement: "Hello, thanks for calling. We are rapidly growing and need energetic people willing to be part of a team and have the drive and ambition to succeed." However you say it, make the interviewee feel welcome and confident that by joining your team, she will be making a good career choice.

Finally, rehearse going through your script or checklist. If someone other than you will be doing the initial phone screenings, be certain she has a good understanding of the job and an overview of the company so she can answer applicants' questions in a helpful way.

Just the facts

- Use screening techniques to limit the number of face-to-face interviews you do.

- Prepare a list of "must haves" before you screen the first resume.

- For a telephone screening, prepare a brief list of points you'll want to cover and any questions raised by the applicant's resume.

- Divide the resumes you receive into Pile A for the most promising; Pile B for promising but questionable candidates; Pile C for the definite rejects.

- Stay focused on what you really need. Rely on your job description to keep you on track.

- Although telephone interviews can be a great convenience, remember their shortcomings (for example, body language is invisible, and some people don't perform as well on the phone as they do in person).

Watch Out!
When you place an ad listing your phone number—even if you ask for resumes and cover letters— be sure you're prepared to handle any calls that come in. Make sure your receptionist knows what to ask job applicants and to whom to transfer calls.

GET THE SCOOP ON...
How to prepare for an interview ▪ How to set
the stage for a good interview ▪ Common interview mistakes—and how to avoid them ▪
Questions to ask at an interview ▪ What to do
after the interview

The Interview

Why is a manhole cover round? If you don't know the answer, that's fine with Tom McElveen, director of administrative service lines at Carilion Health System in Roanoke, Virginia, who asks this question at just about every hiring interview he conducts. He is not looking for the "correct" answer; he just wants to see how you answer it.

Such are the vagaries of the hiring interview, a somewhat mysterious and often trying experience for both interviewee and interviewer—a process in which the way you answer a question can be more important than getting the answer right. The interview is the "moment of truth," the point where you meet and most definitively judge the job applicant, and he or she judges you. The decision of whether to hire or not to hire usually stems directly from the interview. In this chapter, we'll cover how to organize and prepare for a hiring interview, how to conduct an interview, and how to know what to ask.

Unofficially...
According to a study done in 1994 conducted by Bruskin/ Goldring Research and reported in *American Demographics,* the third most anxiety-producing activity is interviewing for a job. Keep this in mind when conducting a job interview: The person you're interviewing is under pressure, so her "performance" in the interview may not be an entirely accurate predictor of her performance on the job.

Prepare, prepare, prepare

I cannot emphasize too strongly the need for careful preparation for the interview. Why is it worth taking the time to prepare? If you don't prepare:

- You won't get all the information you could from the interview.

- You may misinterpret or miss the information you get from the interview—or not get the information you need—which could lead you to hire the wrong person, or decide not to hire the right person.

- The interviewee will pick up on your lack of preparation and likely read this as a lack of interest. You may lose out on the opportunity to hire the person you really want because you didn't do your homework.

Hiring interviews are among the most important duties of managers and business owners. If you believe that the well-being of your business depends largely on the quality of your workforce, then the hiring interview, as the key component to hiring good people, is essential to the overall health and performance of your business. The interview requires a sense of seriousness and attention on the part of the interviewer—as well as a proper valuation of the applicant's time and your own.

Goals of the interview

To make the most of the interview, you should know what your hiring goals are. Start your interview planning by understanding your goals for the interview. General goals for the interview should include:

- Finding out job-related facts and information that you didn't get from the applicant's resume or application so that you can develop a complete and accurate picture of the applicant.

■ Give the applicant a complete and positive picture of your company so he will want to work for you if you offer him a job.

There are also more specific goals, depending on your situation, which could include:

■ If this is to be the only interview with the candidate, your goal is to collect enough information so you can make a choice between him and the other applicants.

■ If this interview is to be the first in a series of two or more, you may want to collect enough information about the applicant to decide whether or not to have her participate in further interviews with you and/or others in your company.

■ If you have more than one position available, this could be an interview to get a better understanding of the person and her goals, strengths, and weaknesses, with the idea that you'll direct her toward certain job openings your company has and away from certain others.

Who will conduct the interview?

In larger organizations, initial interviews are typically conducted by a representative in the human resources department. In smaller firms, the most logical person to do an interview is the immediate supervisor of the position that is open. This is the person who will work most closely with and be most responsible for whoever is hired.

If the position is divided between two or more supervisors, all the supervisors involved should participate in the interview. Jeff Colosimo, CEO of

> **"**
> So many people have no idea what to do when a candidate shows up. We're fairly amazed how inept managers are at interviewing. Instead of asking fact-finding types of questions—how the job candidate would react in certain situations, how they've behaved in work situations—they discuss fly fishing.
> —Vince Webb, vice president of marketing, Management Recruiters International Inc., Cleveland
> **"**

Alternate Solutions Inc., in Camp Hill, Pennsylvania, hired a full-time recruiter for his 50-employee computer reseller business after having a difficult time in finding qualified employees. He puts each candidate through three interviews: The first is with his recruiter, the second with him, and the third with the leader of the team the prospect will be working with. **Vital point:** Make sure that those who will work with the person—both above and below—have input into the hiring decision.

The interview setting

Many interviewers give little thought to the setting where the interview will be held, or to other logistical aspects. These should be considered and prepared before the interview.

- *Hold interviews in the workplace.* Avoid such settings as restaurants or bars. If you're out of town, rent a conference room. Don't hold the interview in your hotel room.

- *Find a setting that is private and quiet.* The interview should not be open to a public audience; this is a personal situation, and the interviewer shows a lack of respect if she holds the interview in view of others. Privacy and quiet also minimize distractions.

- *Place all phone calls on hold.* Either program your telephone or tell your secretary that you do not want to be interrupted during the interview.

- *Make the physical setting as comfortable as possible for the interviewee.* Have a comfortable chair and have a clean place where the interviewee might want to spread out her portfolio or other background materials.

- *Your place of business should look polished and attractive.* Make sure the reception area (which the interviewee will see first) is tidy and attractive—and the same goes for your office. You're selling yourself and your company to the interviewee, so your company's appearance should be appealing. (Also, your personal appearance needs to be neat and clean.)

- *Have all materials you'll need for the interview ready at hand.* Of course, you should have the applicant's resume, job application, and any other material he has provided. You'll probably want to take notes, so have paper and pen available. If you plan to give out information about your company—say, a brochure, catalog, or annual report—have it out and visible so the candidate knows you have prepared for the interview.

- *Allocate sufficient time.* Don't warn the candidate when he or she enters your office that you have only 15 minutes and that you'll have to hurry the interview. If you're rushed, you can't do the candidate justice, you give a poor impression of yourself, and you likely waste everyone's time. If you lack the time to do a proper job, reschedule the interview.

Your own appearance

Yes, you will be judged during the interview just as the interviewee will be. The job candidate will be watching and judging you: your attitude, your appearance, what you say, and how you say it. You may well want to write down the questions you intend to ask to ensure that you ask all the important questions. Some interviewers think it doesn't look good to read from a "script," but if it helps you

Bright Idea
As reported in *Inc. Online*, personnel consultant Ed Ryan of MPR in Chicago recommends audiotaping job interviews. Ryan says candidates answer more thoughtfully and honestly when they know you're recording every word. By law, you must ask interviewees' permission before you start taping. Another user of taped interviews says that recording has improved his own interviewing techniques. He now talks less and listens more, and he has learned to ask more open-ended questions.

" Too many people put value in this deal called experience at a very junior level," warns Gopal K. Kapur, president of the Center for Project Management, San Ramon, California. What I want is someone who is talented, curious, likes to learn, and then actually teach them, rather than insisting that everyone who comes in have experience. We look for too much in technical skills, and not on strategic skills, communication skills." **"**

focus, it's worth doing. Also, as you go through several interviews for the same position, you'll need the crib sheet less and less.

Jerry Jaderholm, president of Northstar Sleep Products Corp., Kent, Washington, makes notes to himself as a reminder of what he wants to accomplish and what he needs to find out during the interview. He often interviews for sales people, of whom he wants to know such things as:

- How long has this person been in sales?

- Is this person familiar with the territory where he or she will sell?

- Is this person familiar with the products he or she will be selling?

Such simple questions help keep him on track and ensure he covers the topics he needs to know about.

Know what you want to say about your company. This is your chance to "sell" your company to the prospect. You want the interviewee to have a positive impression of your company so that if you offer him or her a job, it's accepted. It's very likely that you'll be competing with other employers for strong candidates, so you need to give the candidate reasons for accepting your offer versus the competition's. One way is to paint a positive—but honest—picture of your company and why it is a good place to work (but in highlighting your company's good qualities, be careful not to disparage the competition: ill-considered remarks could risk libel). Among the positive attributes to convey are your company's growth, its reputation, its location, its concern for its employees, its long and illustrious history, its innovative products, its competitive strengths, the length of time that employees stay with the firm, and the large number of job applicants the company receives for each opening. As part of your preparation for the interview, think about the characteristics of your company that would appeal to a job candidate, and be sure to mention them during the interview.

Chick and Paula Hall own two Great Harvest Bread Company bakeries in the Chicago area. When someone comes in to fill out a job application, that person receives a printed copy of the company's mission statement, which includes a history of the company, principles the owners use to guide the company, the need for teamwork, and the importance of having fun. The sheet also "alerts people to the fact that we're not kidding when we say customer service is important," says Chick.

Be open minded

We can get so caught up with a single idea or purpose that we miss out on opportunities. Ron Griffin, senior vice president of information services at the Home Depot, Atlanta, tells the story of a woman who applied for a job as a business analyst. However, the company also had a need for people with people development and training skills. After interviewing her, he found she had a passion for training and had experience in it, so he hired her for that position rather than the one she initially applied for. "Figure out how you might best use [those who apply] and how they might make your whole organization better," he says. "We have a pretty flexible culture."

Interview all candidates

If you've done a good job of screening resumes and job applications, everyone you've asked to come in to be interviewed should have a reasonable chance of being chosen. Give everyone a fair hearing.

Make the most of an interview

Making the most of an interview can be difficult. You may have a good list of questions and ask all the questions, but an interview can still fail if you miss the subtleties or get poor responses from those you interview.

- *Be pleasant.* Set a tone of friendliness and openness. Smile. Shake hands. Ask if the candidate would like something to drink (coffee, tea, water, or a soft drink). Offer her a seat and thank her for coming. Try to put her (and perhaps yourself) at ease. You might do this by engaging in a little chitchat, about the weather or the traffic. You don't want to waste time, but you want to set the stage for a pleasant and productive conversation. If an interviewer's first question is, "Tell me about your failures and why," that does not set a tone conducive to open and relaxed communication. If you put the candidate on the defensive from the beginning, they'll likely stay that way throughout the interview, and you won't be able to learn much about their skills, their personality, or their ability to fit into your organization.

- *Maintain control.* An aggressive candidate may try to take control by making comments about various subjects, going off on tangents, asking questions. As the interviewer, you want to keep control yourself, because you have certain goals and needs that must be met. If the candidate starts going off track, gently bring the discussion back to the subject at hand. If the candidate asks questions to a distracting extent, you might ask that they save their questions for the end, when you will be happy to answer them.

■ *Observe body language.* It has been said that most communication is not limited to what is spoken, but "speaks" through body language and *how* things are said. (This is why telephone interviews are inherently limiting; you miss all those nonverbal clues.) Lots can be said about body language, but what is particularly important to note is a pattern of inconsistencies between what is said and how the person behaves physically. If the interviewee says she likes something, but begins to fidget, that suggests that the answer has caused her stress and perhaps is not entirely true. Pay close attention throughout the interview to physical reactions of candidates.

■ *Effective questioning.* Ask open-ended questions, as suggested at the beginning of this chapter. Instead of inquiring, "Do you like being in sales?," try, "So tell me, how did you first get involved with sales?" Gopal Kapur of the Center for Project Management says don't ask, "Are you a team player?" Rather, ask something like, "When you're on a team of four or five people, what are the problems four or five people can cause? What if three team members don't have the same idea of closure? How would you help solve it?" Open-ended questions require an extended answer, while closed ones can usually be answered with a simple yes or no. Also, try to avoid leading questions, such as, "You don't mind traveling a fair amount, do you?" "You wouldn't mind working on weekends, would you?" "We work long hours here, not nine to five—that's not a problem, is it?" Leading questions foreshadow the desired answer. Instead, you could mention that the job requires X-amount of travel per month or that three days a week on average, you will probably be working until 8:00 p.m. Another approach you could take is to say, "The job involves a fair amount of travel (or work hours). How much travel (or work hours) would you be comfortable with?" You want to know what the applicant really thinks—not what he thinks you want to hear.

▪ *Set the stage.* Good public speakers know that effective speeches begin with an introduction that tells the audience what they will hear, capsulizes what's been covered at various points in the speech, and closes with a summary of what's been said. (Another way to put it is: Tell them what they're going to hear, say it, tell them what they've just heard.) This method can apply to some degree to interviews. Start the interview with an introduction. For example:

> My name is —, and my title is —. What I do here is —. What I'd like to do first is tell you about our company and the position we have open. Then I'd like you to briefly tell me about your work history. I'll follow that with a few questions about each of your previous jobs and why you decided to leave. Then we'll talk about some technical issues. And finally, we'll discuss your goals and how this job may match what you want to achieve.

▪ *Money discussion.* When asking an applicant about salary, take time to discuss how salary figures are counted. For example, if the applicant says she is paid $37K per year, is she counting the salary only, or does that figure include a bonus? The applicant may not be trying to deceive, exactly, if she counts $31,200 + $6,300 bonus as her year's salary of $37K. Still, be sure you and the interviewee are speaking the same language regarding salary.

■ *Reference checks.* Near the end of the interview, if you plan to run informal background checks on candidates' references (as we recommend; see the next chapter), you should let the candidate know that you'll be checking references. Say to the interviewee, "We check all references, so are all these telephone numbers current?" It is best to ask the candidate to sign a waiver indicating that he has been notified that references will be contacted.

■ *Summary.* At the end of the interview, you might give a very brief summary of what was discussed and then let the applicant know what to expect. This might include:

> I will continue to interview for this position during the remainder of this week. You should hear back from me within a week if it is worthwhile for you to come in for a second interview. If you don't hear back by then, please feel free to call, but first let me have a week to narrow down the candidates so we can conduct some further interviews.

■ *Tests.* Depending on the position, you might consider giving a test or assignment. This is a somewhat dicey area. Some companies like to give assignments to candidates or have them take tests *before* the interview. This is asking a lot from a candidate, and you should have a good reason for doing it, or you may lose out on some candidates who balk at spending hours doing an assignment for a job they know little about.

An alternative is to give an assignment *after* an interview to those who you think might make the grade. This is often a good idea because at this point, the candidate has had a chance to learn about the job and to determine whether she wants it, and, if so, she would likely be more favorably disposed to doing the assignment than if asked before the interview.

If you do give a test or assignment, provide very clear written instructions regarding time, references, or resources, and so on. Depending on the complexity of the assignment—particularly if it results in a "work product" that the employer might use—you might also be prepared to pay a modest stipend, or "honorarium," as a way of recompensing the time the applicant spent on the assignment.

You will have to find out for yourself how feasible it is to use assignments as part of the interviewing process.

Questions to ask

The variety of questions that could be and are asked at hiring interviews is almost limitless. To give you an idea of the variety of questions that can be asked, a recent book on interviewing promises "751 Great Interview Questions." (See Appendix C, "Recommended Reading.") Let's look at several questions you might consider asking:

- What specific steps have you used to upgrade your knowledge or skill during the past 12 to 24 months?

- What key contribution could you or would you make to this group or this project? (This question could be broken down into short-term contributions—3 to 6 months—and longer-term—6 to 12 months.)

- Please give an example of a specific problem that arose in a previous job and explain how you devised a solution. (James Essey of TemPositions in New York says that specific, targeted questions, rather than hypothetical scenarios, are best for indications of how an applicant would perform in the job.)

- Ask three or four questions in quick succession (with no time to respond between questions) to test a person's ability to listen, think, organize their thoughts, and communicate back effectively. It almost doesn't matter what you ask. Examples: What job would you like to have in five years? What are the major challenges to setting up a corporate intranet? What are the most important things you look for from an employer?

- What am I likely to hear—both positive and negative—when I call your references? (Dr. Pierre Mornell, a psychiatrist, writes in *Inc.*: "The question is both practical and fair. Practical because it allows the candidates to alert their references to your inquiry. Fair, because it tells the candidates that you will be checking their references in depth, and it gives them a chance to tell their side of the story.")

Watch Out!
The biggest mistake in interviewing by new managers, says Jon Marshal of Robert Half International, is not considering whether the person is a good fit with the company's culture. For example, for a computer company doing client/server technology, is the person really interested in client/server technology? Match the person with the organization, instead of only matching skills to the skills needed.

General background questions reveal something about a person and their experience. For example:

- What were your responsibilities at your previous jobs?

- What aspects of your work do you like the most? The least? And why?

- What do you do to keep up to date in your job?

- Why did you apply for this job?

- What contributions do you think you could make to our organization?

- In what type of environment do you thrive?

- Please describe what you like (disliked) about your last supervisor? (This gives you a feel for personality conflicts.)

- Describe how your experience relates to our products/company.

- Describe for me a project you worked on and what your contribution to it was.

- What do you do in your spare time? (Tom Probert, smelter manager at Kennecott Utah Copper Corp., says, "I use this question at an inopportune time, so they have to think about it and I see how fast they shift their thinking. A balanced person makes the shift easily." By "balanced," Probert means someone who has interests outside of work, as opposed to an "unbalanced," one-dimensional workaholic.)

- Tell me about a supervisor you did not like. This question will probably make most applicants uncomfortable, which lets you see how they deal with stressful situations. Of course, what they say is important. If a candidate talks about how the manager tried to control his every move, it suggests that the candidate likes freedom, and probably is willing to be held accountable. If the candidate complains that the supervisor was the cause of most of the department's problems, then the candidate may not be willing to take responsibility. If the person answers this question well, Tom Probert then asks about a supervisor the person liked.

■ If you came to work for me today, assuming that I offered you a job, and six months from now you woke up and thought, "What have I done? Taking this job was the biggest mistake I ever made." What would cause you to have that reaction? This question will make some people defensive ("that's an impossible question to answer") or reveal what really motivates them ("I could get a better offer"). Keith Bearden, information services manager at A-dec Inc., Newberg, Oregon, who asks this question, found his ideal response from a candidate who said: "Well a lot of things can change, but I can tell you one thing: If I come here and you don't let me do my job, you micro-manage me, I'll leave." That's the kind of answer you're looking for.

■ Why are manhole covers round? Remember this question from Tom McElveen, director of administrative service lines at Carilion Health System, Roanoke, Virginia, that started off this chapter? He's not looking for the correct answer but how logical and articulate is the person's response. (By the way, only two people have given McElveen the correct answer: A round manhole cover cannot fall through its hole as long as there is a small lip around the top of the hole. Few geometric shapes have this quality.)

Closing the interview

Be polite, even if you are not interested in the candidate, and thank him or her for coming.

At the end of the interview, ask the applicant to write a one-page summary of what was discussed during the interview and return it to you within two days. Request that it be handwritten. This will tell you: 1. How interested the person is in the job (if they don't submit the summary, or do so late, or give you a sloppy summary, consider them uninterested); 2. How well the person listened during the interview (don't tell them ahead of time you'll be asking for this); and, 3. What is important to the person.

Interviewing errors to avoid

There are lots of things you can do wrong at an interview. Some are related to the legal issues we discussed in Chapter 2. But here are some others worth watching out for:

"
From listening comes wisdom, and from speaking, repentance.
—Italian proverb
"

- *Talking too much.* Excessive talking by the interviewer is a common problem. Donald H. Weiss, author of *Fair, Square and Legal,* advises, "An interview should consist of 80 percent of job candidates talking and 20 percent of the interviewer talking. Mainly, you should be asking questions." Whether you talk only 20 percent or a bit more, certainly, the applicant should do most of the talking. Just remember that the primary purpose of the interview is for the interviewer to learn about the applicant.

- *Asking generic, predictable questions.* The job-seeking audience today is often fairly sophisticated.

Universities and even high schools are providing counseling on handling job interviews. When an interviewer asks predictable, worn-out questions, such as, "Where would like to be in five years in terms of your career?," she should expect predictable answers. The applicant has likely been coached how to answer this type of question or has at least given it some thought. Not all your questions have to come from left field, but if you ask a stock question, don't be surprised when you get a stock answer.

■ *Promising more than you can deliver.* Perhaps because of the tight labor market, some managers tend to exaggerate their company's good qualities and overpromise to attract an applicant. Do not promise more than you can deliver. First, over promising can get you into legal trouble. In addition, it raises expectations in the job candidate that, when not fulfilled on the job, can cause resentment, hostility, and headaches. For example, do not say that everyone gets a promotion and raise every six months—unless it's true.

■ *Making assumptions.* You may make an assumption about a person based on minimal information and, as a result, jump to false conclusions. Let the applicant speak, and listen to what she says. If you don't understand something or are missing a piece of information, ask for an explanation.

How candidates can be "lost"

You can lose candidates because of how you treat them. Be sure the interviewer is well prepared; a

> 66
> Assumptions are the termites of relationships.
> —Henry Winkler, actor, quoted in *Life Isn't Fair*, by Harold Hill
> 99

poorly organized or informed interviewer reflects poorly on your organization. Looking for work is a full-time job, so be sensitive to the demands you make on candidates, such as calling them back for repeated interviews or asking them to do sample projects. Provide accurate written job descriptions so they understand what the job entails. Keep them abreast of the status of their candidacy. And don't string them along or be indecisive: Make a decision, and do it quickly. In today's job market, you can lose good candidates to other employers who make offers faster than you.

Compensation

Don't discuss it during the first interview. We'll talk about compensation in the next chapter. The exception is if there will be only one interview. In this case, provide the candidate with a salary range, but don't get into negotiations.

After the interview

Take a few minutes after the interview to weigh whether this candidate is worth a second interview. Write down your thoughts and impressions.

Evaluate your own performance. Ask yourself:

- Did I learn from this candidate what I needed to know?

- Did I get my message across to the candidate about the job, about the company?

- Do I have enough information now to make a decision?

- Was the interview conducted in the most efficient way?

- How could I improve my technique?

Multiple interviews

Many small companies and virtually all large ones subject their candidates to multiple interviews, but two or three is usually the maximum. (Some large companies go for a six-to-eight-interview extravaganza, especially for higher-level positions, or for those positions where the employee works with a variety of people; they should have some say as to who they work with.) Multiple interviews are beneficial because the responsibility of hiring doesn't rest on one person, and various people bring different things to interviews so that, when taken together, you usually get a more complete picture of the candidate than if one person did all the interviewing.

If you work in teams, be sure to include team members in the interviewing process. Chick and Paula Hall bring candidates to their current employees in the bakery and let the workers ask questions and get a "feel" for the person. The people in the bakery will have to work with the new hire, so they should have a say in whether or not they want to work with him. "We talk to our crew as to what they are looking for," says Paula. "We ask them to look at people to see if the applicant can carry their weight. They can pick out who will be the hardest workers."

If you use more than one interviewer, be sure that all interviewers ask the same questions, and then compare how the candidate responded. This could provide an indication of how forthright the candidate has been in his answers.

Making a choice

How do you decide whom to pick? If you've done your homework well, this should be relatively easy to answer. You know what you're looking for, and, with good interviewing techniques, you've gotten the information you needed so you could quickly compare and contrast candidates. The problems should only arise if you have two or more highly qualified candidates—or basically no qualified candidates. (If you don't have any, either your market is so tight, you're out of luck, or you haven't done a good job promoting the job, which is more likely.) If you have two or more very good candidates to choose from, consider yourself lucky. Go with the one whose personality seems most compatible. If you can't choose because so many candidates seem alike, it may be that you need to go back to defining what you want and determine how to shape the interview to get the information you need.

Just the facts

- A list of questions to ask and points to cover can help keep the interview on track.

- Conduct the interview in a private, quiet place, to minimize distractions.

- Use open-ended questions almost exclusively— avoid closed and leading questions.

- The interviewer should do most of the listening, while the candidate does most of the talking.

- The interviewer should be careful not to promise more than the company can deliver.

GET THE SCOOP ON...
Why thorough reference checks are essential ▪
How to detect warning signals ▪ Why direct
supervisors are the best references ▪ How to
find knowledgeable references ▪ Why you
should rely on the telephone for references

After the Interview: Checking References

Chapter 13

After the interviews have been completed, it's time to check up on the candidates' references and determine the offer you want to make to your number-one pick. This chapter is about setting the stage for identifying and landing the applicant who will make a contribution to your business.

When you've selected the most promising few of the candidates interviewed, you can contact their references to verify claims of experience and ask about general performance, which we'll discuss in detail below. You can then use these findings to help in deciding on the person to whom you want to offer the job. A general background check may supplement your decision, which should be based primarily on qualifications, performance in the interview, and so on. When you make an offer, explain that the offer is contingent upon satisfactory completion of a background check. This is an

Watch Out!
A survey of information systems employees by *Computerworld* (Oct. 27, 1997) found that 19 businesses have had cases of theft or fraud committed by internal information systems workers, yet only 25 percent of the businesses routinely do criminal history checks on IS applicants. Only 11 percent routinely check credit histories to see whether IS applicants have major financial problems that could spur misconduct.

option the employer may, or may not, choose to pursue, depending on whether any questions remain about the candidate's background. After you have made an offer, you may begin a more detailed background check of previous employers, current supervisor, and, if pertinent to the position (as for someone handling money), a credit check.

Checking references

You might expect that in the tight labor market we have today, where jobs in most fields and most geographic areas are fairly plentiful, job applicants would not sense a need to lie on their resumes or applications or in interviews—but they do. Probably the main factor is a desire for higher salary. And maybe they want a better or more prestigious job than their education, experience, or job performance would honestly get them. Then, too, some job-seekers may be insecure about their qualifications, and so "doctor up" their resumes to make things look better than they are. Whatever the reasons for such deceptions, statistics from recent studies are troubling. According to a report in *Computerworld Online*, "Recruiters estimate that one out of three job applicants misrepresents his or her background" (March 17, 1998). And David Harrell, a principal at Follmer, Rudzewicz and Company, a CPA firm in Sterling Heights, Michigan, says, "Somebody pointed out that 50 percent to 60 percent of people lie on their resumes about their academic credentials."

Observers agree that what many job hunters say and report to employers is not entirely accurate. Conducting reference checks can be time-consuming and something of an annoyance, but it's worthwhile because if you don't properly check references, you significantly increase your chances of making a regrettable selection.

"We advise that you get as thorough a background check as possible," says Stephen Sheinfeld, chairman of the labor and employment department at the New York law firm of Whitman Breed Abbott & Morgan. "It's a lot easier to reject someone because it just doesn't seem right than to have them join you, and then you say, with hindsight, 'We always thought that there was going to be a problem with him or her in this job.'"

Up to now, we've been talking about how to make your hiring process more effective. All your planning and all the time you have invested in interviewing can come to naught if someone lies to you, and you don't realize it and you end up hiring that person. You can easily make your choice based on things told to you that have no more substance than smoke and mirrors. And when you make a wrong hiring choice, as we have seen, the mistake can cost you thousands of dollars.

Start checking now

In the previous chapter, on interviews, I recommended asking applicants to sign a waiver granting permission to conduct reference checks. Of course, you should only check the references of applicants you're seriously interested in. Focus on the best qualified, and get to work immediately. If this person is really as good as you think, you may be in competition with other employers, so the faster you act, the better your chances of getting him or her to work for you.

Watch Out!
If you're uncomfortable with asking for possibly negative information, and if you're reluctant to ask references the hard questions, such as, "Would you rehire Mr. X?," then give the job of reference checking to someone not so squeamish. Such questions are too important to put aside simply because they're difficult to ask.

Unofficially...
Of companies that conduct pre-employment screening, 81 percent verify education, 79 percent check previous employment, 59 percent check references, 37 percent examine criminal records, 50 percent conduct drug testing, and 21 percent inspect motor vehicle records, according to Dannette Evans, president of EMDM, information consultants in Marietta, Georgia (*Black Enterprise*, October 1997).

Have the immediate supervisor do the reference checking

A clerical person might do the credit checks and other relatively simple reference checks, but you want someone who really knows the job and its demands to question former employers and others who can provide insights into the person's professional abilities. Don't consider reference checks to be annoyances better left to underlings. Background checks are important, and management should take them seriously.

Prepare

Throughout this book, as when discussing hiring plans and hiring interview, we've talked about the importance of preparation. Here, also, you need to prepare. Before making a reference call, know exactly what you want to learn from the call and write these points down. Before you hang up, be sure you have gotten answers to all the issues you needed to address.

You can get useful information

The fear of litigation has made many employers shut their mouths tighter than a clam when someone calls for a reference, but don't assume that there's no useful information to be obtained from reference checks. You can get useful information, and we'll discuss some "discovery methods" shortly.

Recognize the differences between references

Not all references are created equal. First, some have better insights into a person's character and abilities than others. Immediate supervisors tend to be the best references. A direct supervisor can usually speak more knowledgeably about a person than can someone far above or below the applicant.

Those lower in the pecking order may have some useful knowledge about the applicant but lack the overview that a supervisor would have. But others can be very useful. Peers can provide valuable insights, as can others who have contact with the person, such as vendors and employees of other departments in the applicant's company. An executive can be useful if he or she really knows the person. From a high-up exec, you'll probably get as honest an appraisal as from anyone, because the executive has too much at stake to be known as a liar; but often the executive has limited knowledge of the applicant, which reduces the value of his or her recommendation. Probably least useful are the "personal" references; they can usually be relied on to say only nice things about the applicant.

Basic questions to ask

There are some basic questions that need to be verified when you check on the candidate's performance at previous jobs. These include:

- *For each previous employer:* The name of the company, the name of the position the candidate held, and the dates of employment. When you get this information, compare it to the resume or job application the candidate submitted, and note any discrepancies.

- *Education:* Call up the college or university listed on the candidate's resume and verify that what is claimed on the resume or job application is true. Did the candidate actually graduate? This is an enticing place for candidates to lie or exaggerate (such as claiming they graduated). Whether your job opening calls for a specific degree is not necessarily the point; you want to

Watch Out!
Percentage of fast-food-restaurant employees who say they have stolen food or money from their employer: 62. Quoted in *What Counts: The Complete Harper's Index*, edited by Charis Conn & Hena Silverman.

make sure the person is being honest. You may not care if she has a college degree, but you should care if the candidate claims a degree she hasn't earned.

■ *The pecking order:* Where was the candidate in the pecking order of the organization? He may claim to have been higher up than he really was. Check the accuracy of the title the person says he had. This helps place him on the corporate hierarchy, but it's hard to know exactly what a title means because different companies use the same titles to mean different things, or have titles you may not be familiar with. Verify who the candidate's supervisor was. An applicant may claim that one person was their supervisor—and even give that person as a reference—when in fact their supervisor was someone else. You need to know who the candidate reported to.

■ *Salary:* Find out the person's salary. Sometimes companies are reluctant to disclose this. For this reason, says Laurie Levenson, it's very important that you get an accurate salary from the candidate during his interview with you. Levenson says: "It's good to ask the candidate what specifically was his income as it was listed on his W2 form. I find that when I interview and I ask what they're making and they give me a dollar amount, I usually have to dig deeper to find out what component of that was in salary, what was in bonus, in stock options, etc., so that you can really compare apples to apples.

"When you mention the W2, many people think you will check up on what they say, so they tend to be more honest. Also, you can have the

person himself verify what he earned by showing you his W2 or his last pay stub." If the candidate does not verify his earnings, then when
you check with his employer, and the employer
says they won't reveal that information, you can
ask, "Did the person earn $XXX?" Usually a
company will let you know if the figure is fairly
accurate.

Even if the candidate verifies his income, be
sure to ask the employer how long he was earning at that level. You may find he got a raise
from $42,000 to $48,000 just last month, and is
now asking you for $55,000, claiming he won't
want to make a move unless he gets a raise of
about 15 percent or more. The "15 percent" figure may be accurate on the surface, but you are
in a better position if you know the candidate
just got a sizable raise. He may be willing to take
less than the $55,000 he says is his minimum.

Some additional questions

Ask the reference if she would rehire the candidate.
Some companies have a policy of never rehiring
someone who has voluntarily left their employ, so
you should ask if this is a factor if the reference says
they would not rehire the candidate. But assuming
this is not a company or personal policy, asking this
question helps reveal what the reference really
thought of the candidate. It's like someone asking
you if you had it to do over again, would you choose
the same car or stereo system you bought?

Asking about rehiring calls for tact and good
judgment. While some companies do not rehire former employees, others have a policy or custom of
rehiring that may not be observed if an employee

left to work for a competitor. In other cases, a company may hold a grudge against or feel "betrayed" by a particularly valuable employee who left for greener pastures. Keep these factors in mind when asking whether the company would rehire the person in question.

Ask about the candidate's reliability. Also, inquire whether there is a particular noteworthy achievement the candidate performed, and could she say something about that? It's telling if the reference cannot come up with any notable achievement. As with asking for a return call if the candidate was judged outstanding, here you learn something negative about the candidate without anything overtly negative being said. (Note, however, that if you're calling a business where the applicant worked a long time ago, the supervisor may honestly not remember. In this case, you can refresh her memory by inquiring about a particular "bullet point" item on the applicant's resume and ask for elaboration.)

And, of course, ask questions specific to the job. If you work in teams, you'll want to know how well the candidate meshes with a team. If you need someone who takes orders, you might ask, "How comfortable is Joe with taking direction from a supervisor?" On the other hand, if you need a self-starter who can make things happen, you might ask, "How well do you think Joe would do in an atmosphere where there is not close supervision, and he is left largely on his own to achieve his goals?"

If there are technical aspects to the job you're seeking to fill, such as running certain machinery, fixing certain equipment, or programming computers, be sure to ask the reference about the candidate's performance here, too.

Beware the phantom reference

Many applicants do not believe you'll contact their references (and they're often right), so they give references who either do not exist or know little about the applicant. If you find you have great trouble in locating references (the applicant should have asked their permission ahead of time, so they should be expecting your call), take that as a red flag. You definitely do not want to hire someone who cannot or will not give you several credible, reachable references. If the job candidate starts making excuses about why his references can't be contacted, start thinking about hiring someone else.

Ways to get behind the camouflage

Here are some techniques for delving deeper into a candidate's past:

Others in the company

"We don't typically take the references given by the employee as the reference we're going to count, because who would give a bad reference?" asks James Essey, president TemPositions in New York. "We ask the employee the name of someone they worked with at their previous company. We then call that individual, talk to them about the employee, but then ask them to give us the name of someone else to talk to as well. That's someone who the applicant has not potentially set up for the reference call, if you will. And that tends to be a very good reference, a sort of unbiased, unexpected call, and it works well for us."

Read between the lines

Don't take everything at face value: Read between the lines, look for discrepancies, troubling patterns, things that don't feel right. Stephen Sheinfeld advises, "Check the applicant's background. Check for gaps in employment on their resume, look for discrepant information when you compare their applicant, their interview and their background check.

"Discrepant information, especially if it's material, can be very important. They told you they resigned to pursue other interests, and you're told that they have been fired. They told you they made $37,500 when they left that job, and you find out it was $31,200. They told you they had an MBA from Harvard; Harvard says they don't. If you find all these things on the way in, you save yourself untold aggravation in terms of your process—not just because you then may have to fire them and deal with that, but because of all the wasted effort."

Ask the right type of questions

In the last chapter, we discussed how to ask the right type of interview questions: the open-ended inquiry versus the closed. The open-ended question generally elicits a response that is detailed and in some sense complete. This holds true with questions asked during reference checks. Rather than asking, "Did Amy make any significant contributions to your company?," put it this way: "What, if any, significant contributions did Amy make to your company?" If you get a curt, vague, or unrevealing response, don't hesitate to follow up with, "Can you expand on that?"

Dealing with the negative

For most of us, confrontation and negative situations cause discomfort. This is especially true of professional, business settings. That's why trying to see if there is significant negative information about an applicant has to be handled gingerly. Deflect the negative by couching some questions into the positive. Instead of asking, "What is Jim's most significant weakness?" (which will likely result in the unhelpful reply, "He has no significant weaknesses," or something trite like, "He's overly enthusiastic"), ask, "What are some areas where Jim can improve?" and ask for an example, and a second example, as a way of exploring his areas of weakness, however slight they may be. Another example: Instead of asking, "Does Jane choke under pressure?," say, "Tell me about a time when Jane had to work under pressure." References are far more likely to give you negative information about a person when a question is couched in the form of how a person reacts to certain circumstances, or how he could improve himself.

Silence speaks loudly

Here's another trick to get around the tendency of references to avoid saying something that's less than positive about a job candidate. This comes from Dr. Pierre Mornell's book, *Hiring Smart!*, as excerpted in *Inc.* magazine (March 1998). Dr. Mornell recommends calling references at a time when you wouldn't normally expect them to be available, such as lunchtime. The idea is to reach a person's voice mail or assistant. Mornell writes that when you call you say: "Jane Jones is a candidate for [the position] in our company. Your name has been given as a reference. Please call me back if the candidate was outstanding." The key here is the last sentence: Call back if the candidate was *outstanding*. According to Mornell, if the candidate is outstanding, the reference will quickly call back. That's a good sign, and you then have the opportunity to query the reference. If most of the references

Unofficially...
One of six workers has a drug problem, and drug use costs companies $7,000 to $10,000 per drug-using employee, because their productivity is only about two-thirds that of non-drug users, reports *Management Review* (Feb. 1997). It's no surprise, then, that 81 percent of major U.S. companies conduct drug tests, according to a study by the American Management Association as reported in *Security Management* (March 1997).

you've been given don't return your call, it's a red flag. This technique works, says Mornell, because no derogatory information has been shared, no libelous statements have been made, and no confidences or laws have been broken. In case the reference may be out of town, it's a good idea to check with the reference's secretary or someone in their department to make sure he or she isn't calling back because they are out of town or otherwise not getting their messages.

Use your network

Surf your network of friends and acquaintances to find anyone who might know the applicant. This is a reference you know and trust, and therefore is likely to be less biased than references provided by the applicant. If possible, don't stick strictly to references given to you—cast a wider net.

The most recent job is not necessarily the most revealing

Many who do reference checks focus on the candidate's most recent job and limit their check to his current or most recent employer. That's a good start, but it may not be enough. The candidate may have done nothing out of the ordinary at his most recent job or may not have worked there very long. If the candidate has had several jobs during the past few years, be sure to check out as many of the employers as possible. At a previous job—possibly in a position or at an organization more akin to yours than the candidate's current job or employer—the candidate may have had responsibilities that might better indicate how he would perform in your company. Of course, if the candidate has been with one employer for the past decade or two, it's not worth checking back further than the most recent job.

(But you need to do some checking just to verify this.)

You want to talk to references

When a job candidate provides the names of his references, be sure to get their phone numbers, not just the post office box or e-mail address. Checking a candidate's references depends on the ability to ask follow-up questions, to hear "little hesitations" or other nuances in the respondent's voice, and other clues that may signal "red lights" or "green lights." If someone gives you a brief answer over the phone, for example, you can come back with the question, "Can you give me an example?" or "Would you please explain that in more detail?" A written list of questions submitted through the mail or via e-mail can provide some information, but the interviewer has little control if the answers are minimal, one- or two-word replies. (If you do use a written format, be sure not to invite one-word answers but ask open-ended questions, as discussed above, that would require a real answer. And be sure to provide a self-addressed, stamped envelope to facilitate a quick reply.)

Take notes

Take as complete a set of notes of each reference interview as you can. Record the questions you ask and the replies, and any names or numbers you may need for follow-up calls.

Careful note-taking will:

1. Give you a picture of the candidate that you can review later, and that you can share with others in your organization so they can see what the references have been saying about the candidate. Your notes can easily be passed around to

those who need to know. (Respect the applicant's privacy, though: Use discretion in what
you include in notes that will be passed around
to others.)

2. Help you distinguish what was said, by whom.
   Keep in mind that you will likely contact several
   references for each of several candidates.

3. Give you a record you can use to back up your
   decision about hiring or not hiring the candidate, in case you were ever to be questioned
   later in a court suit.

Other types of references

We've been focusing primarily on checking the references who are previous employers. But there are
other types of references worth looking into. One of
these is credit reports, which the federal Fair Credit
Reporting Act says can be given to employers by
credit reporting agencies for purposes of making
employment decisions. Why would you want a person's credit history? If the person will be handling
cash or other valuables for you, you may not want to
hire someone currently in financial straits. In fact,
those currently experiencing financial difficulties
may be poor candidates for certain jobs in that they
are under considerable stress, which may affect their
ability to perform on the job.

You might also check criminal records (if any),
current and previous residences, civil records (for
lawsuits, and so on), and motor vehicle records (for
such things as drunk driving convictions). Some
companies test for drugs. Others require physical
examinations (though these can be required only
when directly related to the demands of the job).

In theory, you should do a complete, thorough background check of every person you hire, and in fact, there are companies that conduct these checks for a fee (often a couple of hundred dollars or so apiece). In practice, many companies do not have the time, the human resources, the financial resources, or the will to do thorough investigations. Being trusting is not altogether irrational. After all, when you hire someone, you're trusting them to be honest, diligent, fair, and reliable. You trust that the person will not come to work with a gun and will not try to sabotage your operation. Of course, some people may prove to be your worst nightmares, and a background check may not reveal the person's true character.

But what's important is for you to do everything you possibly can to check references and check the candidate's background. Do as much as you can, and be serious about it, not cursory. You've got an enormous amount riding on your choosing the right employee. And, when making that choice, you leave a great deal to chance if you do little or no reference checking, or do a poor job of the checking you do.

Just the facts

- A general background check of the two or three most promising candidates can help you narrow the field to one; once you've made an offer, you may want to conduct a more thorough check of your number-one pick.

- Before you ever make a reference call, be sure to know what you want to ask—and what you want to learn.

- Take notes during all reference calls; don't rely on your memory.

- The candidate's prospective supervisor, not a clerical worker or assistant, should conduct the reference checks.

- To learn about a person's real income, ask what income he or she reported on the W2 form.

GET THE SCOOP ON...
Why you should concentrate on accomplishments ▪ Why attitude counts ▪ The two basic
methods for choosing between candidates ▪ How
to make an offer the job candidate will appreciate ▪ When "cheap" can prove very expensive

Making a Decision, Making an Offer

Chapter 14

Yᵒu've now interviewed your candidates and checked out their backgrounds. All that's left to do is choose the right one and make that person an offer. Sounds easy, and if you've done your homework, it shouldn't be too hard—unless you're blessed with more than one "perfect candidate" and have to make a choice. (That's an embarrassment of riches, a problem other employers would envy.) What this chapter will show you is how to choose between the candidates you do have and make a fair offer likely to be accepted.

Some tips and traps to keep in mind

The opportunity for errors at this stage of the hiring process are many. Here are some tips—and some traps—to keep in mind:

- *Go with your gut.* You've done all sorts of analyses about what you want and what you need, and checked out the candidates thoroughly, but there's also good reason to listen to the counsel of your "gut instinct." Often our instincts are right. If there is something about a person that bothers you—even if only vaguely—pay attention to that. Don't dismiss your instincts simply because the person looks great on paper. Perhaps there was something at the interview that didn't quite sit well with you. Refer to your notes from the interview and think back to what went on. If you're not sure about the person, try to understand why that may be.

Then, too, the converse can be true: The person's background may seem weak on paper, but there's something about his or her personality, attitude, or energy that makes you think this person could be a solid addition to your team. You've got to pay attention to how you feel. And consider your gut's track record; in the past when you've relied on your instinct for hiring or in other situations, how well has it served you? If you've made good choices based on your instinct before, don't stop now.

■ *Accomplishments are what count.* Yes, credentials— college degrees, professional certificates, job experience—are all important. But there's something even more important, namely the applicant's accomplishments. How well one has done in the past is often a good indicator of how well the person will do in the future. That's why you need to know what the person has *really* accomplished, which you learn from the personal interview and from checking references.

■ *Attitude matters.* A positive attitude is generally ranked at the top of desired characteristics in employees (along with good communication skills). In his book *Learned Optimism,* Martin E. P. Seligman writes: "Our workplaces and our schools operate on the conventional assumption that success results from a combination of talent and desire. When failure occurs, it is because either talent or desire is missing. But failure also can occur when talent and desire are present in abundance but optimism is missing." Optimism, positive attitude—call it what you want—should be present in your candidate. You want someone who thinks in terms of what *can* be done, of what can be improved; in short, someone who believes that she—and your organization—can succeed. If she doesn't believe that, chances are good she won't succeed, no matter how good her credentials or how impressive her list of job titles.

■ *Stay on track.* When in the midst of making a hiring decision, it's easy to get off track and start musing on considerations irrelevant to the job and the work to be done. Stay on track; stay focused on what's important. Keeping the job description and your list of interview questions in front of you is one way to keep your attention focused on the decision at hand. When you wrote the job description, when you started advertising for the position, when you prepared for the hiring interview—at each of these stages, you developed criteria for what the job entailed and what skills, experience, education, and other factors the ideal candidate should possess. Write these out and have this list in front of you as you ponder whom to hire. Now, more than ever, is the time to stay focused on what's important.

- *Remain calm.* It's easy to panic at a time like this—easy, but not advisable. You can remain calm if, as counseled above, you remain focused on the position's requirements and the candidates' qualifications. You'll do the right thing.

- *Think positively (and beware assumptions).* In many ways, about many things, we make assumptions, often without recognizing or acknowledging that they are only assumptions. For example, don't assume that just because a candidate worked for a big company before, and you have a small company, he or she won't consider working for you. They responded to your ad, so they obviously have some interest. Don't reject someone because you think they wouldn't really want to work for your company.

- *Be objective.* You might have a list of criteria you're using to judge each candidate, such as intelligence, communication skills, appearance, attitude, experience, personality, initiative, and being a team player. Then the candidate walks into your office for an interview, is very engaging, and you enjoy his or her company and personality, and, bam, you rank him or her high on all criteria. Slow down. Be objective. An engaging personality might be important (more so in some positions than in others), but don't let that blind you to shortcomings the person may have in other areas. Be objective. Run through your list of criteria for each candidate and realistically analyze each person's strengths and weaknesses for each of your criteria.

- *"Cheap" isn't necessarily a bargain.* Being penny-wise and pound foolish is definitely not the way to choose the candidate who will be the most valuable for you. You might get someone for $5,000 a year less—that's $100 a week—but the more expensive person might be far more productive and give you a return on that $5,000 investment many times over.

- *Don't over-buy.* Be open to hiring someone who is "overqualified," as they may do you a world of good. But in a tight labor market, you'll probably have to pay for the candidate's qualifications, so the more qualifications, the more you have to pay. If you can't put those qualifications to good use, you may be wasting your money. Before making such a person an offer, think about ways you might use such a person to good advantage, such as by having them open a new market for you or developing a new product. If you really cannot use that person's abilities, go with another candidate whose background may not be quite as impressive, but who won't demand as much compensation, either.

The mechanics of selection

I've been discussing what to do and what not to do when selecting a candidate. Now I'll address some of the techniques you can use to choose one person over another.

Have a plan

You need a plan for how you will evaluate all the candidates you interviewed and did references checks on. This plan should include the following steps:

1. Create a list of all those who will take part in the evaluation process. If you have a very small company and you make all the decisions, then this is

easy. More likely, others will take part in the selection. Even in small companies, the owner and the immediate supervisor are usually involved. In larger organizations, the immediate supervisor, department head, and executive could contribute to the decision. You might want to include someone who will be working directly with the prospect. If you use a team approach, the team leader and the immediate supervisor are likely participants. In large organizations, someone from human resources will be involved. Know right from the beginning who will be involved.

2. Schedule a meeting in which everyone who is involved in making a choice can sit down together and discuss the criteria that will be used and how candidates will be rated. You want consistency here, an agreement about what is important and what's not so important. This is not to say that everyone will agree completely but that you all are working from the same page. Both for reasons of basic fairness and consistency, and to prevent any liability of discrimination, the same "decision team" should choose among all the candidates. What you don't want is someone who is judging candidates primarily, say, on their technical expertise, while someone else is putting heavy emphasis on management experience—unless you decide to divide up responsibilities and have one person judge technical competence, another managerial strengths, and a third person business acumen. This approach is perfectly acceptable, as long as everyone understands and agrees to this division of labor.

3. Make copies of all the materials from all the candidates available to everyone who will be involved in the choice. This includes resumes, job applications, tests, supporting materials the candidate provided, notes about interviews, and notes about reference checks. This has to be an organized effort, and providing copies for everyone will help assure that the process works smoothly.

4. Set deadlines for decisions. Don't let the process drag on and on. You lose good candidates that way and waste a lot of people's time. Give all those who are involved with the decision a day or two to come up with a list of, say, three top candidates, and then schedule a meeting where everyone meets and discusses their choices.

5. Make the offer. Later in this chapter, I will discuss the offer you will make to your number-one candidate, but at this meeting, make sure everyone is in agreement with what the chosen candidate will be offered, and what leeway the person who will be making the offer has in raising the job package. You need parameters beyond which the negotiations cannot go. It's not a good idea for the person making the offer to offer a signing bonus, for example, unless the group has agreed that a signing bonus is something they want to propose to the candidate. Again, everyone should be working from the same page.

Mistakes to avoid when selecting

Your hiring strategy should be designed to help you select candidates based on *quality*. This may sound obvious, but companies sometimes do amazing things that lead them to hire employees of less than desirable quality. Among the mistakes to avoid are:

▪ *The desperate approach.* When you take the pick of a middling litter of candidates out of fear you'll never find anyone better, you're choosing out of desperation. When you plan correctly, do your homework, and screen carefully; the talent pool will almost always have several winners in it, and you'll have no need to feel desperate.

▪ *Hiring in haste because you needed someone yesterday.* Astute observers call this the "buy now, pay later" strategy of hiring.

▪ *Hiring in the hope that the employee will change under your tutelage.* This strategy doesn't work in marriage, and it doesn't work with hiring. Most people will not change much, no matter how hard you try to transform them. Take the conservative approach: What you see is what you get, and if that is not acceptable, look elsewhere.

▪ *Letting yourself be enamored by the person's "performance" at the job interview or persistence in pursuing the job.* Those who act dazzling in interviews or who go after a job with all guns blazing may be great at getting hired but may lack the attributes your company needs, such as persistence, a positive and cooperative attitude, and willingness to learn. A glib talker at an interview may be wrong for a computer programming or bookkeeping job, for example. Go beyond the veneer you see during the interview and ask if this person is really right for your company and the position available.

▪ *Being blinded by past performance.* When pitching financial products such as mutual funds, sales people remind customers that past history is no guarantee of future performance. The same can be said of potential employees. A good track record may be a function of a person's abilities, but it also may be the result of luck, or the help of a mentor (who remains unknown to you), or a one-time moment of inspiration. Be realistic when assessing a person's potential.

▪ *Being distracted by the pull of product or technical knowledge.* A candidate may know a great deal about your product or technology, but that may have limited value if the open position does not involve working directly with the product or technology. If you have a financial planning practice, it's great to have people who know the tax laws, but if that is the strength of all of your employees, who will sell or manage your business? Keep your focus on the job's needs and the candidates' qualifications.

▪ *Lowering your standards because employees have nowhere to go.* Some lower their hiring standards because they feel they must; they have nowhere to promote those who excel, so they look for mediocrity. If this is your situation, consider changing your organization and how it's structured, rather than change your selection standards. You harm your company when you hire those not fully qualified.

Making the choice

Two basic methods for evaluating candidates are widely used, and you may want to choose one or both. These are:

▪ **How well the candidate matches your criteria**

One selection method is to match the candidates' strengths and weaknesses to the criteria

> 66
> Hire the strongest people you can possibly find even if they may personally intimidate you a little bit.
> —Richard Lennon, vice president, Brown-Forman Corp., Louisville, Kentucky
> 99

you have established for the job, such as experience, technical know-how, and the like. It's very likely you will not find a candidate that meets 100 percent of your criteria. Mr. or Ms. Perfect probably doesn't exist. So you have to choose among imperfect candidates. A candidate who meets 75 percent of your criteria but is willing and able to learn could be a better choice than a candidate who matches 85 percent of your criteria but is not very flexible or eager to learn. You need to understand how much emphasis you want to place on exact matches to your criteria, and how much "wiggle room" you want to incorporate into your decision-making process.

- **How well the candidates compare to one another**

  The second way to look at candidates is by assessing how well they compare to one another. This approach says, this is the pool of candidates we have; let's take the one who best matches what we need, even if that person isn't a very good match. This differs from the first selection method, which tries to get as good a match as possible, and if a good match isn't available, either starts the search again or adds additional criteria, such as the ability of a candidate to learn.

Pros and cons of the two approaches

There is no right or wrong as to which approach you use. Sports teams often use one or the other when drafting players, depending on their philosophy. For example, a football team may say, "We have an opening for a tight end. Let's pick the prospect who seems to have the best potential as a tight end."

Another team might say, "We need a tight end, but let's pick the best athlete available, no matter which position he plays."

Sticking to your criteria and choosing only those who match your criteria sounds like the best idea, but from a practical viewpoint, it may not work. Given the pool of applicants you have attracted, you may not have anyone who matches your criteria as closely as you would like. Either your criteria were unrealistic or the labor pool is such that you cannot get a good match of people who meet your needs. This school of thought says to choose the best of the bunch.

The other approach says that such a strategy doesn't make much sense because if none of the candidates meet your minimum needs, they won't be productive. Or to choose one of the candidates requires you to lower your standards just to land someone. This school of thought says to go back to square one, start the search again, and work extra hard to get a more qualified pool of candidates so you don't have to settle for inferior choices. If you take this approach, certainly rethink your hiring campaign. *Do not do the exact same thing again and expect different results.* If you decide not to lower your standards and start again, review your hiring plan and see where it can be improved.

As to which approach to take, unfortunately there is no clear right or wrong. Much depends on who applies for the position, how badly (and how quickly) you need someone in the position, how clearly inferior the candidates are, and how stringent are your criteria. Another factor to consider is whether you'll soon have another opening due to turnover.

If you decide to go with a much-less-than-ideal candidate, use a trial period to make sure this person can be productive for you, and it is only fair to make this clear to the candidate. Tell the person in clear language that they are being hired on a trial basis, and state for how long. Consider hiring all employees for a specified trial period—for example, 90 days—to avoid charges of discrimination.

Checklist for evaluating candidates

Here's a 10-point checklist to use when evaluating candidates:

1. What are the applicant's strengths relative to the needs of the job?

2. What are the applicant's weaknesses relative to the needs of the job?

3. Can these weaknesses be made up relatively easily and quickly through training, mentoring, or on-the-job experience?

4. How do the candidate's education, experience, and skills match up with the job's needs?

5. How strong are the candidate's communication skills?

6. How intelligent and creative is the candidate?

7. How much demand in the marketplace is there likely to be for this candidate; what is my competition for this candidate's services?

8. How much money is the candidate likely to require to make the switch to my company? Is the candidate worth this much money—and can we afford it?

9. How does this candidate compare with the other candidates?

10. Does this candidate meet at least the minimum criteria I have set for the job? If not, are there other candidates who do?

Create an evaluation chart

When evaluating candidates, Sara Brown of Sara Brown and Associates recommends setting up a grid chart. Along one side of the chart, say the X or bottom axis, you put the names of all the candidates. Then along the left side or Y axis, place the key characteristics you're looking for, prioritized by importance: intelligence, ability to operate a certain machine, reliability, experience, attitude, ability to work well with others, knowledge of how to make a certain product, supervisory experience, and so on. She covers the basics, including technical abilities, interpersonal skills, work habits, and experience. She then rates each candidate against the key characteristics using a ranking system of 1 to 10. "Without making this really complex," says Brown, "it helps to see all the candidates and how they measure up on these characteristics and how they compare to one another."

Making an offer

Here's a brief list of factors to consider and steps to follow in determining what to offer your "pick of the litter":

- Title of position
- Department/division and location of job
- Date job starts
- Supervisor
- Annual or monthly salary/hourly wage
- Sales or other commissions, if any

- Benefits (life insurance, medical insurance—specify whether it's just for the employee or the employee's family, too—child care, retirement plan, car, car allowance, tuition, and so on)

- Performance bonuses

- Profit sharing

- Signing bonus

- Vacation time (in number of work days)

- Daily hours of work/flex time/telecommuting arrangements

- Any pre-employment tests on which the employment is contingent, such as physical exam or drug test

Computing the salary offer

As I discussed in Chapter 6, "Creating a Job Description," you'll need to know—before you start advertising and interviewing—what kind of money you're willing to pay the new employee. You may simply pay the new hire what you paid the one before. But what if you're seeking to fill a newly created position? Or, in cases where the position has been in your company for a while, what if the previous employee was in the job at a certain pay scale for years, and you're unsure what new employees might be expecting nowadays? As mentioned before, you can contact your professional or trade association for information on what various jobs are paying in different parts of the country. You can also check the going rates listed in similar businesses' help-wanted ads, and during interviews, without showing all your cards, you can ask approximate pay ranges that the applicants would be expecting.

Executive recruiter Laurie Levenson says you should try to "get into the head" of the candidate, to learn what he or she wants. What Levenson is referring to is learning what the candidate is earning, what the candidate wants, and what it would take to get the candidate to make a move to your company. You have to listen carefully during the hiring interview to what the candidate is saying. Maybe the candidate is interested in a move not for money but for something else. For example, the candidate might mention in passing that his boss micro-manages and does not allow subordinates much room for individual initiative. You might land this candidate more through assurances of latitude and flexibility rather than through promises of money.

When your offer is declined

What happens when your first choice says no? First, understand why you were rejected. It may be that you offered an inferior opportunity—pay, responsibilities, job title, security, bonus, and so on— compared with the competition. In this case, see if you can raise your offering without breaking the bank or offending current employees. Maybe the person's current employer countered with a better offer. This is tough to offset. For one thing, the current employer has an advantage you don't: The current employer is a known quantity to the job applicant. Switching jobs represents a higher risk because the applicant doesn't know your company, the job, and your other employees. He or she would be taking a risk by choosing you; so even if the current employer offers a package equal to yours, chances are good the employee will stay put. Also, if you counter with a better offer, you may well find

Bright Idea
If you don't get your first choice, review your criteria. Know the most important must-have qualification, and see if any Number Two candidates have it. Consider providing training or other support for your secondary choice, as long as your most important must-have criterion is met.

yourself in a bidding war, and this could put the candidate beyond your ability to pay.

Levenson has a simple strategy that works well. She tries not to negotiate or get into bidding wars at all. Instead, she does careful research into what the position pays, what the applicant is earning, and what the job is worth, and then offers a "fair" compensation package. She says: "You don't make an offer with the idea that you'll negotiate. If you make a good offer, it will usually be accepted."

She goes on to say: "You make an offer that is competitive with what's in the marketplace and with information as to where that person is at with respect to money and other things." This type of offer is not put forth in take-it-or-leave-it terms. Instead, she says: "Tell the person, 'I'm going to make an offer that is competitive and I'm putting my best foot forward. I'm not doing this with the idea of negotiating, but with the idea of paying you well for your coming to work for us so that we have a good long-term relationship.'"

By the time it gets into writing, the details should have been agreed to by all parties. Work out the offer with the candidate verbally, so that he or she understands everything in the employment package, and then put it all in writing.

Negotiating considerations

Even if you make what you think is a fair offer, there's no guarantee the applicant will accept it. The applicant may just want more than you want to give, or have another idea of what is fair, or have a counteroffer from a competitor that you may consider beyond reach. In this case, you've got some negotiating to do. Here are a few basic tips on negotiating—to be considered *before* you sit down at the table.

- "The one who throws out the first number, loses," says Levenson. Ask the applicant how much money he or she wants before you mention a salary.

- Consider your leverage. Do you have other candidates equally desirable or almost as desirable, or is this the only acceptable one? The more eligible alternates you have, the better your bargaining position.

- Consider the applicant's leverage. Does the applicant have other offers either from his current employer or from other companies? If so, how do these employers and their offers stack up against your company and your offer? You don't negotiate in a vacuum, so you have to consider what your position is and that of the applicant's.

- Consider offering non-financial perks rather than getting into a bidding war. Flextime, telecommuting, responsibility for a project, access to leading-edge technology, child care, medical insurance for the applicant's entire family—these are but some of the perks you could offer that might entice a reluctant applicant to come on board. Don't offer the moon, or you may create resentment among your current employees. If you let this person work on a flex-time basis, and others have asked for this and you've refused, you're asking for trouble within the ranks. Whatever you offer, make it consistent with your current policies relating to your present employees. You don't want to win

Before making your offer in front of the candidate, "rehearse a half-dozen times or even more until you've got the entire process down cold. When you finally do get to negotiate, you'll be more comfortable, more confident, more powerful, and more likely to get what you want.
—John Ilich, *The Complete Idiot's Guide to Winning through Negotiation*

over a new employee only to lose current employees because they think they've been treated unfairly.

▪ Set a deadline for a response to your offer—usually a week, at most. Deadlines are great motivators, and they help you not only by putting pressure on the applicant, but also by bringing a faster resolution to your hiring. Warning: Don't set a deadline unless you're sure you can live with it. Don't say to the applicant, "I need an answer within four working days, or I will have to make an offer to another candidate," unless you're prepared to do so.

Bright Idea
When making an offer, be sure to spell out all aspects of the offer: salary, vacation, insurance, bonus, retirement, stock options, profit sharing, flextime, telecommuting. You want the applicant to be well aware of everything you're offering, so don't be bashful about pointing out the goodies.

10-point recruiters' checklist

This checklist is from Cook Associates Inc., an executive search and recruitment firm in Chicago. It's designed to help you prevent mistakes commonly made in the recruitment process.

1. Define the position (list key tasks, priorities, and expectations).

2. Define candidate characteristics as well as qualifications (to ensure the candidate fits in to your company management culture).

3. Develop a realistic but balanced compensation program (for some, benefits weigh as heavily as salary).

4. Define the role of the recruiter, whether in-house or consultant (include target dates to avoid disappointment later in the process).

5. Prepare for the interview and conduct it promptly and professionally, "selling" the benefits of your company.

6. Be prepared to make a decision (waiting for the "perfect" candidate can be costly).

7. Check references (you'd be surprised how many "masters" bluff their way to the top until their deficiencies begin appearing on the company's balance sheet with increasing regularity).

8. Make a fair offer, based on the value of the position and qualifications of the candidate to fill it (not the current salary of the candidate).

9. Once the offer is made, maintain regular contact with the candidate to avoid or to offset any counteroffers. (A candidate who is unprepared for a counteroffer will be attracted by this flattering but usually empty gesture, and will not realize the mistake before you've lost the executive talent you intended to hire.)

10. Make a commitment to helping the candidate succeed (an orientation program for the first few weeks will keep your new executive in touch with new priorities and better prepared to meet your expectations).

Just the facts

- Value a candidate's attitude when selecting. A good attitude can make up for other shortcomings.

- Don't be penny-wise and pound foolish. The candidate willing to take the least amount of money up front may cost you the most in the long run.

- Don't get caught up in the heat of the moment. Have salary and other parameters set before you negotiate, and don't overstep them.

- Offer a fair compensation package up front; don't try to lowball the applicant with the idea of negotiating and boosting up your offer later.

- If you have to offer more money than you planned, try to make it a sign-up bonus rather than a boost in salary.

- Don't offer an ultimatum. Say to the candidate that you're putting your "best foot forward" with the offer you present.

Firing: How to Do It Right

GET THE SCOOP ON...

How to make a firing easier on yourself—and
the person being fired ▪ Tactics you can use to
help an employee avoid being fired ▪ What
kinds of records you should keep ▪ Management
practices to avoid

When Firing Becomes Necessary

In Chapter 4, "Employee Retention and Problem-Solving," we discussed various ways to work constructively with problem employees, to cooperate and give them another chance, both for the employee's benefit and to spare the company from having to hire a replacement. Sometimes, however, the attempts at repairing a problem simply don't work—for many reasons—and the time comes when the employee must be "let go."

According to *What Counts: The Complete Harper's Index,* an average of 11,800 Americans are fired each work day—about three million a year. And, as reported in *Men's Health* (Nov. 1993), 33 percent of U.S. employees will be fired at some point in their careers. The Onset Study, a research project studying the effects of daily stresses, "found that managers run double their usual risk of a heart attack during the week after they give someone the ax," as reported in the Salt Lake *Tribune* (March 20, 1998).

Chapter 15

"I just hate telling somebody they don't have a job anymore," admits Ray Taggart, vice president of Ikon Office Solutions Technology Services, Salt Lake City. "It's the one thing about managing I dislike the most."

The evidence above provides some glimpses into what might be called "the dark side of the workplace": the firing of employees who aren't performing adequately or are in the wrong place at the wrong time—"downsized" because the company can't afford to keep them anymore. Of all the responsibilities that managers and business owners have, none is likely to be more stressful or distasteful than having to fire someone. And, with our litigious society, a firing improperly handled can cost a company plenty. Yet, there are times when it has to be done. Fire an employee the right way, and the stress is temporary. Fire them the wrong way, and you could experience some serious long-term consequences. In this chapter, we'll discuss how to lay the groundwork for firing an employee—professionally, carefully, and tactfully.

The number of reasons why employees are fired is legion, and includes:

- Dishonesty
- Theft
- Violation of a code of conduct
- Being disruptive
- Being unproductive
- Having non–work-related problems that affect their job performance (for example, marital problems or substance abuse)
- Incompetence
- Breach of rules or policies

- Conflict of interest
- Unreliability
- A business downturn makes them unaffordable
- Your business changes, and you no longer need them
- Personality conflict
- Insolence or insubordination

Any of these situations might make a boss want to send an employee out the door. The big question is how you handle the firing.

The time to start acting is now

Few of us relish doing things we dislike, and when faced with a problem employee, it's not unusual for a supervisor to make a few attempts at repairing the situation while mostly looking the other way. We may ignore the problem, or try to work with a problem employee, vaguely hope things will get better, or put off the day of reckoning because of other chores. Many of us will do just about anything not to fire someone. This in itself is a problem. If you have an employee who is not working out, everyone suffers: management, employees, the business, and even the person who should be fired. The costs of carrying someone who is unproductive, disruptive, antagonizing, or unaffordable are too high not to face the necessity of firing, however unpleasant.

"Those people, the ones who are not performing, will drive you down," says Ray Taggart. "They will drag morale down. They will drag your personal productivity down. They will affect everything you do. That's why we are learning to fire sooner. They're responsible for their actions, so the problems are of their making. I can't take it personally."

Beware of firing precipitously, however, for that can lead to lawsuits, even violence. You have to plan. Never fire someone on the spot for an infraction. Prepare. Throughout this book I have stressed the importance of preparation and having a plan to go by. The need for preparation is never more critical than when dealing with firings. You not only have to prepare yourself psychologically for a firing, but you must also prepare administratively by creating a record of the employee's performance that justifies the firing.

Know what you're doing

Bright Idea
Almost all sizable companies, and many smaller ones, have employee manuals. They can help orient an employee to your company and spell out company policies regarding such topics as the company's right to fire. If you decide to issue an employee handbook, be sure to have a good labor attorney review it carefully. This is too important a document to not be reviewed by an expert.

Before you begin to seriously think of firing someone, be certain you know the facts. Remember that there really are at least two sides to every story. A supervisor should not take at face value one employee's comments about another. Check them out. When something goes wrong and you *think* you know who is at fault, you have a responsibility to get the facts, regardless of what you want to believe.

A subordinate once reported to a superior at a large organization that his immediate supervisor was running a business on the side. That, in itself, wasn't illegal or unethical. But the subordinate further claimed that his supervisor was using resources from the company to run the business, using the company's good name to promote the business, and conducting matters relating to this business on company time. These are serious charges, and the supervisor came very close to being axed. But fortunately for him, a dogged investigator from the company checked all the allegations and determined they were unfounded. In the end, the supervisor was exonerated, and eventually the person making the allegations left the organization.

People say things for many reasons. Jealousy, resentment, insecurity, a desire for promotion or power, mental instability, all contribute to unfounded charges and rumors being made against people. As one manager who wants to remain anonymous told me: "Many times, people want others to be fired because they just don't like them. Often it's a question of personality issues, not performance issues. That's what you have to guard against."

Employment at will

Traditionally, employer and employee who worked together without a contract could end the arrangement at any time for any reason—or no reason. Management's right to fire "at will" has been eroded over the years as federal and state antidiscrimination laws have limited the abilities of management to act as it wants. Title VII of the Civil Rights Act of 1964, for example, prohibits you from dismissing someone because of the individual's race, color, religion, sex, or national origin. It also prohibits discrimination against any employee because he or she opposed an unlawful employment practice, filed a charge or participated in an investigation, proceeding, or hearing under Title VII.

It seems that many employers are afraid to fire because they fear the dismissed person will counter with a lawsuit. And, while plenty of lawsuits have resulted from dismissals, plenty more people are getting fired without resorting to legal redress. As noted above, the number of folks fired each year is in the millions. So, while the laws on the books may restrict and inhibit an employer's ability to fire, they don't prevent you from doing so. Therefore, if you plan properly, you can fire those who need to be

66
Have independent review at all times for termination decisions. Maybe there's a personality problem there. Maybe there's something else going on that management doesn't know about. If somebody's going to be terminated, the person who is the final one to sign off on it should be a level up and a step removed so that they can be objective about whether, in the culture of the given employer, they're comfortable that this is the way to go.
—Stephen Sheinfeld, chairman of Whitman Breed Abbott & Morgan (New York) labor and employment department
99

dismissed and limit the chances of subsequent legal action.

Create a history

Dismissing someone should never be done on the spot. First, you need to warn a problem employee ahead of time that his or her performance is not meeting company standards, for example. Abrupt firing, without warning, not only weakens the employer's legal case, but it increases the chances that the employee will be angry and seek retribution through the legal system or by other means. "We first put a person on probation," says James Essey, president of TemPositions Group of Companies, New York. "Our feeling is that someone should never be fired who doesn't know there was a problem before they were fired."

And to protect yourself further, legally and otherwise, establish a paper trail that shows (1) the steps you have taken to help the employee rectify the situation, and (2) the results of yours and the employee's efforts. "You need as much documentation as possible," recommends Alan M. Johnson, managing director of compensation consultants Johnson and Associates, New York. "Most companies don't document things as well as they should. They praise too much. They haven't warned the person."

To lay the groundwork for a dismissal in case it's needed at a later date, start at the beginning—the day the employee starts working for you. You might say in an employee handbook, or if you lack such a document, in a form the employee signs, that employees are subject to termination at will. For example, a statement might read: "If hired by XYZ Corp., I understand I may terminate my employment at any time without notice or cause, and that

XYZ Corp. can terminate my employment with the company at any time without notice or cause." Of course, this may get the relationship off with the new employee to a somewhat rocky start, but it's one way of setting the stage in the event you have to terminate the employee at a later date. "We have an at-will agreement," says Ray Taggart of Ikon Office Solutions. "We looked over all the alternatives and decided we wanted to be able to let somebody go when we chose. If somebody wants to go, they could go, too. I know of a property management firm where, if someone wants to leave, they have to give a one-year notice. The productivity of those people typically in that one year is very, very low." So the arrangement cuts both ways. The company gives the employee the opportunity to leave at will, and keeps for itself the option of removing that person when removal is deemed necessary.

Conduct regular employee reviews. Although it's a good practice to give praise where appropriate, don't be overly complimentary at these reviews. Keep your eye on the job requirements and the facts of the employee's performance. Employee reviews should be documented: points covered, suggested improvements, steps agreed to, and so on.

Be sure your employees know what is expected of them. Set goals, deadlines, production quotas, and other measurable criteria, and follow the employee's progress. Write notes that are placed in the employee's file as to how well the employee is meeting expectations. Stay on top of the employee's performance problem by monitoring it and taking action early in its development. An employer should not expect that merely setting goals or quotas allows the later firing of an employee who doesn't measure up; the employer has an obligation to monitor the employee's work and give feedback. If you consistently ignore the fact that the employee hasn't met his or her goals, deadlines, or quotas, then you may have trouble if you suddenly decide later that this behavior is unacceptable and fire the employee.

Our discussion here concerns terminations resulting from problems with the employee's performance or behavior. Layoffs, which are not due to any actions of individual employees but are the result of outside economic and market situations, or due to general problems within an organization, are another matter. Here, it's possible that you will surprise employees with their dismissal. The key is to treat equally everyone who must be laid off. Use a reasonable and consistent set of criteria in determining who must be laid off, and be sure that these criteria are applied to all the affected employees equally.

The paper trail

You need a record of trying to turn things around with a problem employee before you fire him or her. Here are three steps to take toward termination, as recommended by an executive at a distribution firm:

1. *Verbal warning:* The employee gets a verbal warning with reference to problem behaviors or the quality of their performance. While the warning is verbal, keep written notes on what you said, the employee's response, and when and where the warning occurred.

2. *Written warning:* This is a more serious warning, given after sufficient time has passed since the verbal warning. How long a "sufficient" time is

depends on the circumstances. For example, if an employee has a problem of frequently showing up late, after you give a verbal warning, you might wait a week or two and see if the tardiness has stopped. If not, then give the employee a written warning.

3. *Written termination:* When all else fails, give a written termination. This is given to the employee at the exit interview, which I will discuss in the next chapter.

Of course, copies of all written as well as verbal communication should be kept in the employee's file. What should be kept? Anything that pertains to the problems that the employee is causing. These could include:

- Notes of supervisor's verbal warnings to the employee.

- Written warnings.

- Complaints by fellow employees (written and/or notes of verbal complaints).

- Complaints by customers or vendors (written and/or notes of verbal complaints).

- Notes of discussions or meetings where problems were addressed. These may not be "warnings," per se, but perhaps performance reviews or informal discussions where you noted that the employee was exhibiting problem behavior or was not performing up to stated expectations, and you requested that the employee start correcting the problem.

- Signed agreements by the employee. This is a technique recommended by consultant Michael Masin. When you want to highlight a problem,

Watch Out!
Nothing can stop a dismissed employee from attempting to sue you. But you can limit the probability of legal trouble if you don't alter the conditions of the person's employment as a means of inducing them to quit; for example, by lowering their wages or cutting back on their hours. Follow your established procedures for disciplining employees, and you'll improve your chances of successfully defending yourself should you be sued.

write it out and include a goal. For example, it has been taking Jack four hours to handle service calls handled by other employees in two hours. State this situation on paper and set a goal: Within three weeks of today, Jack will bring the time it takes him to handle service calls down to an average of two hours. And have the employee sign it so that he shows he has read it. You can't make him sign it, however. "People who won't sign a document typically think they don't have a problem," observes Masin.

▪ Supporting documentation. This could be time sheets, production records, records of missed deadlines, and so on.

These are steps to take in creating a paper trail that will support your claim that the employee was not performing well or was otherwise a problem, and that you worked with the employee and warned the employee that the problem existed. Despite your efforts, though, the employee's behavior or performance did not improve, and you were left with no choice but to fire the individual, as demonstrated by the documentation you have collected. This is the purpose of the documentation, and the more detailed documentation you have, the stronger your case and your legal protection.

Important warning: Do not try to create these documents *after* you have fired the employee. Yes, you can claim you recreated them from memory, but if you have a file of documents created ex post facto, you enter the courtroom or arbitration with diminished credibility.

Communicate

If there is one thing you must do with a problem employee—to try to "save" that employee or to protect yourself if you must fire him or her—it's communicate. Don't ignore the problem; don't assume it will go away. For many managers, this is the most difficult part of managing: communicating, especially communicating unpleasant messages, such as when an employee is not performing adequately. You have to let the employee know:

1. That there is a problem, and what the problem is.

2. What you want to see accomplished that will indicate the problem is being taken care of.

3. When you want to see the accomplishment.

Consider the following scenario as a way to involve the employee in the process. James Essey, president of TemPositions Group of Companies, New York, does this. When there is a problem with a person, the first thing TemPositions does is place the person on probation, which sends a clear message the company isn't happy.

"Once we put them on probation," says Essey, "we don't specifically tell them now to fix their problem, but instead we ask them to come to us with a 'success plan' detailing how they're going to fix the problem themselves." This involves the employee in correcting what needs correcting, and minimizes the feeling the employee might have that management is forcing something on or dictating to them.

And there are also legal benefits to involving the employee in a corrective action plan. In one case where an individual brought suit against the company claiming wrongful discharge, TemPositions was able to show the court the probation notice the employee was given, as well as the success plan that showed what the individual had said she would do to improve her performance. Says Essey: "This

Watch Out!
Have you ever given a positive employee evaluation, only to pull the trigger on the employee a month or two later for poor performance? That's a no-no and can get you into legal hot water. Don't put anything on record you don't sincerely believe.

Watch Out!
Sometimes, in order to sign someone on, employers will say things that create the expectation that the employee will not be terminated except for cause, and that he will have a very long and satisfactory career, says Gilmore F. Diekmann, partner at Bronson, Bronson and McKinnon, San Francisco. You have to avoid vague or misleading promises, says Diekmann, or you might compromise your ability to terminate at will.

individual had problems relating to her fellow workers and, in fact, got into verbal arguments and abuse. In her success plan she had said, 'I recognize I need to take my personal issues outside of the office, and I won't have any of these [arguments] anymore.' The reason we gave for terminating her was that she had faxed a threat of physical harm to an employee." When the arbitrator at the hearing asked the former employee to reconcile her success plan with her actions, she didn't have an answer and lost the case.

In an article that appeared in *Inc. Online,* Lonny H. Dolin of Dolin & Modica, in Rochester, New York, reports that an employer will look bad in court if an employee can show:

- A personnel file that, after the fact of termination, is "papered" with memos written from memory.

- Training, such as giving some people time off to attend seminars but not others, is made available for new or younger workers but not for older employees.

- Different terms and conditions among employees with comparable skills.

- Conflicting records of employee performance. For example: A subordinate is told his project isn't good and ultimately is terminated, while the performance review for the superior lauds the same project.

Gilmore F. Diekmann, partner at Bronson, Bronson and McKinnon, San Francisco, recommends inclusion of the following elements in the firing procedures:

- *Follow the golden rule:* Do unto others as you would have them do unto you. "Jurors want to see employees treated the way that they would expect to be treated by their employer," says Diekmann. So, if you're a supervisor or manager and you want to know how your action is going to be perceived by a jury, bear in mind the golden rule, that you really shouldn't treat anybody any differently than you would expect to be treated under similar circumstances.

■ *Follow company procedures.* Juries are generally biased against the employer, so if a jury believes the employer isn't following its own procedures, it will pounce on the employer.

■ *Treat people consistently.* If you treat somebody differently under similar circumstances from somebody else, it creates a potential impression of race, sex, national origin, or other perceived discrimination. And it might mean you will be perceived by a jury of treating somebody unfairly or inappropriately because you've been more lenient with others in the past.

Diekmann has identified eight bases on which jurors tend to award large verdicts or findings of liability. These include the following:

1. Promises of long-term employment.

2. Failure to investigate properly before reaching a termination decision.

3. Failure to document poor performance or misconduct.

4. Failure to provide clear job descriptions: failure to define an employee's responsibilities and duties and expected levels of performance.

5. Subjective instead of objective evaluation criteria.

6. Inconsistent treatment of employees.

> **66**
> Bill Bradley, former U.S. senator, said this at a graduation ceremony at Trenton State College, and it could apply to those facing having to fire someone: "Woody Allen once offered the following advice to a graduating class: 'Two paths lie ahead of you. One leads to utter despair, and the other to total extinction. May you have the wisdom to choose wisely.'" —Quoted in *Life Isn't Fair* by Harold Hill
> **99**

7. Absence of clear policies and procedures for resolving grievance and employee complaints.

8. Having different people establishing different expectation or performance levels. Have one person ultimately determine the standards. Too many cooks spoil the broth.

The psychology of termination

As noted at the beginning of this chapter, firing is perhaps the most emotionally difficult responsibility for a manager or owner, and it's usually a very trying experience for the person being fired, as well. It's worth noting some of the psychological effects on both parties.

Trauma experienced by the person doing the firing

Some of the things the manager experiences include:

▪ Resentment that he or she has to do this dastardly deed; there might be some self-pity mixed in.

▪ There's guilt about the person who will be terminated, and probably (hopefully) some compassion, as well.

▪ Mixed into all this is likely some anger—possibly anger at upper management, and maybe at the person being fired for forcing the manager into this position.

▪ Add to this some fear, which includes fear of having to face the person who will be fired, and fear of what the person's response will be.

▪ Eventually, the manager resigns him- or herself to the task at hand and goes through with the firing.

Upper management should appreciate not only the financial but the emotional effects of a firing on the supervisor charged with carrying it out. The supervisor may be distracted both before and after the firing. As noted at the top of this chapter, those who conduct a firing are, for a week after the deed is done, twice as likely to suffer a heart attack than they would otherwise. The manager may feel some resentment toward upper management, especially if he or she has some grounds to believe that part of the blame is due to mistakes (or ill-conceived decisions) on the part of upper management. This feeling is likely to be intensified if the manager has had a relatively close, friendly relationship with the employee who is being fired. That makes the manager's job all the more difficult.

Trauma experienced by the person being fired

Recognize that the person being fired will experience a lot of intense emotions during and after the termination interview. These emotions include:

- Shock
- Anger
- Resentment
- Depression
- Mood swings
- Denial

As discussed in Chapter 4, "Employee Retention and Problem-Solving," a manager has a responsibility to help correct an employee's performance, within reasonable bounds, primarily by letting the employee know there's a performance problem and giving him the opportunity to remedy the situation.

Probably more than any other situation in business (with the possible exception of office

> 66
> Before you put someone in their place, you should put yourself in theirs.
> —David Denotaris, quoted in *Bits & Pieces* (June 18, 1998)
> 99

romances), firings are emotional events, and they should be treated with consideration and forethought because the consequences of mishandling a firing can be unfortunate at the least.

Just the facts

- Give the employee a chance to change, and, in case dismissal becomes necessary, create a paper trail to protect your company in the event of a lawsuit.

- Don't make assumptions or believe rumor and innuendo; if something seems amiss, investigate the facts and get everyone's side of the story.

- Don't fire anyone on the spur of the moment; it can lead to lawsuits, even violence.

- Good, honest communication between supervisors and employees is the single best way of preventing firings and, if firing becomes necessary, the best way of handling the dismissal.

The Act of Firing

I n a sense, the hangmen of old had it easier than the firing managers of today: They were allowed to wear a mask to cover their identity. When you fire someone, there's no disguising the fact that you are the bearer of ill tidings. You can't hide from your responsibilities, but you can help create an atmosphere that makes the process as minimally stressful and as little humiliating as possible. That's what this chapter is about: how to set the stage for a firing, how to do the deed, and how to handle the aftermath.

Setting the stage for a firing

After determining that an employee must be fired, a manager should set the stage for the firing by planning who will give the news, the place for the meeting with the employee, the timing of the firing, and who in the company needs to be informed before the firing. It is also necessary to carefully prepare the logistics of the firing and what to say to the employee. I'll discuss each of these points in the sections that follow.

Who will do it?

The first thing to consider when preparing for a firing is who will conduct the firing. This is one responsibility that should not be passed around; the manager has got to do it himself or herself. As a rule, the best person to conduct a firing is the employee's immediate supervisor. Why have the immediate supervisor take this responsibility?

- Generally, it's this person who hired the employee in the first place.

- It is probably the immediate supervisor who initiated the firing action or, at least, was heavily involved in the decision.

- The supervisor has had immediate responsibility for the employee in all other ways during the person's employment at the company, so why would the responsibility for firing be passed to someone else now?

Watch Out!
Many managers view a third party as a backup for them. This is probably not a good reason, as it shows the manager's insecurity and suggests that the third party is there more for the benefit of the manager than for the company or the employee being fired.

There are two schools of thought about whether another person from the company—a neutral party—should be present at the meeting, too. The downside to having a third party in the room is that the "audience" seeing the employee's humiliation at being fired is larger than if just one person were involved. A third person might aggravate the employee. Some might even liken the situation to that of an inquisition. And, you might say, if everyone acts professionally, there should be no particular need to have a witness.

But a firing is virtually always an emotional situation, and even the most professional of people, when being fired, can lose their composure. Which is why having a third party present is often a good idea. This person can be a witness and provide an objective view of what happened at the exit meeting if questions were to arise later in court or arbitration. A third party can also help assure that the procedure goes smoothly by being a calming influence. If the person being fired were to become agitated, the third party could help settle the situation. At the beginning of the meeting, explain why the third party is present: She is there only as a neutral, silent observer, helping to ensure fair, professional treatment.

There is no clear-cut answer to the question of whether it's desirable to have a third party present. In part, it's a function of the manager's style and what works best in a given organization. If you do decide to engage a third party, this participant is frequently someone from human resources in larger companies, and in small companies a department head or business owner.

The place of the firing

Your next decision is where you are going to conduct the firing. Always, *always* conduct the meeting in private. There are no circumstances under which anyone should be fired in front of others. Choose an office or other space that is private, quiet, and free of distractions. There should be seats available for you and the employee (and for a third party if a witness is attending).

Although some recommend conducting the meeting in a neutral location—neither the supervisor's office nor the employee's—I believe that, if possible, the meeting should be done in the employee's office. In this way, when the meeting is over, the employee can regain his composure, if need be, in the familiarity of his own space, without having to face his co-workers just yet. He will be able

Watch Out!
If you have a third party with you at the meeting when you dismiss an employee, be sure that: (1) The third party is neutral—someone with whom the fired employee has neither a close nor an antagonistic relationship; and (2) The third party understands that she is there as an impartial witness, not as a participant. There should be no need for the third party to speak at all.

to collect his things and leave much as he has left on other days. Of course, if his office is an open cubicle or other space that does not provide sufficient privacy, you need to find a more private setting—preferably as close to the employee's cubicle as possible in order to spare him the embarrassment of contact with co-workers whom he probably will not want to see just yet.

Generally, I don't recommend using your office. Holding the meeting in the employee's office or at a neutral site lets you easily end the meeting when you want, rather than waiting for the employee to leave or asking the employee to leave.

Timing the firing

This is another area of disagreement. Some prefer to hold firings in the mornings, others at the end of the day. Friday seems to be a common preference, but others find the beginning of the week better. The rationale for firing on Friday is that it's the end of the week, and the weekend gives the person time to regroup. Those who prefer to fire early in the week think that the open weekdays give the person time to get things moving toward finding another job; also, it spares him from having to sit around during the weekend with nothing to do but stew about his termination. I read of one CEO who prefers to fire on Thursdays because "it's depressing to go home Friday without a job." (And a Thursday's better?)

If I have to fire someone, I prefer to do it at the end of the day, as I think it makes it easier for the employee to leave with as little disruption to the office as possible. The office is emptying, so the fired employee has less chance of running into now-former colleagues and being embarrassed, or badmouthing his ex-boss or the company. For some managers, the afternoon approach is difficult because all through the day, the manager knows he or she has to fire the person, somebody they probably will see frequently during the course of the day. This makes it harder on the manager than if the firing was conducted in the morning, but the issue here isn't how to make the situation easier for the manager, but how to make it as easy as possible for the employee.

Whom to tell

Certain people or departments will need to know about the firing ahead of time. But, first, recognize that the fewer the people who know, the better. Tell only those who really need to know, such as the personnel department, the manager's supervisor, the heads of other departments where the employee works, and the head of the company (depending on the size of the company). Word will spread quickly once the firing is done, but you definitely do not want the employee to hear about it ahead of time through the grapevine. Limiting the number of people who know up front minimizes the chances that you will be sued later for defamation of character. Furthermore, it is not anyone's business except for a few who have a need to know. Who should be advised? It depends on your organization. If you are not the ultimate boss, then your boss should certainly know and perhaps his or her boss, too. If you have a human resources department, they must be told. Accounting will have to be told because a check will have to be cut, and any severance package that may be offered will have to be worked out. Other than select representatives of departments that need to be informed for practical reasons, no one else needs to know until after the employee has been told directly. Show respect for the employee—and protect the company from litigation: Keep it under wraps.

Preparation: the logistics

You'll need some logistical preparations to pull off the termination interview smoothly. Make sure the place you want to hold the meeting is available. Check to be sure the employee will be in the office or factory, and not off-site or at a meeting. Have the last paycheck ready. If there is a severance package, retirement issues, and so on, be sure to have all the information needed at hand. Also provide a package of any printed information the terminated employee can take with him or her, such as brochures about the company's retirement package, material about any medical benefits being extended, and even brochures published by the state's unemployment department that describe state unemployment services. If you are offering outplacement services, include information about these in the package. Provide a checklist of things the employee needs to return, such as keys, customer lists, product samples, and laptop computers. If you have a computer network that employees access with their password, notify the information services department that this person's password is to be deactivated by a certain time that day, which should be by the time of the interview. Not to be alarmist, but if there is any chance that the employee might become unstable, have the building's security stationed nearby (but not in sight of the employee)—and call it in *only* if needed.

Also, have the employee's personnel file with you. You don't want to get into a debate, but if the terminated employee makes a statement that you need to correct, you'll want some evidence to back you up.

Preparation: what to say

Just as you need to prepare for a hiring interview, you need to get ready for a termination meeting. Know what you want to say before you meet. Write down your thoughts. Rehearse once or twice what you will say and how you will say it (how you say it is very important, since this is an emotional situation). What should you say and not say?

Tell the employee, politely but in no uncertain terms, that he is being terminated. This may sound simple, but because a firing is so difficult for many managers, they sometimes skirt the topic and leave some question in the employee's mind as to what the manager said or meant. One manager told me she fired someone and expected her to collect her things and leave, yet a half hour later, the manager saw the employee working at her desk, as usual. The manager admits she may have been less than clear about the employee's termination and there may have been some cause for confusion. The *New York Times* (Dec. 7, 1997) published an article that told of a similar situation: "The words were so vague that my friend did not realize he had been given the ax . . . . He continued to come to work for several weeks, and one day he bumped into the personnel manager who asked him what arrangements he had made for health insurance after termination. Only then did the man realize that he was no longer an employee." Firing an employee is not an occasion for hemming and hawing. You absolutely must make clear that the person is being terminated, that this decision is irrevocable and not open to negotiation, and that there is no chance of the person being kept on. Do not use words like "layoff," unless it really is a layoff, because this implies that the person may be rehired at a later date when economic circumstances change.

In Hollywood, if you want to sell a screenplay, the advice that writers are given is that they need to be able to summarize the storyline in a sentence or two. Likewise, a manager should be able to say directly and economically why it is that the person is being fired. You should only need a few sentences. Steven Sheinfeld, chairman of the labor and employment department at Whitman Breed Abbott & Morgan in New York, advises, "You should be able to pretty succinctly explain why it is someone was let go, and feel that your reasons are persuasive, because if you can't be persuasive before you do it, it's too late afterward. What I tell my clients is, be your own best devil's advocate. Put yourself in the employee's place." Sheinfeld goes on to say: "Be honest with them. Be candid. Don't make up a story or sugarcoat it."

Also, do not make promises you can't keep. Don't promise you'll try to get them a job if you won't, or say you'll try to get them a larger severance package. And don't compare or contrast the employee with other employees. Just state that they are being let go. Don't get into an argument. Don't apologize; you have nothing to apologize for. If you have done your homework, the reason for firing the employee was that he or she didn't perform, and if you've given them the proper support, their inability to perform is not your fault. If the employee says, "I think you're wrong for firing me," say something like, "Well, I respect your opinion, but we have carefully thought this through and have decided this is best for both of us."

Make the meeting brief, 10 to 15 minutes. This is not a time for extended discussion.

Follow these guidelines at all times:

- Be straightforward. Be clear and succinct about why you decided to terminate the person, and don't backtrack by saying this "seems" the best choice, or some other equivocation. Just make clear that your reasons are not based on personal matters. Also, be careful not to mention any reason for termination that the employee may use later against you.

- Be supportive. Here's an opportunity to be positive. Couch the dismissal in terms like, "This is an opportunity for you to find work more suitable to your skills and desires."

- Give the employee a chance to speak, but don't get drawn into long discussions or arguments. Make clear the decision is final.

- Let the employee know, very clearly, what you expect him or her to do next: to clear out his or her desk and leave now, and not to return the next day to pick up their things. If they have to return things, like a laptop or keys, make it clear they will get their severance package when everything is returned.

- Provide a clear, concise rundown on perks being given to the employee, such as severance, insurance, outplacement services, and other assistance.

- Immediately after the interview, after you and the employee have parted, write down what happened. Place these notes of the meeting in

Bright Idea
Don't be cheap. The person may have been incompetent, but unless they were really out to take advantage of the company, it is probably worthwhile to offer even newer employees a week or two of severance. This sends a message to the remaining employees that you care about your workers, and it takes away some of the sting of the termination to the fired employee, which may dissuade him or her from suing you later. Be fair and be considerate.

the employee's file. If a third party witnessed the meeting, they should write down what they saw, too.

Consider the employee

It's not enough to think about yourself and what you will say; at all times you must consider the employee. Safeguard the person's self-esteem. That's why you hold the meeting in private. That's why you should be understanding and considerate at the termination interview, and not behave in a belittling or dismissive manner. Be diplomatic, firm, but compassionate. Firing someone is hard on you, but it's harder on the person being terminated. A manager once told me, "When I've fired someone, all I could think about was their family and what its effect would have on all of them." You'll get over the firing pretty quickly. Depending on the employee's ego and ability to land another job, the effects of firing the person who is terminated can last for weeks, even months.

If you can truthfully say positive things about the employee, you might offer to be a reference. Give generalities when called upon for references, and don't say negative things. Don't stand in the way of the employee getting another job. There is no need to take revenge for real or imagined slights. (Besides, an employed ex-employee is less likely to sue you than one who can't find a job.) Employees might sue you claiming you discriminated on any number of different bases, such as age, race, gender, sexual orientation, or pregnancy.

Discharge checklist

The following checklist was created by Richard DuRose, the leader of the employment group in the

Orlando, Florida, office of the national law firm, Foley & Lardner. This checklist is for managers with the responsibility to terminate employees. Managers might want to review it before each termination. It assumes the employee is "at will" (as most employees are), with no employment contract.

Before the termination

Before the final meeting between the employee and the manager, several preliminary matters should be checked.

1. Has the employee been told that the employer is not happy? Unless the employee's conduct is extreme, the employer should tell the employee that he or she is not pleased with his conduct before "pulling the plug." An employee will accept termination more readily if the decision is not unexpected.

2. Has the employee's conduct been documented? Every termination should be treated as if it will end up in a lawsuit or before an administrative agency. It is much easier to obtain a good statement concerning the situation when it is still fresh in the memory of supervision. After just a few weeks, the recollection of details will fade to an astonishing degree.

3. Was the employee given a fair opportunity to correct his behavior? As a general rule, employees should be given an opportunity to correct their behavior prior to being terminated. The morale of your remaining employees may be damaged if the employer is perceived to be unfairly harsh. For example, employees may seek employment elsewhere if they believe that their fellow employee was treated poorly.

Employees with long service should be given more time to correct unacceptable behavior than new employees. Accordingly, even though an employer is legally permitted to terminate an employee for any reason, it is not healthy to the organization to do so unless there are good reasons for such action.

4. Does the employee know that termination is a probability? Employees should be told that termination is the probable result of their continued problem behavior. This can be done generally through written rules, or by being specifically told through verbal or written warnings. Employees should be told ahead of time that their conduct will lead to termination.

5. Is the conduct so serious that immediate discharge is appropriate? Theft, fraud, drug use, sabotage, fighting, and reckless, dangerous behavior are some of the reasons that might call for immediate termination with no advance warning.

6. Has the employee been given an opportunity to present his side of the story? Even when the conduct is unquestionably unacceptable, the employee should be given an opportunity to give his side. For instance, he may demonstrate remorse to such a degree that another chance is granted. When the unacceptable conduct is not so clear, the employee's statement may clarify the situation. It is awkward to conduct a discharge meeting only to learn that the facts are not what they were reported to be. This meeting with the employee should precede the discharge meeting, and the decision to terminate should normally be made only after the

employee has stated his case. Of course, the termination can take place immediately after hearing the employee's side of the story.

7. Greater care should be taken in dealing with high-salaried executives than with low-paid hourly workers. The higher-paid employees are more likely to find a way to litigate their dismissal. The low-paid worker is less likely to bring a suit, and the back-pay consequences are far less serious.

The termination meeting

The meeting should be conducted privately by two members of management and the employee. The meeting should be held at a time and place convenient to the managers.

To the extent they apply, the following items should be considered prior to the actual meeting and discussed at the termination meeting in accordance with the wishes of management:

- *Discharge is clearly stated:* The employee must be told in clear and unmistakable terms that he/she is being terminated.

- *Reasons for termination:* The reasons for the termination should be conveyed in general terms. There is no necessity to cite details or to invite a discussion about those reasons. If the employee attempts such a discussion, fall back on the reasoning that "we have decided that it is not in the employer's best interest to continue the employment relationship."

- *Reasons for termination in writing:* Sometimes employees want the reasons for discharge in writing. This is usually a tip-off that he wants to use those reasons against the employer with an attorney or governmental agency. Generally, there is no legal necessity to do so. However, a few states, such as Missouri and Wisconsin, require employers upon written request to provide reasons for discharge. If the reasons are given in writing, they should be very broadly drafted; for example, "your overall performance and absentee record were not satisfactory."

- *Last paycheck:* Delivering the last paycheck helps to establish the finality of the decision. However, there is no legal requirement that an employee be given a final paycheck upon termination. It should be distributed no later than the next pay day after the termination.

- *Vacation pay:* Any vacation pay due should be included in the last paycheck.

- *Severance pay:* Severance pay is to provide a cushion for the employee during the time that he/she must hunt for a new position. There is no legal obligation to pay severance pay. However, if you do pay severance pay, it should be on the condition that the employee executes a release of claims against the employer. There are requirements that have to be met for this release to be binding on the employee, especially if the employee is over the age of 40 (the age when age discrimination laws kick in), and thus it should be drafted and presented carefully.

Severance pay does not necessarily extend the employment of the terminated employee. For example, just because an employee continues to receive a paycheck for some number of weeks after his termination, it does not automatically extend vacation or insurance benefits. If the intent is to extend any benefits, then such should be specifically mentioned in an agreement or letter.

- *Letters of reference:* Some employees will want a letter of reference. These should be freely given, although it is not a good idea to paint too rosy a picture. Letters of reference can be as positive as is honestly possible.

- *Option of quitting:* Employees would sometimes prefer to have their records show that they have quit rather than that they were fired. Here, again, this request should be freely granted. Under some circumstances, the employer may want to take the initiative and offer this option, but in most cases, it is best to agree to it after the employee has requested it. Legally, if the matter comes under scrutiny by a court or agency, a forced quit will not be considered voluntary and will be treated the same as a termination.

- *Ground rules:* The employee should be instructed as to when he should leave, when and how he should gather personal possessions, and whom in the organization to contact in the future should there be any questions.

- *Leaving:* The employee should be instructed to leave as quickly as possible. It is generally not a good idea to permit the employee to continue working even for a short period of time. Neither the employee who has been fired nor his fellow workers will be very productive once they know of the termination.

- *Personal possessions:* Human nature is such that it is probably best to have the gathering of personal possessions done on a supervised basis. The tightness of the security will differ from case to case. But many employers have been surprised to find customer lists, product information, and other confidential material missing once the employee has left.

Another problem of recent vintage is access to computers. Employees can quickly scramble or erase necessary company information on their way out the door. Have computer access codes changed during the termination meeting.

- *Return of company property:* Make arrangements for the return of keys, badges, personal computers, automobiles, employer handbooks, codebooks, and so on.

- *Non-compete agreement:* If there is one, a copy of it should be given at the termination meeting. However, if you don't intend to enforce it (and sometimes you don't), you can use the non-compete agreement as a bargaining chip when negotiating the employee's separation agreement.

- *Insurance:* The employee should be given pertinent information regarding benefits. What insurance benefits are there? How long will they continue? What continuation rights are there?

- *Pension:* What pension rights are there? What does the employee have to do to collect any pension?

- *Unpaid commissions:* A review of any written policies regarding commissions should be thoroughly conducted *prior to* the discharge meeting. How will these be handled? How much and for how long?

- *Appeal rights:* If the employee has any right to appeal the termination through company policy or union contract, that procedure should be explained.

■ *Announcement:* Decide what if anything should be announced to the remaining staff (or, in some cases, to the press).

■ *Miscellaneous:* Take the employee's name off directories, name plates, telephone lists, and so on, and change locks, access codes, and so on.

■ *Unemployment compensation:* If the employee files for unemployment compensation, fill out the forms received in a straightforward, honest way. The fact that the employee was terminated does not automatically bar the employee from receiving benefits. For instance, if the employee is not guilty of bad conduct, but could not handle the job, he is probably going to receive benefits. Normally, when only a small number of employees are awarded unemployment benefits, it does not materially affect the rate at which the employer must contribute to the state fund.

If you want to seriously contest a claim, be sure to have firsthand witnesses at the unemployment compensation hearing, and give the referee any pertinent documents, even if the hearing is conducted by telephone. There is usually no second opportunity to offer evidence except after the initial hearing.

The survivors

The effects of a termination extend beyond the person who is terminated, his or her family, and the person doing the terminating; your company's other employees are affected, too.

There is no need to dodge your staff. Think about what you will tell them and then face the music. If you fire the person late one day, first thing the next morning, make an announcement of what action you took. There is no need to be too specific about why a person was terminated: just state the facts. But you have to appear ready to deal with your employees. If you appear to be in hiding until the clouds pass, you will be viewed as weak and perhaps as having fired someone you don't have a strong case against. Look confident when you walk through the office after the firing.

Ask your staff if anyone has any questions or comments. This gives them a chance to express their reactions. Be sure to convey to your staff that you appreciate their concern and you know how they feel, and explain that you did everything you could to help the person. But, as when terminating the employee, don't get into debates about your decision, and don't say anything that could get back to the terminated employee and be used against you. Just state the facts, briefly. By no means should a supervisor badmouth a dismissed employee; diminishing the terminated person in the eyes of others incurs a risk of a defamation suit.

Just the facts

- Prepare for the firing just as you would prepare for a hiring interview: have your facts and statements ready.

- It is sometimes appropriate and advisable to have a neutral, silent third-party witness to the termination meeting.

- Maintain the employee's dignity; hold the meeting in private, treat the person with respect, and do not belittle the employee during the interview or badmouth him afterward.

- Be clear and direct: dismissal of an employee is not a time for "beating around the bush."

- Be clear about what the employee must return: keys, car, customer lists, and so on.

Glossary

Age Discrimination in Employment Act of 1967 (ADEA)   Prohibits age discrimination against individuals who are forty (40) years of age or older. The ADEA applies to employers with twenty (20) or more employees.

"At will" employment   When the employer can fire a worker at any time for any cause.

Americans With Disabilities Act (ADA)   The Americans with Disabilities Act gives civil rights protections to individuals with disabilities similar to those provided to individuals on the basis of race, color, sex, national origin, age, and religion. It guarantees equal opportunity for individuals with disabilities in public accommodations, employment, transportation, state and local government services, and telecommunications.

Benefits   Services and other things received other than salary or wages, including child care, insurance (health, medical, life, disability, et al), sick leave, pension and retirement plans, tuition reimbursement.

Bonus Compensation or something else of value that is in addition to a worker's regular compensation, such as a sign-up bonus, which is a one-time payment given when an employee agrees to be hired.

Classifieds Employment Ads These are advertisements in publications that list available job openings. Likely the most widely used means for employers to advertise what job openings they have.

Consolidated Omnibus Budget Reconciliation Act of 1985 (COBRA) Gives participants and beneficiaries the right to maintain, at their own expense, coverage under their health plan that would be lost due to a triggering event, such as termination of employment at a cost that is comparable to what it would be if they were still members of the employer's group.

Disability A mental or physical condition that limits a person's ability to conduct one or more major life activities, such as walking, seeing, learning.

Discrimination To give unfair treatment, to treat someone with prejudice.

Due process The U.S. Constitution states the government cannot take away the right to life, liberty or property, without due process of law. Due process is essentially the idea the law has to be just and fair, as must the government's legal proceedings.

Employee Someone hired by another (either a person or business entity) for a wage or salary. This person must not provide services as part of an independent business.

Employee Stock Ownership Plan (ESOP) Created by Congress, these are employee benefit plans which make the employees of a company owners of stock in that company

Employer   A person or business who pays a wage or salary to another in exchange for services.

Employment agency   An organization that locates, screens, and recommends employees to an employer. Works on contingency fees: gets paid only if a candidate it recommends is hired. Generally deals with lower- and mid-level employees.

Employment agreement   When an employer and employee agree with regards to rights and obligations relating to employment.

Equal Employment Opportunity Commission (EEOC)   A U.S. government agency, it enforces the federal laws that prohibit employment discrimination on the basis of an individual's race, color, religion, sex, national origin, age, or disability.

Executive search firms (also called headhunters)   Firms that locate, screen, and recommend job candidates. They are paid a retainer (which they receive whether or not their search is successful). They deal with upper level employees, such as executives and professionals.

Exempt employees   Employees not entitled to overtime pay. They are generally "white collar" workers, such as executives, middle managers, professionals.

Fair Labor Standards Act (FLSA)   Requires that most employees in the United States be paid at least a minimum wage and overtime pay at time and one-half the regular rate of pay after 40 hours in a workweek. In addition, the law includes child labor and recordkeeping provisions.

Flex-time   When an employee is able to choose the hours he or she works, at least to some degree. An example is when an employee can take time off one day and make it up at another time.

Headhunters   see Executive search firms.

Human resources (HR)   The function within a corporation, government agency, or other organization that deals with employees and employment issues.

Independent contractor   A person or business which provides services to another person or business but is not under that person's or business' direct control.

Job fair   Organized by various types of organizations, including local government agencies, companies, local, regional or national trade groups. These are places where employers have a presence and talk with job prospects, "selling" the prospects on the benefits of working for them.

Job sharing   When two or more persons share the same job. For example, if two share a job, one might work Monday and Tuesday all day, and Wednesday morning, and the second person would work the remainder of the week.

Labor dispute   A dispute or controversy concerning the terms or conditions of a person's employment.

Layoff   When a job is eliminated because of economic situations, not the performance of the employee.

Non-exempt   Workers entitled to overtime pay after a certain number of hours (generally 40). Includes many "blue collar" and "pink collar" employees, such as factory workers and secretaries, and just about anyone paid by the hour.

Offer of employment   When an employer offers a job candidate employment while specifying the terms of the employment agreement.

Open house   When an employer (corporation, government agency), invites prospective job applicants to a place (usually the organization's place of business) to learn about the employer, to learn about job openings and, if the applicant wants, usually to fill out a job application and, in some cases, have a job interview.

Outplacement services   When an employee loses a job (usually because of a layoff), an employer may hire a firm to provide outplacement services, which include career counseling, job-hunting, training, and sometimes facilities the laid off employee can use for looking for work, such as use of a desk, phone, and copy machine.

Part-time employee   Generally, an employee working for an employer less than 20 hours per week.

Probation   A period of time (often three months), during which the employer sees if the new employee is a good fit with the organization. During this time, the employee can be let go without the more formal procedures associated with firing "permanent" employees.

Professional employee   Employee involved with predominately intellectual or creative work, versus more routine mental or physical labor. Often requires advanced knowledge of a field and university degree(s).

Recruiting   The process of identifying and signing on job prospects to fill an employer's human resources needs.

Reference   Information given an employer about a prospective employee by a former employer of the prospect and/or others who know the person.

Resignation   When someone quits their job.

Severance pay   Pay given to an employee when he or she leaves an employer—in addition to any salary or wages due for work completed.

Telecommuting   Those who work at home at least one day a week; usually interact with the business via technology, such as computers, Internet, telephone, fax.

Termination   When an employee is fired for reasons relating to such factors as performance.

Turnover rate   The rate at which employees quit or are fired. For example, if a business has had a steady 100 employment positions during a year, and it has had to replace 25 employees during that year, it's turnover rate is 25 percent. Note: Turnover rate can exceed 100 percent, if many employees stay less than one year.

Unemployment insurance   In general, insurance provided through the states for those who "involuntarily" leave their jobs.

Work made for hire   Work that is done by an employee as part of his or her job or specifically asked for.

Worker's compensation   When a worker receives payment for a work-related injury or illness.

Resource Guide

This appendix supplies you with a guide to numerous resources about hiring and firing:

- Associations for human resources professionals
- Web sites with human resources and jobs information
- Human resources software
- State labor offices
- Small business regional contacts
- Child labor resource guide

Associations for Human Resources Professionals

Academy of Human Resource Development
P.O. Box 25113
Baton Rouge, LA 70894-5113
(504) 334-1874
www.ahrd.org

American Compensation Association
1404 N. Northsight Blvd.
Scottsdale, AZ 85260
(602) 922-2020
www.acaonline.org

American Society for Training and Development
1640 King St.
Box 1443
Alexandria, VA 22313-2043
(703) 683-8100
www.astd.org

**Canadian Council of Human Resources
 Associations**
P.O. Box 1227
Station 'B'
Ottawa, Ont. K1P 5R3 Canada
(403) 290-4128
www.chrpcanada.com

Human Resource Certification Institute
1800 Duke St.
Alexandria, VA 22314-3499
(703) 548-3440
www.shrm.org

Human Resource Planning Society
317 Madison Ave., Ste. 1509
New York, NY 10017
(212) 490-6387
www.hrps.org

Institute for International Human Resources
1800 Duke St.
Alexandria, VA 22314-3499
(703) 548-3440
www.shrm.org

International Association of Human Resource Information Management
401 N. Michigan Ave.
Chicago, IL 60611-4267
(312) 321-5141
(formerly Association of Human Resource Systems Professionals)
www.ihrim.org

International Personnel Management Association
1617 Duke St.
Alexandria, VA 22314
(703) 549-7100
www.ipma-hir.org

National Human Resource Association
6767 W. Greenfield Ave.
Milwaukee, WI 53214
(414) 453-7499
www.humanresources.org

Society for Human Resource Management
1800 Duke St.
Alexandria, VA 22314-3499
(703) 548-3440
www.shrm.org

Web Sites with Human Resources and Jobs Information

4Work

www.4work.com

All Business Network

www.all-biz.com/human.html

American Jobs

www.americanjobs.com

America's Job Bank

www.adb.dni.us

Career Builder

www.careerbuilder.com

CareerCity

www.careercity.com

Career.com

www.career.com

Career Magazine

www.careermag.com

CareerMosaic

www.careermosaic.com

Career Path

www.careerpath.com

Career Site

www.careeersite.com

CareerWeb

www.cweb.com

CarPeople

(automotive jobs in Pacific Northwest)

www.carpeople.com

Chase Professionals

www.chasepro.com/cp

Contract Employment
www.ceweekly.com

E-Span
www.espan.com

Federal Government Jobs/U.S. Office of Personnel Management
www.usajobs.opm.gov

Global HR Village (Human Resource Planning Society)
www.hr-global-village.org

Headhunter
www.headhunter.com

HiTech Career (Canada)
www.hitechcareer.com

HR OnLine
www.HR2000.com

Human Resource Connection
www.hrconnection.com

IntelliMatch
www.intellimatch.com

International Association for Human Resource Information Management
www.ihrim.org

Internet Business Network
www.interbiznet.com

JobBank USA
www.jobbankusa.com

JobCenter
www.jobcenter.com

JobSmart Home
jobsmart.org

Jobtrack
www.jobtrak.com

Lycos Careers & Jobs
a2z.lycos.com/Business_and_Investing/
Careers_and_Jobs

MedSearch
www.medsearch.com

The Monster Board
www.monsterboard.com

National Association of Colleges and Employers
(formerly College Placement Council)
www.jobweb.org/NACE

NationJob Network
www.nationjob.com

Occupational Outlook Handbook
(U.S. Bureau of Labor Statistics)
stats.bls.gov/ocohome.htm

Online Career Center
www.occ.com

Recruiters Online Network
www.recruitersonline.com

Recruiting-Links.com
www.recruiting-links.com

SelectJOBS
www.selectjobs.com

Society for Human Resource Management
www.shrm.org

Strive Magazine
www.strivemag.com

USJobLink
www.usjoblink.com

Womens Work
wwork.com

Yahoo Employment
www.yahoo.com/Business_and_Economy/
Employment

Human Resources Software

Employee Appraiser
Price: $129
Designed to help managers write accurate and thorough employee appraisals.

> Austin-Hayne Corp.
> 2000 Alameda de las Pulgas, Ste. 242
> San Mateo, CA 94403
> (888) 850-3566/(650) 655-3800
> www.austin-hayne.com

Employee File Maker
Price: $99
Tools for managing employee information.

Employee Manual Maker
Price: $99
Helps you create an employee manual.

> Jian Sales
> 1975 W. El Camino Real
> Mountain View, CA 94040
> (800) 346-5426/(650) 254-5600
> www.jian.com

Greentree Employment System
Price: Starts at $21,070
Made up of modules, including applicant tracking (applicant information, applicant searching and retrieval, follow-up), requisition tracking (job requisitions, printed and Web-ready job postings, requisition status tracking), and resume processing

(automatic extraction and data loading of key items from e-mailed and scanned resumes).

> Greentree Systems Inc.
> 3131 S. Bascom Ave., #200
> Campbell, CA 95008
> (800) 348-8845/(408) 879-1410
> www.greentreesystems.com

Hire Standards and Team Building
Price: $795
According to the company, this software "allows you to step beyond the typical individual assessment to evaluate specific teams which you assemble."

> Tri-Tech Associates Inc.
> 330 Carr Dr.
> Brookville, OH 45309-0459
> (800) 334-1630/(937) 833-5595
> www.tri-techceg.com

HR Power Guide
A listing of various human resources software.
www.cam.org/~steinbg/hurepg.htm

Job Description
Has information about various occupations and over 12,800 unique job descriptions.

Job Manager
Used to computerize job classification and pay categorization.

LawCruit for Windows
Price: Starts at $2,850
Specifically designed for recruiting for law firms and legal departments.

Micron Systems Corp.
P.O. Box 605
Washington Crossing, PA 18977
(215) 321-1810
www.micronsystems.com

Merit Matrix

Provides the ability to computerize merit increases
for all employees based on a performance appraisal
rating, total salary budget, and/or a targeted average percent increase.

Workscience Corp.
P.O. Box 528
Chincoteague, VA 23336
(757) 336-1109
www.workscience.com

Recruiter

Price: Starts at $30,000
According to the company, this software "captures
great candidates as they browse your Web site. It
attracts and holds onto interested passive as well as
active job seekers. A candidate answers key qualifying questions and a hiring manager is notified
instantly of a match."

World.hire
6101 Balcones Dr.
Austin, TX 78731
(800) WLD-HIRE/(512) 406-3330
world.hire.com

RecruitFinder

Price: Starts at $1,200
Described by the company as an Internet-based
online recruiting system that allows recruiting

companies and human resources personnel to post positions on the Internet and allows prospective employees to browse the jobs posted.

> LinkedPlanet Media Corp.
> 14901 Quorum, Ste. 525
> Dallas, TX 75240
> (888) 333-3064/(972) 789-1572
> www.recruitfinder.com

Safari Head Hunting System
Price: Starts at $3,895
Applicant tracking, search and retrieval system, including scanning, contact managers, mail merge.

> Safari Software Products
> 420 E. Lake St.
> Horicon, WI 53032
> (920) 485-4100
> www.safarisoftproducts.com

Sourcer
Price: Starts at $1,795
Keeps track of correspondence, schedules, database of candidates and job orders.

Talent Scout
Price: $1,295
Imports resumes into database, searches resume for key words.

> Young Associates Inc.
> 9805 SE Evergreen Highway
> Vancouver, WA 98664
> (360) 993-4527
> www.sourcer.com

State Labor Offices

Source: U.S. Department of Labor

Alabama

Commissioner
Alabama Department of Labor
100 N. Union St., Ste. 620
P.O. Box 303500
Montgomery, AL 36130-3500
Phone: (334) 242-3460
Fax: (334) 240-3417

Director
Department of Industrial Relations
Industrial Relations Bldg.
649 Monroe St., Rm. 204
Montgomery, AL 36130
Phone: (334) 242-8990
Fax: (334) 242-3960

Alaska

Commissioner
Department of Labor
P.O. Box 21149
Juneau, AK 99802-1149
Phone: (907) 465-2700
Fax: (907) 465-2784

Arizona

Chairman
Industrial Commission
800 W. Washington St., 3rd Fl.
P.O. Box 19070
Phoenix, AZ 85005-9070
Phone: (602) 542-4411
Fax: (602) 542-3070

Director
State Labor Department
800 W. Washington St., Ste. 403
P.O. Box 19070
Phoenix, AZ 85005-9070
Phone: (602) 542-4515
Fax: (602) 542-3104

Arkansas
Director
Department of Labor
10421 W. Markham
Little Rock, AR 72205
Phone: (501) 682-4500
Fax: (501) 682-4535

California
Director
Department of Industrial Relations
45 Fremont St., Ste. 3270
P.O. Box 420603
San Francisco, CA 94015
Phone: (415) 972-8835
Fax: (415) 972-8848

State Labor Commissioner
Division of Labor Standards Enforcement
Department of Industrial Relations
45 Fremont St., Ste. 3250
San Francisco, CA 94105
Phone: (415) 975-2080
Fax: (415) 975-0772

Colorado
Executive Director
Department of Labor and Employment
2 Park Central, Ste. 400
1515 Arapahoe St.
Denver, CO 80202-2117
Phone: (303) 620-4701
Fax: (303) 620-4714

Labor Standards Office
Phone: (303) 572-2272
Fax: (303) 620-4599

Connecticut
Commissioner
Labor Department
200 Folly Brook Blvd.
Wethersfield, CT 06109-1114
Phone: (860) 566-4384
Fax: (860) 566-1520

Delaware
Secretary
Department of Labor
4425 N. Market St.
4th Fl.
Wilmington, DE 19802
Phone: (302) 761-8001
Fax: (302) 761-6621

District of Columbia
Director
Department of Employment Services
Employment Security Building
500 "C" St., NW, Ste. 600
Washington, D.C. 20001
Phone: (202) 724-7100
Fax: (202) 724-5683

Florida

Secretary
Department of Labor and Employment Security
2012 Capitol Circle, SE
Hartman Building, Ste. 303
Tallahassee, FL 32399-2152
Phone: (850) 922-7021
Fax: (904) 488-8930

Georgia

Commissioner
Department of Labor
Sussex Place, Rm. 600
148 International Blvd., NE
Atlanta, GA 30303
Phone: (404) 656-3011
Fax: (404) 656-2683

Guam

Director
Department of Labor
Government of Guam
P.O. Box 9970
Tamuning, GU 96931-9970
Phone: (671) 475-0101
Fax: (671) 477-2988

Hawaii

Director
Department of Labor and Industrial Relations
830 Punchbowl St., Rm. 321
Honolulu, HI 96813
Phone: (808) 586-8844
Fax: (808) 586-9099

Idaho
Administrator
Division of Building Safety
P.O. Box 83720
Boise, ID 83720
Phone: (208) 334-3950
Fax: (208) 334-6430

Illinois
Director
Department of Labor
160 N. LaSalle St.
13th Fl., Ste. C-1300
Chicago, IL 60601
Phone: (312) 793-2800
Fax: (312) 793-5257

Indiana
Commissioner
Department of Labor
402 W. Washington St.
Rm. W195
Indianapolis, IN 46204-2739
Phone: (317) 232-2378
Fax: (317) 233-5381

Iowa
Director
Iowa Workforce Development
1000 E. Grand Ave.
Des Moines, IA 50319-0209
Phone: (515) 281-5365
Fax: (515) 281-4698

Labor Commissioner
Division of Labor Services
1000 E. Grand Ave.
Des Moines, IA 50319
Phone: (515) 281-3447
Fax: (515) 281-4698

Kansas
Secretary
Department of Human Resources
401 SW Topeka Blvd.
Topeka, KS 66603
Phone: (913) 296-7474
Fax: (785) 368-6294

Kentucky
Secretary
Labor Cabinet
1047 U.S. Hwy. 127 South, Ste. 4
Frankfort, KY 40601
Phone: (502) 564-3070
Fax: (502) 564-5387

Louisiana
Secretary
Department of Labor
P.O. Box 94094
Baton Rouge, LA 70804-9094
Phone: (504) 342-3011
Fax: (504) 342-3778

Maine

Commissioner
Department of Labor
20 Union St.
P.O. Box 309
Augusta, ME 04332
Phone: (207) 287-3788
Fax: (207) 287-5292
Director
Bureau of Labor Standards
Department of Labor
State House Station #45
Augusta, ME 04333
Phone: (207) 624-6400
Fax: (207) 624-6449

Maryland

Secretary
Department of Labor, Licensing and Regulation
500 N. Calvert St.
Baltimore, MD 21202
Phone: (410) 333-1393
Fax: (410) 333-0853
Assistant Secretary
Department of Labor, Licensing and Regulation
Commissioner
Division of Labor and Industry
500 N. Calvert St.
Baltimore, MD 21202
Phone: (410) 333-4179
Fax: (410) 767-2986

Massachusetts
Director
Department of Labor & Work Force Development
1 Ashburton Place, Rm. 1402
Boston, MA 02108
Phone: (617) 727-6573
Fax: (617) 727-1090

Michigan
Director
Department of Consumer & Industry Services
P.O. Box 30004
Lansing, MI 48909
Phone: (517) 373-7230
Fax: (517) 373-2129

Minnesota
Commissioner
Department of Labor and Industry
443 Lafayette Rd.
St. Paul, MN 55155
Phone: (612) 296-2342
Fax: (612) 282-5405

Mississippi
Chairman
Workers' Compensation Commission
1428 Lakeland Dr.
P.O. Box 5300
Jackson, MS 39296
Phone: (601) 987-4258
Fax: (601) 987-4233

Missouri
Chairman
Labor and Industrial Relations Commission
P.O. Box 599
3315 W. Truman Blvd.
Jefferson City, MO 65102
Phone: (573) 751-2461
Fax: (573) 751-7806

Commissioner
Labor and Industrial Relations Commission
P.O. Box 599
Jefferson City, MO 65102
Phone: (573) 751-2461
Fax: (573) 751-7806

Acting Director
Department of Labor & Industrial Relations
P.O. Box 504
Jefferson City, MO 65102
Phone: (573) 751-9691
Fax: (573) 751-4135

Montana
Commissioner
Department of Labor and Industry
P.O. Box 1728
Helena, MT 59624-1728
Phone: (406) 444-9091
Fax: (406) 444-1394

Nebraska
Commissioner
Department of Labor
550 S. 16th St.
Box 94600
Lincoln, NE 68509-4600
Phone: (402) 471-9792
Fax: (402) 471-2318

Nevada
Commissioner
Labor Commission
555 E. Washington Ave., Ste. 4100
Las Vegas, NV 89101
Phone: (702) 486-2650
Fax: (702) 486-2660

New Hampshire
Commissioner
Department of Labor
95 Pleasant St.
Concord, NH 03301
Phone: (603) 271-3171
Fax: (603) 271-7064 *or* 271-6852

New Jersey
Commissioner
New Jersey Dept. of Labor
P.O. Box CN 110
Trenton, NJ 08625-0110
Phone: (609) 292-2323
Fax: (609) 633-9271

New Mexico
Secretary
Department of Labor
P.O. Box 1928
401 Broadway, NE
Albuquerque, NM 87103-1928
Phone: (505) 841-8409
Fax: (505) 841-8491

New York
Commissioner
Department of Labor
State Campus, Building 12
Albany, NY 12240
Phone: (518) 457-2741
Fax: (518) 457-6908
–or–
345 Hudson St.
New York, NY 10014-0675
Phone: (212) 352-6000

North Carolina
Commissioner
Department of Labor
4 W. Edenton St.
Raleigh, NC 27601-1092
Phone: (919) 733-0360
Fax: (919) 733-6197

North Dakota
Commissioner
Department of Labor
State Capitol Building
600 E. Blvd., Dept. 406
Bismark, ND 58505-0340
Phone: (701) 328-2660
Fax: (701) 328-2031

Ohio
Administrator
Bureau of Employment Services
145 S. Front St.
Columbus, OH 43215
Phone: (614) 466-2100
Fax: (614) 466-5025

Oklahoma
Commissioner
Department of Labor
4001 N. Lincoln Blvd.
Oklahoma City, OK 73105-5212
Phone: (405) 528-1500, ext. 200
Fax: (405) 528-5751

Oregon
Commissioner
Bureau of Labor and Industries
800 NE Oregon St. #32
Portland, OR 97232
Phone: (503) 731-4070
Fax: (503) 731-4103

Pennsylvania
Secretary
Department of Labor and Industry
1700 Labor and Industry Building
7th and Forster Sts.
Harrisburg, PA 17120
Phone: (717) 787-3756
Fax: (717) 787-8826

Puerto Rico
Secretary
Department of Labor & Human Resources
Edificio Prudencio Rivera Martinez
505 Munoz Rivera Ave.
G.P.O. Box 3088
Hato Rey, PR 00918
Phone: (787) 754-2119 or 2120
Fax: (787) 753-9550

Rhode Island
Director
Department of Labor
610 Manton Ave.
Providence, RI 02909
Phone: (401) 457-1701
Fax: (401) 457-1769

South Carolina
Director
Dept. of Labor, Licensing & Regulations
Koger Center – King St. Building
110 Center View Dr.
P.O. Box 11329
Columbia, SC 29210
Phone: (803) 896-4300
Fax: (803) 896-4393

South Dakota
Secretary
Department of Labor
700 Governors Dr.
Pierre, SD 57501-2291
Phone: (605) 773-3101
Fax: (605) 773-4211

Tennessee
Commissioner
Department of Labor
Andrew Johnson Tower
710 James Robertson Pky., 2nd Fl.
Nashville, TN 37243-0655
Phone: (615) 741-2582
Fax: (615) 741-5078

Texas
Acting Executive Director
Texas Workforce Commission
101 E. 15th St., Rm. 618
Austin, TX 78778
Phone: (512) 463-0735
Fax: (512) 475-2321

Commissioner Representing Labor
Texas Employment Commission
101 E. 15th St., Rm. 674
Austin, TX 78778
Phone: (512) 463-2829
Fax: (512) 475-2152

Utah
Commissioner
Utah Labor Commission
General Administration Building
P.O. Box 146600
Salt Lake City, UT 84114-6600
Phone: (801) 530-6880
Fax: (801) 530-6390

Vermont
Commissioner
Department of Labor & Industry
National Life Building
Draw #20
Montpelier, VT 05620-3401
Phone: (802) 828-2288
Fax: (802) 828-2195

Virgin Islands
Commissioner of Labor
Department of Labor
2303 Church St., Christiansted
St. Croix, U.S. VI 00820-4612
Phone: (340) 773-1994, Ext. 230
Fax: (340) 773-1858

Virginia
Commissioner
Dept. of Labor and Industry
Powers-Taylor Building
13 S. 13th
Richmond, VA 23219
Phone: (804) 786-2377
Fax: (804) 371-6524

Washington
Director
Department of Labor & Industries
7273 Linderson Way
P.O. Box 44001
Olympia, WA 98504-4001
Phone: (360) 902-4213
Fax: (360) 902-4202

West Virginia
Commissioner
Division of Labor
Bureau of Commerce
State Capitol Complex
Building #3, Rm. 319
Charleston, WV 25305
Phone: (304) 558-7890
Fax: (304) 558-3797

Wisconsin
Secretary
**Department of Industry, Labor and Human
  Relations**
201 E. Washington Ave., #400 x
P.O. Box 7946
Madison, WI 53707-7946
Phone: (608) 266-7552 *Robot*
Phone: (608) 266-6928 *Main Number*
Fax: (608) 266-1784

Wyoming
Director
Department of Employment
Herschler Building, 2-East
122 W. 25th St.
Cheyenne, WY 82002
Phone: (307) 777-7672
Fax: (307) 777-5805

Administrator
Labor Standards
Department of Employment
U.S. West Building, Rm. 259C
6101 Yellowstone Rd.
Cheyenne, WY 82002
Phone: (307) 777-7261
Fax: (307) 777-5633

Small Business Regional Contacts

Small Business Regulatory Enforcement Fairness
 Act of 1996
Agency Regional Contacts (as of March 26, 1997)

SBA Region I—Boston, Massachusetts
Employment Standards Administration
Office of Federal Contract Compliance Programs
(ESA-OFCCP)
James R. Turner
Acting Regional Director
JFK Federal Building, Rm. E-235
Boston, MA 02203
(617) 565-2055

Employment Standards Administration
Office of Labor Management Standards
(ESA-OLMS)
Eric Feldman
Regional Director, Atlantic Regional Office
801 Arch St., Rm. 415
Philadelphia, PA 19107
(215) 597-4960

Employment Standards Administration
Office of Workers' Compensation Programs
(ESA-OWCP)
Charity Benz
Regional Director
JFK Federal Building, Rm. E-260
Boston, MA 02203
(617) 565-2137

Employment Standards Administration
Wage and Hour Division
Tom Johnson
Chief of Operations, Northeast Region
3535 Market St., Rm. 15210
Philadelphia, PA 19104-3309
(215) 596-1193

Employment and Training Administration (ETA)
Robert J. Semler
Regional Administrator
U.S. Department of Labor/ETA
JFK Federal Building, Rm. E-350
Boston, MA 02203
(617) 565-3630

Mine Safety and Health Administration (MSHA)
James Petrie, District Manager
Richard Duncan, Assistant District Manager
230 Executive Dr.
Cranberry Township, PA 16046-9812
(412) 772-2333

Office of the Assistant Secretary for Administration and Management (OASAM)
Janis Carreiro, Regional Administrator
JFK Federal Center Building
Boston, MA 02203
(617) 565-1991

Occupational Safety and Health Administration (OSHA)
Cynthia Coe, Deputy Regional Administrator
JFK Federal Center Building
Boston, MA 02203
(617) 565-9860

Pension and Welfare Benefits Administration (PWBA)
James Benages, Regional Director
One Bowdoin Square, 7th Fl.
Boston, MA 02114
(617) 424-4950

Office of the Solicitor (SOL)
Frank V. McDermott
Regional Solicitor
JFK Federal Building, Rm. E-375
Boston, MA 02203
(617) 565-2500

Veterans' Employment and Training Service (VETS)
Paul Desmond
JFK Federal Building
Boston, MA 02203
(617) 565-2080

SBA Region II—New York, New York
Employment Standards Administration
Office of Federal Contract Compliance Programs
(ESA-OFCCP)
James R. Turner
201 Varick St.
Rm. 670
New York, NY 10014
(212) 337-2378

Employment Standards Administration
Office of Labor Management Standards
(ESA-OLMS)
Eric Feldman
Regional Director
801 Arch St., Rm. 415
Philadelphia, PA 19107
(215) 597-4960

Employment Standards Administration
Office of Workers' Compensation Programs
(ESA-OWCP)
Kenneth Hamlett
Regional Director
201 Varick St., Rm. 740
New York, NY 10014
(212) 337-2075

Employment Standards Administration
Wage and Hour (ESA-WH)
Tom Johnson
Chief of Operations
3535 Market St., Rm. 15210
Philadelphia, PA 19104-3309
(215) 596-1193

Employment and Training Administration (ETA)
Marilyn K. Shea
Regional Administrator
U.S. Department of Labor
201 Varick St., Rm. 755
New York, NY 10014
(212) 337-2139

Mine Safety and Health Administration (MSHA)
James Petrie, District Manager
Richard Duncan, Assistant District Manager
230 Executive Dr.
Cranberry Township, PA 16046-9812
(412) 772-2333

Office of the Assistant Secretary for Administration and Management (OASAM)
Janis Carreiro (Acting)
Regional Administrator
U.S. Department of Labor
201 Varick St.
New York, NY 10014
(212) 337-2254

Occupational Safety and Health Administration (OSHA)
Nancy Adams, Deputy Regional Administrator
201 Varick St.
New York, NY 10014-4811
(212) 337-2325

Pension and Welfare Benefits Administration (PWBA)
John E. Wehrum, Jr., Regional Director
1633 Broadway, Rm. 226
New York, NY 10019
(212) 399-5191

Solicitor of Labor (SOL)
Patricia M. Rodenhausen, Regional Solicitor
201 Varick St., Rm. 707
New York, NY 10014
(212) 337-2078

Veterans' Employment and Training Service (VETS)
Dan Friedman
201 Varick St.
New York, NY 10014
(718) 797-7441

SBA Region III—Philadelphia, Pennsylvania
Employment Standards Administration
Office of Federal Contract Compliance Programs (ESA-OFCCP)
Joseph DuBray, Jr.
Regional Director
Gateway Building, Rm. 15340
3535 Market St.
Philadelphia, PA 19104
(215) 596-6168

Employment Standards Administration
Office of Labor Management Standards
(ESA-OLMS)
Eric Feldman, Regional Director
801 Arch St., Rm. 415
Philadelphia, PA 19107
(215) 597-4960

Employment Standards Administration
Office of Workers' Compensation Programs
(ESA-OWCP)
David Lotz
Regional Director
Gateway Building, Rm. 15200
3535 Market St.
Philadelphia, PA 19104
(215) 596-1457

Employment Standards Administration
Wage and Hour (ESA-WH)
Tom Johnson
Chief of Operations, Northeast Region
3535 Market St., Rm. 15210
Philadelphia, PA 19104-3309
(215) 596-1193

Employment and Training Administration (ETA)
Edwin G. Strong, Jr.
Regional Administrator
U.S. Department of Labor
P.O. Box 8796
3535 Market St., Rm. 13300
Philadelphia, PA 19104
(215) 596-6336

Mine Safety and Health Administration (MSHA)
Glenn R. Tinney, District Manager
Penn Place, 20 N. Pennsylvania Ave.
Wilkes-Barre, PA 18701
(717) 826-6321

**Office of the Assistant Secretary for
 Administration and Management (OASAM)**
Gerald Jensen, Regional Administrator
U.S. Department of Labor
3535 Market St.
Philadelphia, PA 19104
(215) 596-6560

**Occupational Safety and Health Administration
(OSHA)**
Richard Soltan, Deputy Regional Administrator
Gateway Building, Ste. 2100
3535 Market St.
Philadelphia, PA 19104
(215) 596-1201

**Pension and Welfare Benefits Administration
(PWBA)**
Virginia Smith, Regional Director
Gateway Building
3535 Market St., Rm. M300
Philadelphia, PA 19104
(215) 596-1134

Solicitor of Labor (SOL)
Deborah Pierce-Shields, Regional Solicitor
14480 Gateway Building
3535 Market St.
Philadelphia, PA 19104
(215) 596-5158

**Veterans' Employment and Training Service
(VETS)**
Irvin Pope
Gateway Building
3535 Market St.
Philadelphia, PA 19104
(215) 596-1664

SBA Region IV—Atlanta, Georgia
Employment Standards Administration
Office of Federal Contract Compliance Programs
(ESA-OFCCP)
Carol A. Gaudin
Regional Director
1375 Peachtree St., NE, Ste. 678
Atlanta, GA 30367
(404) 347-0335

Employment Standards Administration
Office of Labor Management Standards
(ESA-OLMS)
Ronald Lehman
Regional Director
1365 Peachtree St., NE, Rm. 600
Atlanta, GA 30367
(404) 347-7267

Employment Standards Administration
Office of Workers' Compensation Programs
(ESA-OWCP)
Nancy Ricker
Regional Director
214 N. Hogan St., Rm. 1026
Jacksonville, FL 32202
(904) 232-1270

Employment Standards Administration
Wage and Hour (ESA-WH)
Randall Davis
Chief, Labor Standards Enforcement
61 Forsyth St., SW, Rm. 7M40
Atlanta, GA 30303
(404) 562-2202

Employment and Training Administration (ETA)
Toussaint L. Hayes
Regional Administrator
U.S. Department of Labor
1371 Peachtree St., NE, Rm. 400
Atlanta, GA 30367
(404) 347-4411

Mine Safety and Health Administration (MSHA)
Martin Rosta, District Manager
Gary Manwarring, Assistant District Manager
135 Gemini Circle, Ste. 212
Birmingham, AL 35209
(205) 290-7294

Office of the Assistant Secretary for
Administration and Management (OASAM)
Alfred Holston, Regional Administrator
U.S. Department of Labor
1371 Peachtree St., NE
Atlanta, GA 30367
(404) 347-3898

Occupational Safety and Health Administration (OSHA)
Karen Mann, Deputy Regional Administrator
1375 Peachtree St., NE, Rm. 587
Atlanta, GA 30367
(404) 347-3573

Pension and Welfare Benefits Administration (PWBA)
Howard Marsh, Regional Director
61 Forsyth St., SW, Ste. 7B54
Atlanta, GA 30303
(404) 562-2156

Solicitor of Labor (SOL)
Jaylynn K. Fortney, Regional Solicitor
1371 Peachtree St., NE, Rm. 339
Atlanta, GA 30367
(404) 347-4811

Veterans' Employment and Training Service (VETS)
Bernard Wroble
U.S. Department of Labor
1371 Peachtree St., NE
Atlanta, GA 30367
(404) 347-3673

SBA Region V—Chicago, Illinois
Employment Standards Administration
Office of Federal Contract Compliance Programs
(ESA-OFCCP)
Halcolm Holliman
Regional Director
Kluczynski Federal Building, Rm. 570
230 S. Dearborn St.
Chicago, IL 60604
(312) 353-0335

Employment Standards Administration
Office of Labor Management Standards
(ESA-OLMS)
Kamil Bishara
Regional Director
1100 Main St., Rm. 950
Center City Square
Kansas City, MO 64105-2112
(816) 426-2547

Employment Standards Administration
Office of Workers' Compensation Programs
(ESA-OWCP)
Deborah Sanford
Regional Director
230 S. Dearborn St., 8th Fl.
Chicago, IL 60604
(312) 886-5656

Employment Standards Administration
Wage and Hour (ESA-WH)
Anne Hayes, Special Assistant to the
Regional Administrator
1100 Main St., Ste. 700
Kansas City, MO 64106
(816) 426-5424

Employment and Training Administration (ETA)
Joseph Juarez, Regional Administrator
U.S. Department of Labor
230 S. Dearborn St., Rm. 628
Chicago, IL 60604
(312) 353-0313

Mine Safety and Health Administration (MSHA)
James Salois, District Manager
John Radomsky, Assistant District Manager
515 W. 1st St., Ste. 228
Duluth, MN 55802-1302
(218) 720-5448

Office of the Assistant Secretary for
  Administration and Management (OASAM)
Darlene Lorman, Regional Administrator
U.S. Department of Labor
Federal Building, 10th Fl.
230 S. Dearborn St.
Chicago, IL 60604
(312) 353-8373

Occupational Safety and Health Administration (OSHA)

Sandy Taylor, Deputy Regional Administrator
230 S. Dearborn St., Rm. 3244
Chicago, IL 60604
(312) 353-2220

Pension and Welfare Benefits Administration (PWBA)

Kenneth Bazar, Regional Director
200 W. Adams St., Ste. 1600
Chicago, IL 60606
(312) 353-0900

Solicitor of Labor (SOL)

Richard J. Fiore, Regional Solicitor
Federal Office Building
230 S. Dearborn St., 8th Fl.
Chicago, IL 60604
(312) 353-5744

Veterans' Employment and Training Service (VETS)

Cheryl Santilli
Federal Office Building
230 S. Dearborn St.
Chicago, IL 60604
(312) 353-4932

SBA Region VI—Dallas, Texas
Employment Standards Administration
Office of Federal Contract Compliance Programs
(ESA-OFCCP)
Albert C. Padilla
Acting Regional Director
Federal Building, Rm. 840
525 S. Griffin St.
Dallas, TX 75202
(214) 767-2804

Employment Standards Administration
Office of Labor Management Standards (ESA-
OLMS)
Ronald Lehman
Regional Director
1365 Peachtree St., NE, Rm. 600
Atlanta, GA 30367
(404) 347-7267

Employment Standards Administration
Office of Workers' Compensation Programs
(ESA-OWCP)
Thomas Bouis, Regional Director
525 S. Griffin St., Rm. 407
Dallas, TX 75202
(214) 767-4707

Employment Standards Administration
Wage and Hour (ESA-WH)
Randy O'Neal, Director of Regional Operations
525 Griffin St., Ste. 800
Dallas, TX 75202-5028
(214) 767-6895

Employment and Training Administration (ETA)
Joseph Juarez, Regional Administrator
U.S. Department of Labor
Federal Building, Rm. 317
525 Griffin St.
Dallas, TX 75202
(214) 767-8263

Mine Safety and Health Administration (MSHA)
Doyle Fink, District Manager
Felix Quintana, Assistant District Manager
1100 Commerce St., Rm. 4C50
Dallas, TX 57242-0499
(214) 767-8401

**Office of the Assistant Secretary for
  Administration and Management (OASAM)**
Phil House, Regional Administrator
U.S. Department of Labor
Federal Building
525 Griffin St.
Dallas, TX 75202
(214) 767-6800

**Occupational Safety and Health Administration
(OSHA)**
Glen Williamson
525 Griffin St., Rm. 602
Dallas, TX 75202
(214) 767-4731

Pension and Welfare Benefits Administration (PWBA)
Bruce Ruud, Regional Director
525 Griffin St., Rm. 707
Dallas, TX 75202-5025
(214) 767-6831

Office of the Solicitor (SOL)
James E. White, Regional Solicitor
525 S. Griffin St., Ste. 501
Dallas, TX 75202
(214) 767-4902

Veterans' Employment and Training Service (VETS)
Sharon Harrison
U.S. Department of Labor
Federal Building
525 Griffin St.
Dallas, TX 75202
(214) 767-4987

SBA Region VII—Kansas City, Missouri
Employment Standards Administration
Office of Federal Contract Compliance Programs (ESA-OFCCP)
Halcolm Holliman, Regional Director
Kluczynski Federal Building, Rm. 570
230 S. Dearborn St.
Chicago, IL 60604
(312) 353-0335

Employment Standards Administration
Office of Labor Management Standards
(ESA-OLMS)
Kamil Bishara, Regional Director
1100 Main St., Rm. 950
Center City Square
Kansas City, MO 64105-2112
(816) 426-2547

Employment Standards Administration
Office of Workers' Compensation Programs
(ESA-OWCP)
Charles Ketcham, Regional Director
City Center Square, Ste. 750
1100 Main St.
Kansas City, MO 64105
(816) 426-2195

Employment Standards Administration
Wage and Hour (ESA-WH)
Anne Hayes, Special Assistant to the Regional
Administrator
1100 Main St., Ste. 700
Kansas City, MO 64106
(816) 426-5424

Employment and Training Administration (ETA)
William H. Hood
Regional Administrator
U.S. Department of Labor
City Center Square
1100 Main St., Ste. 1050
Kansas City, MO 64105
(816) 426-3796

Mine Safety and Health Administration (MSHA)
Robert Friend, District Manager
Jake DeHerrera, Assistant District Manager
P.O. Box 25367, DFC
Denver, CO 80225
(303) 231-5469

**Office of the Assistant Secretary for
  Administration and Management (OASAM)**
Darlene Lorman, Acting Regional Administrator
U.S. Department of Labor, Center City Square
Building, 1100 Main St.
Kansas City, MO 64105
(816) 426-3891

**Occupational Safety and Health Administration
(OSHA)**
Marcia Drumm, Deputy Regional Administrator
City Center Square
1100 Main St., Ste. 800
Kansas City, MO 64105
(816) 425-5861

**Pension and Welfare Benefits Administration
(PWBA)**
Gregory Egan, Regional Director
City Center Square
1100 Main St., Ste. 1200
Kansas City, MO 64105-2112
(816) 426-5131

Solicitor of Labor (SOL)
Tedrick A. Housh, Regional Solicitor
Federal Office Building
1100 City Center Square, Ste. 1210
Kansas City, MO 64105
(816) 426-6441

**Veterans' Employment and Training Service
(VETS)**
Ricardo Martinez
Center City Square Building
1100 Main St.
Kansas City, MO 64105
(816) 426-7151

SBA Region VIII—Denver, Colorado
Employment Standards Administration
**Office of Federal Contract Compliance Programs
(ESA-OFCCP)**
Albert C. Padilla, Acting Regional Director
Federal Building, Rm. 840
525 S. Griffin St.
Dallas, TX 75202
(214) 767-2804

Employment Standards Administration
**Office of Labor Management Standards
(ESA-OLMS)**
Russell Rock
Regional Director
71 Stevenson St., Rm. 725
San Francisco, CA 94105
(415) 975-4020

Employment Standards Administration
Office of Workers' Compensation Programs
(ESA-OWCP)
Robert Mansanares, Regional Director
1801 California St., Rm. 915
Denver, CO 80202-2614
(303) 844-1223

Employment Standards Administration
Wage and Hour (ESA-WH)
Anne Hayes, Special Assistant to the Regional
Administrator
1100 Main St., Ste. 700
Kansas City, MO 64106
(816) 426-5424

Employment and Training Administration (ETA)
Peter E. Rell, Regional Administrator
U.S. Department of Labor
1999 Broadway St., Ste. 1780
Denver, CO 80202-5716
(303) 844-1650

Mine Safety and Health Administration (MSHA)
Robert Friend, District Manager
Jake DeHerrera, Assistant District Manager
P.O. Box 25367, DFC
Denver, CO 80225
(303) 231-5469

**Office of the Assistant Secretary for
  Administration and Management (OASAM)**
Phil House
Regional Administrator
U.S. Department of Labor
Federal Building, 525 Griffin St.
Dallas, TX 75202
(214) 767-6800

**Occupational Safety and Health Administration
(OSHA)**
Greg Baxter, Regional Administrator
U.S. Department of Labor
1999 Broadway St., Ste. 1690
Denver, CO 80202-5716
(303) 844-1600

**Pension Benefits and Welfare Administration
(PWBA)**
Gregory Egan, Regional Director
City Center Square
1100 Main St., Ste. 1200
Kansas City, MO 64105-2112
(816) 426-5131

Solicitor of Labor (SOL)
Tedrick A. Housh, Regional Solicitor
Federal Office Building
1100 City Center Square, Ste. 1210
Kansas City, MO 64105
(816) 426-6441

Veterans' Employment and Training Service (VETS)
Bill Belz
U.S. Department of Labor
1999 Broadway St.
Denver, CO 80202-5716
(303) 844-1175

SBA Region IX—San Francisco, California
Employment Standards Administration
Office of Federal Contract Compliance Programs (ESA-OFCCP)
Helen Haase, Regional Director
71 Stevenson St., Ste. 1700
San Francisco, CA 94105-2614
(415) 975-4720

Employment Standards Administration
Office of Labor Management Standards (ESA-OLMS)
Russell Rock, Regional Director
71 Stevenson St., Rm. 725
San Francisco, CA 94105
(415) 975-4020

Employment Standards Administration
Office of Workers' Compensation Programs (ESA-OWCP)
Donna Onodera, Regional Director
71 Stevenson St., Rm. 1705
San Francisco, CA 94105
(415) 975-4162

Employment Standards Administration
Wage and Hour (ESA-WH)
George Friday, Deputy Regional Administrator
71 Stevenson St., Rm. 930
San Francisco, CA 94105
(415) 975-4552

Employment and Training Administration (ETA)
Armando Quiroz
Regional Administrator
U.S. Department of Labor
71 Stevenson St., Rm. 830
P.O. Box 193767
San Francisco, CA 94119-3767
(415) 975-4610

Mine Safety and Health Administration (MSHA)
Fred Hansen, District Manager
Garry Day, Assistant District Manager
3333 Vaca Valley Parkway, Ste. 600
Vacaville, CA 95688
(707) 447-9844

Office of the Assistant Secretary for
  Administration and Management (OASAM)
Felix Contreras, Regional Administrator
U.S. Department of Labor
71 Stevenson St.
San Francisco, CA 94105
(415) 975-4057

Occupational Safety and Health Administration (OSHA)
Chris Lee, Regional Administrator
71 Stevenson St., Rm. 420
San Francisco, CA 94105
(415) 975-4310

Pension and Welfare Benefits Administration (PWBA)
Leonard Garafolo, Regional Director
71 Stevenson St., Ste. 915
P.O. Box 190250
San Francisco, CA 94119-0250
(415) 975-4600

Solicitor of Labor (SOL)
Susanne Lewald, Counsel
71 Stevenson St., Ste. 1110
San Francisco, CA 94105
(415) 975-4492

Veterans' Employment and Training Service (VETS)
John Giannelli
U.S. Department of Labor
71 Stevenson St.
San Francisco, CA 94105
(916) 654-8178

SBA Region X—Seattle, Washington
Employment Standards Administration
Office of Federal Contract Compliance Programs (ESA-OFCCP)
John Checkett, Regional Director
1111 Third Ave., Ste. 610
Seattle, WA 98101-3212
(206) 553-4508

Employment Standards Administration
Office of Labor Management Standards
(ESA-OLMS)
Russell Rock, Regional Director
71 Stevenson St., Rm. 725
San Francisco, CA 94105
(415) 975-4020

Employment Standards Administration
Office of Workers' Compensation Programs
(ESA-OWCP)
Thomas Morgan, Regional Director
1111 Third Ave., Ste. 615
Seattle, WA 98101-3212
(206) 553-5521

Employment Standards Administration
Wage and Hour (ESA-WH)
George Friday, Deputy Regional Administrator
71 Stevenson St., Rm. 930
San Francisco, CA 94105
(415) 975-4552

Employment and Training Administration (ETA)
Bill Janes, Regional Executive
U.S. Department of Labor
1111 Third Ave., Ste. 900
Seattle, WA 98101-3212
(206) 553-7700

Mine Safety and Health Administration (MSHA)
Fred Hansen, District Manager
Garry Day, Assistant District Manager
3333 Vaca Valley Parkway, Ste. 600
Vacaville, CA 95688
(707) 447-9844

**Office of the Assistant Secretary for
 Administration and Management (OASAM)**
Felix Contreras, Acting Regional Administrator
1111 Third Ave.
Seattle, WA 98101-3212
(206) 553-0100

**Occupational Safety and Health Administration
(OSHA)**
Richard Terrill, Acting Regional Administrator
1111 Third Ave., Ste. 715
Seattle, WA 98101-3212
(206) 553-5930

**Pension and Welfare Benefits Administration
(PWBA)**
Leonard Garafolo, Regional Director
71 Stevenson St., Ste. 915
P.O. Box 190250
San Francisco, CA 94119-0250
(415) 975-4600

Solicitor of Labor (SOL)
Susanne Lewald, Counsel
71 Stevenson St., Ste. 1110
San Francisco, CA 94105
(415) 975-4492

**Veterans' Employment and Training Service
(VETS)**
John Giannelli
U.S. Department of Labor
1111 Third Ave., Ste. 715
Seattle, WA 98101-3212
(916) 654-8178

Child Labor Resource Guide

Source: University of California, Berkeley, National Center for Research in Vocational Education Web site.

Here are the state agencies to contact for information concerning your state child labor laws.

Alabama
Child Labor Agency
Department of Industrial Relations
Industrial Relations Building
Montgomery, AL 36130
(205) 242-8265

Alaska
Labor Standards & Safety Division
Department of Labor
P.O. Box 0630
Juneau, AK 99802
(907) 465-4855

Arizona
Department of Labor
800 W. Washington St.
Phoenix, AZ 85007
(602) 542-4515

Arkansas
Arkansas Department of Labor
10421 N. Markham
Little Rock, AR 72205
(501) 682-4500

California
Department of Labor
P.O. 420603
San Francisco, CA 94142
(415) 744-6625

Colorado
Division of Labor
Labor Standards Unit
1120 Lincoln St., Ste. 1302
Denver, CO 80203-2140
(303) 894-7541

Connecticut
Working Conditions Division
Department of Labor
200 Folly Brook Blvd.
Wethersfield, CT 06109
(203) 566-5160

Delaware
Delaware Department of Labor
State Office Bldg., 6th Fl.
820 N. French St.
Wilmington, DE 19801
(302) 577-2882

District of Columbia
Branch of Child Labor and Polygraph Standards
Wage & Hour Division
Department of Labor
200 Constitution Ave., NW
Rm. S3510
Washington, DC 20210
(202) 219-8305

Florida
Child Labor Section
Department of Labor
P.O. Box 5436
Tallahassee, FL 32314
(800) 226-2536

Georgia
Child Labor Section
Georgia Department of Labor
148 International Blvd., NE Ste. 700
Atlanta, GA 30303-1751
(404) 656-3613

Hawaii
Child Labor, Wage Claim Office
Department of Labor Enforcement Division
830 Punchbowl St., Rm. 340
Honolulu, HI 96813
(808) 586-8778

Idaho
Wage and Hour Division
Department of Labor and Industrial Services
277 N. 6th, Statehouse Mall
Boise, ID 83720-6000
(208) 334-2327

Illinois
Child Labor Division
Illinois Department of Labor
160 N. Lasalle, Ste. C-1300
Chicago, IL 60601
(312) 793-2800

Indiana
Bureau of Child Labor
Department of Labor
Indianapolis Government Center South
402 W. Washington St., Rm. W195
Indianapolis, IN 46204
(317) 232-2675

Iowa
Division of Labor Services
1000 E. Grand
Des Moines, IA 51309
(515) 281-3606

Kansas
Human Resources Department
Kansas Department of Labor
512 SW 6th St.
Topeka, KS 66603
(913) 296-4062

Kentucky
Division of Employment Standards and Mediation
Kentucky Labor Cabinet
1047 US 127 South, Ste. 4
Frankfort, KY 40601
(502) 564-3070

Louisiana
Louisiana Department of Labor
P.O. Box 94094
Baton Rouge, LA 70804-9094
(504) 342-7824

Maine
Employment Standards
Bureau of Labor Standards
State House Station 45
Augusta, ME 04333
(207) 287-3788

Maryland
Department of Labor and Industry
501 St. Paul Place
Baltimore, MD 21202
(410) 962-2822

Massachusetts
Office of Attorney General
100 Cambridge St., Ste. 1101
Boston, MA 02202
(617) 727-3464

Michigan
Michigan Department of Labor
Employment Standards Bureau
Wage & Hour Division
P.O. Box 50015
7150 Harris Dr.
Lansing, MI 48909
(517) 322-1825

Minnesota
Department of Labor and Industry
Labor Standards Division
443 Lafayette Rd.
St. Paul, MN 55155-4304
(612) 297-3351

Missouri
Labor & Industrial Relations Department
P.O. Box 449
Jefferson City, MO 65102
(314) 751-3403

Montana
Labor Standards Bureau
Labor and Industry Department
P.O. Box 1728
Helena, MT 59624
(406) 444-5600

Nebraska
Division of Safety
Department of Labor & Labor Standards
State Office Building
P.O. Box 95024
Lincoln, NE 68509
(402) 471-2239

Nevada
Nevada Department of Labor
Labor Commission
1445 Hot Springs Rd.
Carson City, NV 89710
(702) 687-4850

New Hampshire
New Hampshire Department of Labor
Wage & Hour Division
P.O. Box 2076
Concord, NH 03302
(603) 271-2597

New Jersey
New Jersey Department of Labor
Division of Workplace Standards
Office of Wage & Hour Compliance
Trenton, NJ 08625
(609) 292-2337

New Mexico
New Mexico Department of Labor
Labor & Industry Division
Student Labor Section
1596 Pacheco St.
Santa Fe, NM 87501
(505) 827-6875

New York
New York State Department of Labor
Labor Standards Division
65 Court St., Rm. 402
Buffalo, NY 14202
(716) 847-7141

North Carolina
North Carolina Department of Labor
Wage & Hour Division
4 W. Edenton St.
Raleigh, NC 27601
(919) 733-7166

North Dakota
Labor Standards Division
State Capital
600 E. Blvd., 6th Fl.
Bismarck, ND 58505
(701) 224-2660

Ohio
Department of Industrial Relations
Division of Prevailing Wages
Minimum Wage & Minors
2323 W. 5th Ave.
P.O. Box 825
Columbus, OH 43216
(614) 644-2239

Oklahoma
Wage and Hour Division
Oklahoma Department of Labor
4001 N. Lincoln Blvd.
Oklahoma City, OK 73105
(405) 528-1500 x229

Oregon
Bureau of Labor and Industries
Wage & Hour Division
800 NE Oregon #32
Portland, OR 97232
(503) 229-5737

Pennsylvania
Department of Labor & Industries
Labor Standards Bureau
Harrisburg, PA 17120
(717) 787-4671

Puerto Rico
Department of Human Resources
Labor Standards Bureau
505 Munoz Rivera Ave.
Hato Rey, PR 00918
(809) 754-5353

Rhode Island
Labor Standards Chief Examiner
Rhode Island Department of Labor
220 Elmwood Ave.
Providence, RI 02907
(401) 457-1800

South Carolina
S.C. Department of Labor
Employment Standards Division
3600 Forest Dr.
P.O. Box 1129
Columbia, SC 29211
(803) 734-9603

South Dakota
South Dakota Department of Labor
Kneip Building
700 Governors Dr.
Pierre, SD 57501
(605) 773-3682

Tennessee
Labor Department
Labor Standards Division
710 James Robertson Pkwy.
Gate Way Plaza Bldg., 2nd Fl.
Nashville, TN 37243
(615) 781-5343

Texas
Texas Department of Labor
Employment Commission
Labor Law Department
101 E. 15th St.
Austin, TX 78778
(512) 463-2222

Utah
Industrial Commission Labor Division
160 E. 300 South
P.O. Box 146640
Salt Lake City, UT 84114
(801) 530-6801

Vermont
Vermont Department of Labor
Labor & Industry Department
Chief of Wage & Hour Division
Drawer 20
Montpelier, VT 05602
(802) 828-2157

Virgin Islands
Attorney General
Department of Justice
St. Thomas, VI 00801
(809) 776-3700

Virginia
Virginia Department of Labor
Labor & Industry Department
Labor Division
Powers-Taylor Building
13 S. Thirteenth St.
Richmond, VA 23219
(804) 786-2386

Washington
Employment Standards
Department of Labor & Industries
P.O. Box 44510
Olympia, WA 98504
(800) 547-8367

West Virginia
Department of Labor
Labor Division
Wage and Hour Division
Building 3, Rm. 319
Charleston, WV 25305
(304) 558-7890

Wisconsin
Wisconsin Equal Rights Division
201 E. Washington Ave, Rm. 407
Northern Building, 2nd Fl.
Madison, WI 53708
(608) 266-6860

Wyoming
Employment Division
Department of Labor
6101 N. Yellowstone Rd.
Cheyenne, WY 82002
(307) 777-7261

Recommended Reading

Periodicals

There are many good articles about hiring and firing in the general-interest magazines. Among the business-oriented publications readily available at newsstands and libraries are: *Inc., Computerworld, Entrepreneur, Harvard Business Review, Fortune, Fast Company.*

Compensation & Benefits Review
American Management Association
$169/year
P.O. Box 319
Saranac Lake, NY 12983-9988
(800) 262-9699/(518) 891-1500
www.amanet.org

Employee Benefit News
$94/year
Enterprise Communications Inc.
1165 Northchase Parkway
Suite 350

Marietta, GA 30067
(800) 966-3976
www.benefitnews.com

Executive Recruiter News
$187/year
Kennedy Information
Kennedy Place
Route 12 South
Fitzwilliam, NH 03447
(800) 531-1026/(603) 585-6544
www.kennedypub.com

HRfocus
American Management Association
$69.95/year
P.O. Box 57969
Boulder, CO 80322-7969
(800) 759-8520/(303) 678-0439
www.amanet.org

HRMagazine
Society for Human Resource Management
1800 Duke Street
Alexandria, VA 22314-3499
(703) 548-3440
www.shrm.org

Human Resource Development Quarterly
Sponsored by the American Society for Training
and Development and the Academy of Human
Resource Development
$55/year
Jossey-Bass Inc.
350 Sansome Street, Fifth Floor
San Francisco, CA 94104
(800) 956-7739
www.jbp.com

Human Resource Management News
$295/year
Kennedy Information
Kennedy Place
Route 12 South
Fitzwilliam, NH 03447
(800) 531-1026/(603) 585-6544
www.kennedypub.com

The IHRIM Journal
$120/year
International Association for Human Resource
Information Management
P.O. Box 809119
Chicago, IL 60680-9119
(800) 946-6363/(972) 661-3727
www.ihrim.org

Management Review
American Management Association
$39.95/year
P.O. Box 319
Saranac Lake, NY 12983-9988
(800) 262-9699/(518) 891-1500
www.amanet.org

Staffing Industry Report
$315/year
SI Review
$79
Staffing Industry Resources
P.O. Box 1240
Cupertino, CA 95015
(800) 950-9496
www.sireport.com

Workplace Visions
$149/year
Society for Human Resource Management
1800 Duke Street
Alexandria, VA 22314-3499
(703) 548-3440
www.shrm.org

Books

Note: "Widely available" indicates that the book is available in general-interest bookstores or through online booksellers. A few titles below not found online at the time of publication include ordering information.

Applied Measurement Methods in Industrial Psychology
By Deborah L. Whetzel, George R. Wheaton
$54.95
Publisher: Davies-Black
Widely available

Beyond Multiple Choice: Evaluating Alternatives to Traditional Testing for Selection
By Milton D. Hakel
$59.95
Publisher: Lawrence Erlbaum Associates
Widely available

Canadian Directory of Search Firms
By Mediacorp Canada Inc.
$39.95
Publisher: Mediacorp Canada Inc.
Widely available

CareerXroads: The 1998 Directory to Jobs, Resumes and Career Management on the World Wide Web
By Gerry Crispin, Mark Mehler
475 job, resume and career management Web sites
$22.95
Publisher: IEEE
Widely available

Compensation Management: In a Knowledge-Based World
By Richard I. Henderson, Richard J. Henderson
$79
Publisher: Prentice Hall

Competency-Based Recruitment and Selection
By Robert Wood, Tim Wood
$49.95
Publisher: John Wiley & Sons

The Directory of Executive Recruiters
$44.95
Publisher: Kennedy Publications
Widely available

The Directory of Executive Temporary Placement Firms
$24.95
Publisher: Kennedy Publications
Widely available

Directory of Independent Research Consultants
By The Executive Search Roundtable Inc.
Professionals who provide compensation surveys,
reference checks, written candidate assess-
ments, etc.
$65
Order from:
Kennedy Information
Kennedy Place
Route 12 South
Fitzwilliam, NH 03447
(800) 531-1026/(603) 585-6544
www.kennedypub.com

*Directory of Outplacement and Career Management
Firms*
$129.95
By James H. Kennedy
Publisher: Kennedy Publications
Widely available

*Don't Fire Them, Fire Them Up: Motivate Yourself &
Your Team*
By Frank Pacetta, Roger Gittines
$13
Publisher: Simon & Schuster Trade
Widely available

Employee Benefits
By Burton T. Beam, John J. McFadden
$62.95
Publisher: Dearborn Trade
Widely available

Employer's Guide to Recruiting on the Internet
by Ray Schreyer
$24.95
Publisher: Impact Publications
Widely available

Executive's & Professional Employment Contracts
By Ari Cowan
$39.50
Publisher: LEXIS Law
Widely available

Executive Employment Contracts
By Executive Compensation Reports
$592
Order from:
Kennedy Information
Kennedy Place
Route 12 South
Fitzwilliam, NH 03447
(800) 531-1026/(603) 585-6544
www.kennedypub.com

*Executive Search Firms and Employment Agencies in
Seattle: Job-Search Resources for the Executive, Manager
and Professional*
By Linda Carlson
$21.95
Publisher: Barrett
Widely available

The Handbook of Executive Benefits
By Towers Perrin
$75
Publisher: Irwin Professional Publishers
Widely available

High-Impact Hiring: A Comprehensive Guide to
Performance-Based Hiring
By Joseph G. Rosse, Robert A. Levin
$34.95
Jossey-Bass Publishers

Hiring Independent Contractors: The Employers'
Legal Guide
By Stephen Fishman
$29.95
Publisher: Nolo Press
Widely available

How to Design & Implement a Results-Oriented Variable
Pay System
By John G. Belcher, Jr.
$55
Publisher: AMACOM
Widely available

Human Resource Champions: The Next Agenda for
Adding Value and Delivering Results
By David Ulrich
$29.95
Publisher: Harvard Business School Press
Widely available

Human Resource Selection
By Robert D. Gatewood, Hubert Field
$89
Publisher: Dryden Press
Widely available

Innovative Reward Systems for the Changing Workplace
By Thomas B. Wilson, Rosabeth Moss Kanter
$32.95
Publisher: McGraw-Hill
Widely available

J.K. Lasser's Employee Benefits for Small Business
By Jane White, Bruce Pyenson
$12
Publisher: Macmillan General Reference
Widely available

JobSeekers SourceBooks
By Donald D. Walker, Valerie A. Shipe
These come in various geographically-oriented editions, including the Southwest, Mid-Atlantic, Chicago and Illinois, and Pacific Northwest
Prices: $13.95 to $15.95
Publisher: Net Research
Widely available

Kennedy's Pocket Guide to Working With Executive Recruiters
$9.95
Publisher: Kennedy Publications
Widely available

The Manager's Book of Questions: 751 Great Interview Questions for Hiring the Best Person
By John Kaor
$12.95
Publisher: McGraw-Hill
Widely available

Maximizing the Value of 360-Degree Feedback: A Process for Successful Individual and Organizational Development
By Walter W. Tornow, London Manuel
$42.95
Publisher: Jossey Bass Management Series
Widely available

The National Job Line Directory
By Robert Schmidt
$7.95
Publisher: Adams Publishing
Lists over 2,000 employment hotlines
Widely available

People, Performance and Pay: Dynamic Compensation for Changing Organizations
By Thomas P. Flannery, David A. Hofrichter, Paul E. Platten
$27
Publisher: Free Press
Widely available

Personnel Selection and Assessment: Individual and Organizational Perspectives
By Heinz Schuler, James L. Farr
$89.95
Lawrence Erlbaum Associates
Widely available

Personnel Selection and Classification
By Michael G. Rumsey, Clinton B. Walker, James H. Harris
$55
Publisher: Lawrence Erlbaum Associates
Widely available

Power Interviews: Job-Winning Tactics from Fortune
500 Recruiters
By Neil Yeager
$14.95
Publisher: John Wiley & Sons
Widely available

The Principles and Practice of Recruitment Advertising:
A Guide for Personnel Professionals
By Bernard Hodes
$29.95
Publisher: Lifetime Books
Widely available

Staff the Contemporary Organization: A Guide to
Planning, Recruiting and Selecting for Human Resource
Professionals
By Donald L. Caruth, Gail D. Handlogten
$24.95
Publisher: Quorum Books

Staffing the New Workplace: Selecting and Promoting for
Quality Improvement
By Ronald B. Morgan, Jack E. Smith
$40
Publisher: American Society for Quality
Widely available

The Thirteenth Mental Measurements Yearbook (13th
Edition)
By James C. Impara, Barbara S. Plake
$165
Publisher: Buros Institute
Widely available

Workplace Testing: An Employer's Guide to Policies and Practices
By Diane Arthur
$49.95
Publisher: AMACOM
Widely available

Important Documents

This appendix includes verbatim copies of (or pertinent selections from) the following documents:

- The Americans with Disabilities Act of 1990
- The Americans with Disabilities Act: Questions and Answers
- EEOC Recordkeeping Requirements
- Title VII of the Civil Rights Act of 1964
- Immigration Reform and Control Act (IRCA)
- Age Discrimination in Employment Act (ADEA)
- Occupational Safety and Health Act (OSHA)
- Fair Labor Standards Act (minimum wage)
- Employment Retirement Income Security Act (ERISA)
- Consolidated Omnibus Budget Reconciliation Act (COBRA)

The Americans with Disabilities Act of 1990

Below is a portion of the Americans with Disabilities Act (ADA) that applies to many employers (other sections deal other concerns, such as public transportation).

SEC. 302. PROHIBITION OF DISCRIMINATION BY PUBLIC ACCOMMODATIONS.

(a) General Rule.—No individual shall be discriminated against on the basis of disability in the full and equal enjoyment of the goods, services, facilities, privileges, advantages, or accommodations of any place of public accommodation by any person who owns, leases (or leases to), or operates a place of public accommodation.

(b) Construction.—

(1) General prohibition.—

(A) Activities.—

(i) Denial of participation.—It shall be discriminatory to subject an individual or class of individuals on the basis of a disability or disabilities of such individual or class, directly or through contractual, licensing, or other arrangements, to a denial of the opportunity of the individual or class to participate in or benefit from the goods, services, facilities, privileges, advantages, or accommodations of an entity.

(ii) Participation in unequal benefit.—It shall be discriminatory to afford an individual or class of individuals, on the basis of a disability or disabilities of such individual or class, directly, or through contractual, licensing, or other arrangements with the opportunity to participate in or benefit from a good, service, facility, privilege, advantage, or accommodation that is not equal to that afforded to other individuals.

(iii) Separate benefit.—It shall be discriminatory to provide an individual or class of individuals, on the basis of a disability or disabilities of such individual or class, directly, or through contractual, licensing, or other arrangements with a good, service, facility, privilege, advantage, or accommodation that is different or separate from that provided to other individuals, unless such action is necessary to provide the individual or class of individuals with a good, service, facility, privilege, advantage, or accommodation, or other opportunity that is as effective as that provided to others.

(iv) Individual or class of individuals.—For purposes of clauses (i) through (iii) of this subparagraph, the term "individual or class of individuals" refers to the clients or customers of the covered public accommodation that enters into the contractual, licensing or other arrangement.

(B) Integrated settings.—Goods, services, facilities, privileges, advantages, and accommodations shall be afforded to an individual with a disability in the most integrated setting appropriate to the needs of the individual.

(C) Opportunity to participate.—Notwithstanding the existence of separate or different programs or activities provided in accordance with this section, an individual with a disability shall not be denied the opportunity to participate in such programs or activities that are not separate or different.

(D) Administrative methods.—An individual or entity shall not, directly or through contractual or other arrangements, utilize standards or criteria or methods of administration—

(i) that have the effect of discriminating on the basis of disability; or

(ii) that perpetuate the discrimination of others who are subject to common administrative control.

(E) Association.—It shall be discriminatory to exclude or otherwise deny equal goods, services, facilities, privileges, advantages, accommodations, or other opportunities to an individual or entity because of the known disability of an individual with whom the individual or entity is known to have a relationship or association.

(2) Specific prohibitions.—

(A) Discrimination.—For purposes of subsection (a), discrimination includes—

(i) the imposition or application of eligibility criteria that screen out or tend to screen out an individual with a disability or any class of individuals with disabilities from fully and equally enjoying any goods, services, facilities, privileges, advantages, or accommodations, unless such criteria can be shown to be necessary for the provision of the goods, services, facilities, privileges, advantages, or accommodations being offered;

(ii) a failure to make reasonable modifications in policies, practices, or procedures, when such modifications are necessary to afford such goods, services, facilities, privileges, advantages, or accommodations to individuals with disabilities, unless the entity can demonstrate that making such modifications would fundamentally alter the nature of such goods, services, facilities, privileges, advantages, or accommodations;

(iii) a failure to take such steps as may be necessary to ensure that no individual with a disability is excluded, denied services, segregated or otherwise treated differently than other individuals because of the absence of auxiliary aids and services, unless the entity can demonstrate that taking such steps would fundamentally alter the nature of the good, service, facility, privilege, advantage, or accommodation being offered or would result in an undue burden;

(iv) a failure to remove architectural barriers, and communication barriers that are structural in nature, in existing facilities, and transportation barriers in existing vehicles and rail passenger cars used by an establishment for transporting individuals (not including barriers that can only be removed through the retrofitting of vehicles or rail passenger cars by the installation of a hydraulic or other lift), where such removal is readily achievable; and

(v) where an entity can demonstrate that the removal of a barrier under clause (iv) is not readily achievable, a failure to make such goods, services, facilities, privileges, advantages, or accommodations available through alternative methods if such methods are readily achievable.

(B) Fixed route system.—

(i) Accessibility.—It shall be considered discrimination for a private entity which operates a fixed route system and which is not subject to section 304 to purchase or lease a vehicle with a seating capacity in excess of 16 passengers (including the driver) for use on such system, for which a solicitation is made after the 30th day following the effective date of this subparagraph, that is not readily accessible to and usable by individuals with disabilities, including individuals who use wheelchairs.

(ii) Equivalent service.—If a private entity which operates a fixed route system and which is not subject to section 304 purchases or leases a vehicle with a seating capacity of 16 passengers or less (including the driver) for use on such system after the effective date of this subparagraph that is not readily accessible to or usable by individuals with disabilities, it shall be considered discrimination for such entity to fail to operate such system so that, when viewed in its entirety, such system ensures a level of service to individuals with disabilities, including individuals who use wheelchairs, equivalent to the level of service provided to individuals without disabilities.

(C) Demand responsive system.—For purposes of subsection (a), discrimination includes—

(i) a failure of a private entity which operates a demand responsive system and which is not subject to section 304 to operate such system so that, when viewed in its entirety, such system ensures a level of service to individuals with disabilities, including individuals who use wheelchairs, equivalent to the level of service provided to individuals without disabilities; and

(ii) the purchase or lease by such entity for use on such system of a vehicle with a seating capacity in excess of 16 passengers (including the driver), for which solicitations are made after the 30th day following the effective date of this subparagraph, that is not readily accessible to and usable by individuals with disabilities (including individuals who use wheelchairs) unless such entity can demonstrate that such system, when viewed in its entirety, provides a level of service to individuals with disabilities equivalent to that provided to individuals without disabilities.

(D) Over-the-road buses.—

(i) Limitation on applicability.—Subparagraphs (B) and (C) do not apply to over-the-road buses.

(ii) Accessibility requirements.—For purposes of subsection

(a), discrimination includes (I) the purchase or lease of an over-the-road bus which does not comply with the regulations issued under section 306(a)(2) by a private entity which provides transportation of individuals and which is not primarily engaged in the business of transporting people, and (II) any other failure of such entity to comply with such regulations.

(3) Specific Construction.—Nothing in this title shall require an entity to permit an individual to participate in or benefit from the goods, services, facilities, privileges, advantages and accommodations of such entity where such individual poses a direct threat to the health or safety of others. The term "direct threat" means a significant risk to the health or safety of others that cannot be eliminated by a modification of policies, practices, or procedures or by the provision of auxiliary aids or services.

SEC. 303. NEW CONSTRUCTION AND ALTERATIONS IN PUBLIC ACCOMMODATIONS AND COMMERCIAL FACILITIES.

(a) Application of Term.—Except as provided in subsection (b), as applied to public accommodations and commercial facilities, discrimination for purposes of section 302(a) includes—

(1) a failure to design and construct facilities for first occupancy later than 30 months after the date of enactment of this Act that are readily accessible to and usable by individuals with disabilities, except where an entity can demonstrate that it is structurally impracticable to meet the requirements of such subsection in accordance with standards set forth or incorporated by reference in regulations issued under this title; and

(2) with respect to a facility or part thereof that is altered by, on behalf of, or for the use of an establishment in a manner that affects or could affect the usability of the facility or part thereof, a failure to make alterations in such a manner that, to the maximum extent feasible, the altered portions of the facility are readily accessible to and usable by

individuals with disabilities, including individuals who use wheelchairs. Where the entity is undertaking an alteration that affects or could affect usability of or access to an area of the facility containing a primary function, the entity shall also make the alterations in such a manner that, to the maximum extent feasible, the path of travel to the altered area and the bathrooms, telephones, and drinking fountains serving the altered area, are readily accessible to and usable by individuals with disabilities where such alterations to the path of travel or the bathrooms, telephones, and drinking fountains serving the altered area are not disproportionate to the overall alterations in terms of cost and scope (as determined under criteria established by the Attorney General).

(b) Elevator.—Subsection (a) shall not be construed to require the installation of an elevator for facilities that are less than three stories or have less than 3,000 square feet per story unless the building is a shopping center, a shopping mall, or the professional office of a health care provider or unless the Attorney General determines that a particular category of such facilities requires the installation of elevators based on the usage of such facilities.

The Americans with Disabilities Act

Questions and Answers

Revised September 1992

This information has been compiled to assist the general public in understanding and complying with the Americans with Disabilities Act. It does not constitute a determination by the Department of Justice of your rights and responsibilities, and it is not binding on the Department.

Introduction: Barriers to employment, transportation, public accommodations, public services, and telecommunications have imposed staggering economic and social costs on American society and have undermined our well-intentioned efforts to educate, rehabilitate, and employ individuals with disabilities. By breaking down these barriers, the Americans with Disabilities Act will enable society to benefit from the skills and talents of individuals with disabilities, will allow us all to gain from their increased purchasing power and ability to use it, and will lead to fuller, more productive lives for all Americans.

The Americans with Disabilities Act gives civil rights protections to individuals with disabilities similar to those provided to individuals on the basis of race, color, sex, national origin, age, and religion. It guarantees equal opportunity for individuals with disabilities in public accommodations, employment, transportation, State and local government services, and telecommunications.

Fair, swift, and effective enforcement of this landmark civil rights legislation is a high priority of the Federal Government. This booklet is designed to provide answers to some of the most often asked questions about the new law.

This publication was printed with the generous support of the National Institute on Disability and Rehabilitation Research

Employment

Q. What employers are covered by title I of the ADA, and when is the coverage effective?

A. The title I employment provisions apply to private employers, State and local governments, employment agencies, and labor unions. Employers with 25 or more employees are covered as of July 26, 1992. Employers with 15 or more employees will be covered two years later, beginning July 26, 1994.

Q. What practices and activities are covered by the employment nondiscrimination requirements?

A. The ADA prohibits discrimination in all employment practices, including job application procedures, hiring, firing, advancement, compensation, training, and other terms, conditions, and privileges of employment. It applies to recruitment, advertising, tenure, layoff, leave, fringe benefits, and all other employment-related activities.

Q. Who is protected from employment discrimination?

A. Employment discrimination is prohibited against "qualified individuals with disabilities." This includes applicants for employment and employees. An individual is considered to have a "disability" if s/he has a physical or mental impairment that substantially limits one or more major life activities, has a record of such an impairment, or is regarded as having such an impairment. Persons discriminated against because they have a known association or relationship with an individual with a disability also are protected.

The first part of the definition makes clear that the ADA applies to persons who have impairments and that these must substantially limit major life activities such as seeing, hearing, speaking, walking, breathing, performing manual tasks, learning, caring for oneself, and working. An individual with epilepsy, paralysis, HIV infection, AIDS, a substantial hearing or visual impairment, mental retardation, or a specific learning disability is covered, but an individual with a minor, nonchronic condition of short duration, such as a sprain, broken limb, or the flu, generally would not be covered.

The second part of the definition protecting individuals with a record of a disability would cover, for example, a person who has recovered from cancer or mental illness.

The third part of the definition protects individuals who are regarded as having a substantially limiting impairment, even though they may not have such an impairment. For example, this provision would protect a qualified individual with a severe facial disfigurement from being denied employment because an employer feared the "negative reactions" of customers or co-workers.

Q. Who is a "qualified individual with a disability"?

A. A qualified individual with a disability is a person who meets legitimate skill, experience, education, or other requirements of an employment position that s/he holds or seeks, and who can perform the "essential functions" of the position with or without reasonable accommodation. Requiring the ability to perform "essential" functions assures that an individual with a disability will not be considered unqualified simply because of inability to perform marginal or incidental job functions. If the individual is qualified to perform essential job functions except for limitations caused by a disability, the employer must consider whether the individual could perform these functions with a reasonable accommodation. If a written job description has been prepared in advance of advertising or interviewing applicants for a job, this will be considered as evidence, although not conclusive evidence, of the essential functions of the job.

Q. Does an employer have to give preference to a qualified applicant with a disability over other applicants?

A. No. An employer is free to select the most qualified applicant available and to make decisions based on reasons unrelated to a disability. For example, suppose two persons apply for a job as a typist and an essential function of the job is to type 75 words per minute accurately. One applicant, an individual with a disability, who is provided with a reasonable accommodation for a typing test, types 50 words per minute; the other applicant who has no disability accurately types 75 words per minute. The employer can hire the applicant with the higher typing speed, if typing speed is needed for successful performance of the job.

Q. What limitations does the ADA impose on medical examinations and inquiries about disability?

A. An employer may not ask or require a job applicant to take a medical examination before making a job offer. It cannot make any pre-employment inquiry about a disability or the nature or severity of a disability. An employer may, however, ask questions about the ability to perform specific job functions and may, with certain limitations, ask an individual with a disability to describe or demonstrate how s/he would perform these functions.

An employer may condition a job offer on the satisfactory result of a post-offer medical examination or medical inquiry if this is required of all entering employees in the same job category. A post-offer examination or inquiry does not have to be job-related and consistent with business necessity.

However, if an individual is not hired because a post-offer medical examination or inquiry reveals a disability, the reason(s) for not hiring must be job-related and consistent with business necessity. The employer also must show that no reasonable accommodation was available that would enable the individual to perform the essential job functions, or that accommodation would impose an undue hardship. A post-offer medical examination may disqualify an individual if the employer can demonstrate that the individual would pose a "direct threat" in the workplace (i.e., a significant risk of substantial harm to the health or safety of the individual or others) that cannot be eliminated or reduced below the "direct threat" level through reasonable accommodation. Such a disqualification is job-related and consistent with business necessity. A post-offer medical examination may not disqualify an individual with a disability who is currently able to perform essential job functions because of speculation that the disability may cause a risk of future injury.

After a person starts work, a medical examination or inquiry of an employee must be job-related and consistent with business necessity. Employers may conduct employee medical examinations where there is evidence of a job performance or safety problem, examinations required by other Federal laws, examinations to determine current "fitness" to perform a particular job, and voluntary examinations that are part of employee health programs.

Information from all medical examinations and inquiries must be kept apart from general personnel files as a separate, confidential medical record, available only under limited conditions.

Tests for illegal use of drugs are not medical examinations under the ADA and are not subject to the restrictions of such examinations.

Q. When can an employer ask an applicant to "self-identify" as having a disability?

A. Federal contractors and subcontractors who are covered by the affirmative action requirements of section 503 of the Rehabilitation Act of 1973 may invite individuals with disabilities to identify themselves on a job application form or by other pre-employment inquiry, to satisfy the section 503 affirmative action requirements. Employers who request such information must observe section 503 requirements regarding the manner in which such information is requested and used, and the procedures for maintaining such information as a separate, confidential record, apart from regular personnel records.

A pre-employment inquiry about a disability is allowed if required by another Federal law or regulation such as those applicable to disabled veterans and veterans of the Vietnam era. Pre-employment inquiries about disabilities may be necessary under such laws to identify applicants or clients with disabilities in order to provide them with required special services.

Q. Does the ADA require employers to develop written job descriptions?

A. No. The ADA does not require employers to develop or maintain job descriptions. However, a written job description that is prepared before advertising or interviewing applicants for a job will be considered as evidence along with other relevant factors. If an employer uses job descriptions, they should be reviewed to make sure they accurately reflect the actual functions of a job. A job description will be most helpful if it focuses on the results or outcome of a job function, not solely on the way it customarily is performed. A reasonable accommodation may enable a person with a disability to accomplish a job function in a manner that is different from the way an employee who is not disabled may accomplish the same function.

Q. What is "reasonable accommodation"?

A. Reasonable accommodation is any modification or adjustment to a job or the work environment that will enable a qualified applicant or employee with a disability to participate in the application process or to perform essential job functions. Reasonable accommodation also includes adjustments to assure that a qualified individual with a disability has rights and privileges in employment equal to those of employees without disabilities.

Q. What are some of the accommodations applicants and employees may need?

A. Examples of reasonable accommodation include making existing facilities used by employees readily accessible to and usable by an individual with a disability; restructuring a job; modifying work schedules; acquiring or modifying equipment; providing qualified readers or interpreters;

or appropriately modifying examinations, training, or other programs. Reasonable accommodation also may include reassigning a current employee to a vacant position for which the individual is qualified, if the person is unable to do the original job because of a disability even with an accommodation. However, there is no obligation to find a position for an applicant who is not qualified for the position sought. Employers are not required to lower quality or quantity standards as an accommodation; nor are they obligated to provide personal use items such as glasses or hearing aids.

The decision as to the appropriate accommodation must be based on the particular facts of each case. In selecting the particular type of reasonable accommodation to provide, the principal test is that of effectiveness, i.e., whether the accommodation will provide an opportunity for a person with a disability to achieve the same level of performance and to enjoy benefits equal to those of an average, similarly situated person without a disability. However, the accommodation does not have to ensure equal results or provide exactly the same benefits.

Q. When is an employer required to make a reasonable accommodation?

A. An employer is only required to accommodate a "known" disability of a qualified applicant or employee. The requirement generally will be triggered by a request from an individual with a disability, who frequently will be able to suggest an appropriate accommodation. Accommodations must be made on an individual basis, because the nature and extent of a disabling condition and the requirements of a job will vary in each case. If the individual does not request an accommodation, the employer is not obligated to provide one except where an individual's known disability impairs his/her ability to know of, or effectively communicate a need for, an accommodation that is obvious to the employer. If a person with a disability requests, but cannot suggest, an appropriate accommodation, the employer and the individual should work together to identify one. There are also many public and private resources that can provide assistance without cost.

Q. What are the limitations on the obligation to make a reasonable accommodation?

A. The individual with a disability requiring the accommodation must be otherwise qualified, and the disability must be known to the employer. In addition, an employer is not required to make an accommodation if it would impose an "undue hardship" on the operation of the employer's business. "Undue hardship" is defined as an "action requiring significant difficulty or expense" when considered in light of a number of factors. These factors include the nature and cost of the accommodation in relation to the size, resources, nature, and structure of the employer's operation. Undue hardship is determined on a case-by-case basis. Where the facility making the accommodation is part of a larger entity, the structure and overall resources of the larger organization would be considered, as well as the financial and administrative relationship of the facility to the larger organization. In general, a larger employer with greater resources would be expected to make accommodations requiring greater effort or expense than would be required of a smaller employer with fewer resources.

If a particular accommodation would be an undue hardship, the employer must try to identify another accommodation that will not pose such a hardship. Also, if the cost of an accommodation would impose an undue hardship on the employer, the individual with a disability should be given the option of paying that portion of the cost which would constitute an undue hardship or providing the accommodation.

Q. Must an employer modify existing facilities to make them accessible?

A. The employer's obligation under title I is to provide access for an individual applicant to participate in the job application process, and for an individual employee with a disability to perform the essential functions of his/her job, including access to a building, to the work site, to needed equipment, and to all facilities used by employees. For example, if an employee lounge is located in a place inaccessible to an employee using a wheelchair, the lounge might be modified or relocated, or comparable facilities might be provided in a location that would enable the individual to take a break with co-workers. The employer must provide such access unless it would cause an undue hardship.

Under title I, an employer is not required to make its existing facilities accessible until a particular applicant or employee with a particular disability needs an accommodation, and then the modifications should meet that individual's work needs. However, employers should consider initiating changes that will provide general accessibility, particularly for job applicants, since it is likely that people with disabilities will be applying for jobs. The employer does not have to make changes to provide access in places or facilities that will not be used by that individual for employment-related activities or benefits.

Q. Can an employer be required to reallocate an essential function of a job to another employee as a reasonable accommodation?

A. No. An employer is not required to reallocate essential functions of a job as a reasonable accommodation.

Q. Can an employer be required to modify, adjust, or make other reasonable accommodations in the way a test is given to a qualified applicant or employee with a disability?

A. Yes. Accommodations may be needed to assure that tests or examinations measure the actual ability of an individual to perform job functions rather than reflect limitations caused by the disability. Tests should be given to people who have sensory, speaking, or manual impairments in a format that does not require the use of the impaired skill, unless it is a job-related skill that the test is designed to measure.

Q. Can an employer maintain existing production/performance standards for an employee with a disability?

A. An employer can hold employees with disabilities to the same standards of production/performance as other similarly situated employees without disabilities for performing essential job functions, with or without reasonable accommodation. An employer also can hold employees with disabilities to the same standards of production/performance as other employees regarding marginal functions unless the disability affects the person's ability to perform those marginal functions. If the ability to perform marginal functions is affected by the disability, the employer must provide some type of reasonable accommodation such as job restructuring but may not exclude an individual with a disability who is satisfactorily performing a job's essential functions.

Q. Can an employer establish specific attendance and leave policies?

A. An employer can establish attendance and leave policies that are uniformly applied to all employees, regardless of disability, but may not refuse leave needed by an employee with a disability if other employees get such leave. An employer also may be required to make adjustments in leave policy as a reasonable accommodation. The employer is not obligated to provide additional paid leave, but accommodations may include leave flexibility and unpaid leave.

A uniformly applied leave policy does not violate the ADA because it has a more severe effect on an individual because of his/her disability. However, if an individual with a disability requests a modification of such a policy as a reasonable accommodation, an employer may be required to provide it, unless it would impose an undue hardship.

Q. Can an employer consider health and safety when deciding whether to hire an applicant or retain an employee with a disability?

A. Yes. The ADA permits employers to establish qualification standards that will exclude individuals who pose a direct threat — i.e., a significant risk of substantial harm — to the health or safety of the individual or of others, if that risk cannot be eliminated or reduced below the level of a "direct threat" by reasonable accommodation. However, an employer may not simply assume that a threat exists; the employer must establish through objective, medically supportable methods that there is significant risk that substantial harm could occur in the workplace. By requiring employers to make individualized judgments based on reliable medical or other objective evidence rather than on generalizations, ignorance, fear, patronizing attitudes, or stereotypes, the ADA recognizes the need to balance the interests of people with disabilities against the legitimate interests of employers in maintaining a safe workplace.

Q. Are applicants or employees who are currently illegally using drugs covered by the ADA?

A. No. Individuals who currently engage in the illegal use of drugs are specifically excluded from the definition of a "qualified individual with a disability" protected by the ADA when the employer takes action on the basis of their drug use.

Q. Is testing for the illegal use of drugs permissible under the ADA?

A. Yes. A test for the illegal use of drugs is not considered a medical examination under the ADA; therefore, employers may conduct such testing of applicants or employees and make employment decisions based on the results. The ADA does not encourage, prohibit, or authorize drug tests.

If the results of a drug test reveal the presence of a lawfully prescribed drug or other medical information, such information must be treated as a confidential medical record.

Q. Are alcoholics covered by the ADA?

A. Yes. While a current illegal user of drugs is not protected by the ADA if an employer acts on the basis of such use, a person who currently uses alcohol is not automatically denied protection. An alcoholic is a person with a disability and is protected by the ADA if s/he is qualified to perform the essential functions of the job. An employer may be required to provide an accommodation to an alcoholic. However, an employer can discipline, discharge or deny employment to an alcoholic whose use of alcohol adversely affects job performance or conduct. An employer also may prohibit the use of alcohol in the workplace and can require that employees not be under the influence of alcohol.

Q. Does the ADA override Federal and State health and safety laws?

A. The ADA does not override health and safety requirements established under other Federal laws even if a standard adversely affects the employment of an individual with a disability. If a standard is required by another Federal law, an employer must comply with it and does not have to show that the standard is job related and consistent with business necessity. For example, employers must conform to health and safety requirements of the U.S. Occupational Safety and Health Administration. However, an employer still has the obligation under the ADA to consider whether there is a reasonable accommodation, consistent with the standards of other Federal laws, that will prevent exclusion of qualified individuals with disabilities who can perform jobs without violating the standards of those laws. If an employer can comply with both the ADA and another Federal law, then the employer must do so.

The ADA does not override State or local laws designed to protect public health and safety, except where such laws conflict with the ADA requirements. If there is a State or local law that would exclude an individual with a disability from a particular job or profession because of a health or safety risk, the employer still must assess whether a particular individual would pose a "direct threat" to health or safety under the ADA standard. If such a "direct threat" exists, the employer must consider whether it could be eliminated or reduced below the level of a "direct threat" by reasonable accommodation. An employer cannot rely on a State or local law that conflicts with ADA requirements as a defense to a charge of discrimination.

Q. How does the ADA affect workers' compensation programs?

A. Only injured workers who meet the ADA's definition of an "individual with a disability" will be considered disabled under the ADA, regardless of whether they satisfy criteria for receiving benefits under workers' compensation or other disability laws. A worker also must be "qualified" (with or without reasonable accommodation) to be protected by the ADA. Work-related injuries do not always cause physical or mental impairments severe enough to "substantially limit" a major life activity. Also, many on-the-job injuries cause temporary impairments which heal within a short period of time with little or no long-term or permanent impact. Therefore, many injured workers who qualify for benefits under workers' compensation or other disability benefits laws may not be protected by the ADA. An employer must consider work-related injuries on a case-by-case basis to know if a worker is protected by the ADA.

An employer may not inquire into an applicant's workers' compensation history before making a conditional offer of employment. After making a conditional job offer, an employer may inquire about a person's workers' compensation history in a medical inquiry or examination that is required of all applicants in the same job category. However, even after a conditional offer has been made, an employer cannot require a potential employee to have a medical examination because a response to a medical inquiry (as opposed to results from a medical examination) shows a previous on-the-job injury unless all applicants in the same job category are required to have an examination. Also, an employer may not base an employment decision on the speculation that an applicant may cause increased workers' compensation costs in the future. However, an employer may refuse to hire, or may discharge an individual who is not currently able to perform a job without posing a significant risk of substantial harm to the health or safety of the individual or others, if the risk cannot be eliminated or reduced by reasonable accommodation.

An employer may refuse to hire or may fire a person who knowingly provides a false answer to a lawful post-offer inquiry about his/her condition or worker's compensation history.

An employer also may submit medical information and records concerning employees and applicants (obtained after a conditional job offer) to state workers' compensation offices and "second injury" funds without violating ADA confidentiality requirements.

Q. What is discrimination based on "relationship or association" under the ADA?

A. The ADA prohibits discrimination based on relationship or association in order to protect individuals from actions based on unfounded assumptions that their relationship to a person with a disability would affect their job performance, and from actions caused by bias or misinformation concerning certain disabilities. For example, this provision would protect a person whose spouse has a disability from being denied employment because of an employer's unfounded assumption that the applicant would use excessive leave to care for the spouse. It also would protect an individual who does volunteer work for people with AIDS from a discriminatory employment action motivated by that relationship or association.

Q. How are the employment provisions enforced?

A. The employment provisions of the ADA are enforced under the same procedures now applicable to race, color, sex, national origin, and religious discrimination under title VII of the Civil Rights Act of 1964, as amended, and the Civil Rights Act of 1991. Complaints regarding actions that occurred on or after July 26, 1992, may be filed with the Equal Employment Opportunity Commission or designated State human rights agencies. Available remedies will include hiring, reinstatement, promotion, back pay, front pay, restored benefits, reasonable accommodation, attorneys' fees, expert witness fees, and court costs. Compensatory and punitive damages also may be available in cases of intentional discrimination or where an employer fails to make a good faith effort to provide a reasonable accommodation.

Q. What financial assistance is available to employers to help them make reasonable accommodations and comply with the ADA?

A. A special tax credit is available to help smaller employers make accommodations required by the ADA. An eligible small business may take a tax credit of up to $5,000 per year for accommodations made to comply with the ADA. The credit is available for one-half the cost of "eligible access expenditures" that are more than $250 but less than $10,250.

A full tax deduction, up to $15,000 per year, also is available to any business for expenses of removing qualified architectural or transportation barriers. Expenses covered include costs of removing barriers created by steps, narrow doors, inaccessible parking spaces, restroom facilities, and transportation vehicles. Information about the tax credit and the tax deduction can be obtained from a local IRS office, or by contacting the Office of Chief Counsel, Internal Revenue Service.

Tax credits are available under the Targeted Jobs Tax Credit Program (TJTCP) for employers who hire individuals with disabilities referred by State or local vocational rehabilitation agencies, State Commissions on the Blind, or the U.S. Department of Veterans Affairs, and certified by a State Employment Service. Under the TJTCP, a tax credit may be taken for up to 40 percent of the first $6,000 of first-year wages of a new employee with a disability. This program must be reauthorized each year by Congress, and currently is extended through June 30, 1993. Further information about the TJTCP can be obtained from the State Employment Services or from State Governors' Committees on the Employment of People with Disabilities.

Q. What are an employer's recordkeeping requirements under the employment provisions of the ADA?

A. An employer must maintain records such as application forms submitted by applicants and other records related to hiring, requests for reasonable accommodation, promotion, demotion, transfer, lay-off or termination, rates of pay or other terms of compensation, and selection for training or apprenticeship for one year after making the record or taking the action described (whichever occurs later). If a charge of discrimination is filed or an action is brought by EEOC, an employer must save all personnel records related to the charge until final disposition of the charge.

Q. Does the ADA require that an employer post a notice explaining its requirements?

A. The ADA requires that employers post a notice describing the provisions of the ADA. It must be made accessible, as needed, to individuals with disabilities. A poster is available from EEOC summarizing the requirements of the ADA and other Federal legal requirements for nondiscrimination for which EEOC has enforcement responsibility. EEOC also provides guidance on making this information available in accessible formats for people with disabilities.

Q. What resources does the Equal Employment Opportunity Commission have available to help employers and people with disabilities understand and comply with the employment requirements of the ADA?

A. The Equal Employment Opportunity Commission has developed several resources to help employers and people with disabilities understand and comply with the employment provisions of the ADA.

Resources include:

1. A Technical Assistance Manual that provides "how-to" guidance on the employment provisions of

the ADA as well as a resource directory to help individuals find specific information.

2. A variety of brochures, booklets, and fact sheets.

State and Local Governments

Q. Does the ADA apply to State and local governments?

A. Title II of the ADA prohibits discrimination against qualified individuals with disabilities in all programs, activities, and services of public entities. It applies to all State and local governments, their departments and agencies, and any other instrumentalities or special purpose districts of State or local governments. It clarifies the requirements of section 504 of the Rehabilitation Act of 1973 for public transportation systems that receive Federal financial assistance, and extends coverage to all public entities that provide public transportation, whether or not they receive Federal financial assistance. It establishes detailed standards for the operation of public transit systems, including commuter and intercity rail (AMTRAK).

Q. When do the requirements for State and local governments become effective?

A. In general, they became effective on January 26, 1992.

Q. How does title II affect participation in a State or local government's programs, activities, and services?

A. A state or local government must eliminate any eligibility criteria for participation in programs, activities, and services that screen out or tend to screen out persons with disabilities, unless it can establish that the requirements are necessary for the provision of the service, program, or activity. The State or local government may, however, adopt legitimate safety requirements necessary for safe operation if they are based on real risks, not on stereotypes or generalizations about individuals with disabilities. Finally, a public entity must reasonably modify its policies, practices, or procedures to avoid discrimination. If the public entity can demonstrate that a particular modification would fundamentally alter the nature of its service, program, or activity, it is not required to make that modification.

Q. Does title II cover a public entity's employment policies and practices?

A. Yes. Title II prohibits all public entities, regardless of the size of their work force, from discriminating in employment against qualified individuals with disabilities. In addition to title II's employment coverage, title I of the ADA and section 504 of the Rehabilitation Act of 1973 prohibit employment discrimination against qualified individuals with disabilities by certain public entities.

Q. What changes must a public entity make to its existing facilities to make them accessible?

A. A public entity must ensure that individuals with disabilities are not excluded from services, programs, and activities because existing buildings are inaccessible. A State or local government's programs, when viewed in their entirety, must be readily accessible to and usable by individuals with disabilities. This standard, known as "program accessibility," applies to facilities of a public entity that existed on January 26, 1992. Public entities do not necessarily have to make each of their existing facilities accessible. They may provide program accessibility by a number of methods including alteration of existing facilities, acquisition or construction of additional facilities, relocation of a service or program to an accessible facility, or provision of services at alternate accessible sites.

Q. When must structural changes be made to attain program accessibility?

A. Structural changes needed for program accessibility must be made as expeditiously as possible, but no later than January 26, 1995. This three-year time period is not a grace period; all alterations must be accomplished as expeditiously as possible. A public entity that employs 50 or more persons must have developed a transition plan by July 26, 1992, setting forth the steps necessary to complete such changes.

Q. What is a self-evaluation?

A. A self-evaluation is a public entity's assessment of its current policies and practices. The self-evaluation identifies and corrects those policies and practices that are inconsistent with title II's requirements. All public entities must complete a self-evaluation by January 26, 1993. A public entity that employs 50 or more employees must retain its self-evaluation for three years. Other public entities are not required to retain their self-evaluations, but are encouraged to do so because these documents evidence a public entity's good faith efforts to comply with title II's requirements.

Q. What does title II require for new construction and alterations?

A. The ADA requires that all new buildings constructed by a State or local government be accessible. In addition, when a State or local government undertakes alterations to a building, it must make the altered portions accessible.

Q. How will a State or local government know that a new building is accessible?

A. A State or local government will be in compliance with the ADA for new construction and alterations if it follows either of two accessibility standards. It can choose either the Uniform Federal Accessibility Standards or the Americans with Disabilities Act Accessibility Guidelines for Buildings and Facilities, which is the standard that must be used for public accommodations and commercial facilities under title III of the ADA. If the State or local government chooses the ADA Accessibility Guidelines, it is not entitled to the elevator exemption (which permits certain private buildings under three stories or under 3,000 square feet per floor to be constructed without an elevator).

Q. What requirements apply to a public entity's emergency telephone services, such as 911?

A. State and local agencies that provide emergency telephone services must provide "direct access" to individuals who rely on a TDD or computer modem for telephone communication. Telephone access through a third party or through a relay service does not satisfy the requirement for direct access. Where a public entity provides 911 telephone service, it may not substitute a separate seven-digit telephone line as the sole means for access to 911 services by nonvoice users. A public entity may, however, provide a separate seven-digit line for the exclusive use of nonvoice callers in addition to providing direct access for such calls to its 911 line.

Q. Does title II require that telephone emergency service systems be compatible with all formats used for nonvoice communications?

A. No. At present, telephone emergency services must only be compatible with the Baudot format.

Until it can be technically proven that communications in another format can operate in a reliable and compatible manner in a given telephone emergency environment, a public entity would not be required to provide direct access to computer modems using formats other than Baudot.

Q. How will the ADA's requirements for State and local governments be enforced?

A. Private individuals may bring lawsuits to enforce their rights under title II and may receive the same remedies as those provided under section 504 of the Rehabilitation Act of 1973, including reasonable attorney's fees. Individuals may also file complaints with eight designated Federal agencies, including the Department of Justice and the Department of Transportation.

Public Accommodations

Q. What are public accommodations?

A. A public accommodation is a private entity that owns, operates, leases, or leases to, a place of public accommodation. Places of public accommodation include a wide range of entities, such as restaurants, hotels, theaters, doctors' offices, pharmacies, retail stores, museums, libraries, parks, private schools, and day care centers. Private clubs and religious organizations are exempt from the ADA's title III requirements for public accommodations.

Q. Will the ADA have any effect on the eligibility criteria used by public accommodations to determine who may receive services?

A. Yes. If a criterion screens out or tends to screen out individuals with disabilities, it may only be used if necessary for the provision of the services. For instance, it would be a violation for a retail store to have a rule excluding all deaf persons from entering the premises, or for a movie theater to exclude all individuals with cerebral palsy. More subtle forms of discrimination are also prohibited. For example, requiring presentation of a driver's license as the sole acceptable means of identification for purposes of paying by check could constitute discrimination against individuals with vision impairments. This would be true if such individuals are ineligible to receive licenses and the use of an alternative means of identification is feasible.

Q. Does the ADA allow public accommodations to take safety factors into consideration in providing services to individuals with disabilities?

A. The ADA expressly provides that a public accommodation may exclude an individual, if that individual poses a direct threat to the health or safety of others that cannot be mitigated by appropriate modifications in the public accommodation's policies or procedures, or by the provision of auxiliary aids. A public accommodation will be permitted to establish objective safety criteria for the operation of its business; however, any safety standard must be based on objective requirements rather than stereotypes or generalizations about the ability of persons with disabilities to participate in an activity.

Q. Are there any limits on the kinds of modifications in policies, practices, and procedures required by the ADA?

A. Yes. The ADA does not require modifications that would fundamentally alter the nature of the services provided by the public accommodation. For example, it would not be discriminatory for a physician specialist who treats only burn patients to refer a deaf individual to another physician for treatment of a broken limb or respiratory ailment. To require a physician to accept patients outside of his or her specialty would fundamentally alter the nature of the medical practice.

Q. What kinds of auxiliary aids and services are required by the ADA to ensure effective communication with individuals with hearing or vision impairments?

A. Appropriate auxiliary aids and services may include services and devices such as qualified interpreters, assistive listening devices, notetakers, and written materials for individuals with hearing impairments; and qualified readers, taped texts, and brailled or large print materials for individuals with vision impairments.

Q. Are there any limitations on the ADA's auxiliary aids requirements?

A. Yes. The ADA does not require the provision of any auxiliary aid that would result in an undue burden or in a fundamental alteration in the nature of the goods or services provided by a public accommodation. However, the public accommodation is not relieved from the duty to furnish an alternative auxiliary aid, if available, that would not result in a fundamental alteration or undue burden. Both of these limitations are derived from existing regulations and caselaw under section 504 of the Rehabilitation Act and are to be determined on a case-by-case basis.

Q. Will restaurants be required to have brailled menus?

A. No, not if waiters or other employees are made available to read the menu to a blind customer.

Q. Will a clothing store be required to have brailled price tags?

A. No, not if sales personnel could provide price information orally upon request.

Q. Will a bookstore be required to maintain a sign language interpreter on its staff in order to communicate with deaf customers?

A. No, not if employees communicate by pen and notepad when necessary.

Q. Are there any limitations on the ADA's barrier removal requirements for existing facilities?

A. Yes. Barrier removal needs be accomplished only when it is "readily achievable" to do so.

Q. What does the term "readily achievable" mean?

A. It means "easily accomplishable and able to be carried out without much difficulty or expense."

Q. What are examples of the types of modifications that would be readily achievable in most cases?

A. Examples include the simple ramping of a few steps, the installation of grab bars where only routine reinforcement of the wall is required, the lowering of telephones, and similar modest adjustments.

Q. Will businesses need to rearrange furniture and display racks?

A. Possibly. For example, restaurants may need to rearrange tables and department stores may need to adjust their layout of racks and shelves in order to permit access to wheelchair users.

Q. Will businesses need to install elevators?

A. Businesses are not required to retrofit their facilities to install elevators unless such installation is readily achievable, which is unlikely in most cases.

Q. When barrier removal is not readily achievable, what kinds of alternative steps are required by the ADA?

A. Alternatives may include such measures as in-store assistance for removing articles from inaccessible shelves, home delivery of groceries, or coming to the door to receive or return dry cleaning.

Q. Must alternative steps be taken without regard to cost?

A. No, only readily achievable alternative steps must be undertaken.

Q. How is "readily achievable" determined in a multisite business?

A. In determining whether an action to make a public accommodation accessible would be "readily achievable," the overall size of the parent corporation or entity is only one factor to be considered. The ADA also permits consideration of the financial resources of the particular facility or facilities involved and the administrative or fiscal relationship of the facility or facilities to the parent entity.

Q. Who has responsibility for ADA compliance in leased places of public accommodation, the landlord or the tenant?

A. The ADA places the legal obligation to remove barriers or provide auxiliary aids and services on both the landlord and the tenant. The landlord and the tenant may decide by lease who will actually make the changes and provide the aids and services, but both remain legally responsible.

Q. What does the ADA require in new construction?

A. The ADA requires that all new construction of places of public accommodation, as well as of "commercial facilities" such as office buildings, be accessible. Elevators are generally not required in facilities under three stories or with fewer than 3,000 square feet per floor, unless the building is a shopping center or mall; the professional office of a health care provider; a terminal, depot, or other public transit station; or an airport passenger terminal.

Q. Is it expensive to make all newly constructed places of public accommodation and commercial facilities accessible?

A. The cost of incorporating accessibility features in new construction is less than one percent of construction costs. This is a small price in relation to the economic benefits to be derived from full accessibility in the future, such as increased employment and consumer spending and decreased welfare dependency.

Q. Must every feature of a new facility be accessible?

A. No, only a specified number of elements such as parking spaces and drinking fountains must be made accessible in order for a facility to be "readily accessible." Certain nonoccupiable spaces such as elevator pits, elevator penthouses, and piping or equipment catwalks need not be accessible.

Q. What are the ADA requirements for altering facilities?

A. All alterations that could affect the usability of a facility must be made in an accessible manner to the maximum extent feasible. For example, if during renovations a doorway is being relocated, the new doorway must be wide enough to meet the new construction standard for accessibility. When alterations are made to a primary function area, such as the lobby of a bank or the dining area of a cafeteria, an accessible path of travel to the altered area must also be provided.

The bathrooms, telephones, and drinking fountains serving that area must also be made accessible.

These additional accessibility alterations are only required to the extent that the added accessibility costs do not exceed 20% of the cost of the original alteration. Elevators are generally not required in facilities under three stories or with fewer than 3,000 square feet per floor, unless the building is a shopping center or mall; the professional office of a health care provider; a terminal, depot, or other public transit station; or an airport passenger terminal.

Q. Does the ADA permit an individual with a disability to sue a business when that individual believes that discrimination is about to occur, or must the individual wait for the discrimination to occur?

A. The ADA public accommodations provisions permit an individual to allege discrimination based on a reasonable belief that discrimination is about to occur. This provision, for example, allows a person who uses a wheelchair to challenge the planned construction of a new place of public accommodation, such as a shopping mall, that would not be accessible to individuals who use wheelchairs. The resolution of such challenges prior to the construction of an inaccessible facility would enable any necessary remedial measures to be incorporated in the building at the planning stage, when such changes would be relatively inexpensive.

Q. How does the ADA affect existing State and local building codes?

A. Existing codes remain in effect. The ADA allows the Attorney General to certify that a State law, local building code, or similar ordinance that establishes accessibility requirements meets or exceeds the minimum accessibility requirements for public accommodations and commercial facilities. Any State or local government may apply for certification of its code or ordinance. The Attorney General can certify a code or ordinance only after prior notice and a public hearing at which interested people, including individuals with disabilities, are provided an opportunity to testify against the certification.

Q. What is the effect of certification of a State or local code or ordinance?

A. Certification can be advantageous if an entity has constructed or altered a facility according to a certified code or ordinance. If someone later brings an enforcement proceeding against the entity, the certification is considered "rebuttable evidence" that the State law or local ordinance meets or exceeds the minimum requirements of the ADA. In other words, the entity can argue that the construction or alteration met the requirements of the ADA because it was done in compliance with the State or local code that had been certified.

Q. When are the public accommodations provisions effective?

A. In general, they became effective on January 26, 1992.

Q. How will the public accommodations provisions be enforced?

A. Private individuals may bring lawsuits in which they can obtain court orders to stop discrimination. Individuals may also file complaints with the Attorney General, who is authorized to bring lawsuits in cases of general public importance or where a "pattern or practice" of discrimination is alleged. In these cases, the Attorney General may seek monetary damages and civil penalties.

Civil penalties may not exceed $50,000 for a first violation or $100,000 for any subsequent violation.

Miscellaneous

Q. Is the Federal government covered by the ADA?

A. The ADA does not cover the executive branch of the Federal government. The executive branch continues to be covered by title V of the Rehabilitation Act of 1973, which prohibits discrimination in services and employment on the basis of handicap and which is a model for the requirements of the ADA. The ADA, however, does cover Congress and other entities in the legislative branch of the Federal government.

Q. Does the ADA cover private apartments and private homes?

A. The ADA does not cover strictly residential private apartments and homes. If, however, a place of public accommodation, such as a doctor's office or day care center, is located in a private residence, those portions of the residence used for that purpose are subject to the ADA's requirements.

Q. Does the ADA cover air transportation?

A. Discrimination by air carriers in areas other than employment is not covered by the ADA but rather by the Air Carrier Access Act (49 U.S.C. 1374 (c)).

Q. What are the ADA's requirements for public transit buses?

A. The Department of Transportation has issued regulations mandating accessible public transit vehicles and facilities. The regulations include requirements that all new fixed-route, public transit buses be accessible and that supplementary paratransit services be provided for those individuals with disabilities who cannot use fixed-route bus service. For information on how to contact the Department of Transportation, see page 30.

Q. How will the ADA make telecommunications accessible?

A. The ADA requires the establishment of telephone relay services for individuals who use telecommunications devices for deaf persons (TDD's) or similar devices. The Federal Communications Commission has issued regulations specifying standards for the operation of these services.

Q. Are businesses entitled to any tax benefit to help pay for the cost of compliance?

A. As amended in 1990, the Internal Revenue Code allows a deduction of up to $15,000 per year for expenses associated with the removal of qualified architectural and transportation barriers.

The 1990 amendment also permits eligible small businesses to receive a tax credit for certain costs of compliance with the ADA. An eligible small business is one whose gross receipts do not exceed $1,000,000 or whose workforce does not consist of more than 30 full-time workers. Qualifying businesses may claim a credit of up to 50 percent of eligible access expenditures that exceed $250 but do not exceed $10,250. Examples of eligible access expenditures include the necessary and reasonable costs of removing architectural, physical, communications, and transportation barriers; providing readers, interpreters, and other auxiliary aids; and acquiring or modifying equipment or devices.

Telephone Numbers for ADA Information

This list contains the telephone numbers of Federal agencies that are responsible for providing information to the public about the Americans with Disabilities Act and organizations that have been funded by the Federal government to provide information through staffed information centers.

The agencies and organizations listed are sources for obtaining information about the law's requirements and informal guidance in understanding and complying with the ADA. They are not, and should not be viewed as, sources for obtaining legal advice or legal opinions about your rights or responsibilities under the ADA.

Architectural and Transportation Barriers
  Compliance Board
1-800-872-2253 (voice and TDD)

Equal Employment Opportunity Commission
For questions and documents 1-800-669-3362
  (voice)
1-800-800-3302 (TDD)
Alternate number for ordering documents (print and other formats)
202/663-7110 (TDD) 202/663-4264 (voice)

Federal Communications Commission
For ADA documents and general information
202/632-7260 (voice)
202/632-6999 (TDD)

Job Accommodation Network 1-800-526-7234
(voice)
1-800-526-7234 (TDD)
Within West Virginia 1-800-526-4698 (voice & TDD)

President's Committee on Employment of People with Disabilities withDisabilities Information Line:
ADA Work
1-800-232-9675 (voice and TDD)

U.S. Department of Justice 202/514-0301 (voice) 202/514-0383 (TDD)

U.S. Department of Transportation
Federal Transit Administration for ADA documents and information
202/366-1656 (voice) 202/366-2979 (TDD)

Office of the General Counsel (for legal questions)
202/366-9306 (voice) 202/755-7687 (TDD)

Federal Aviation Administration 202/376-6406 (voice)

Rural Transit Assistance Program (for information and assistance on public transportation issues)
1-800-527-8279 (voice & TDD)

Regional Disability and Business Technical Assistance Centers

ADA information, assistance, and copies of ADA documents supplied by the Equal Employment Opportunity Commission and the Department of Justice, which are available in standard print, large print, audio cassette, braille, and computer disk, may be obtained from any of the ten Regional Disability and Business Technical Assistance Centers.

Toll-free number for reaching any of the following Centers
1-800-949-4232 (voice & TDD)

Region I (Maine, New Hampshire, Vermont, Massachusetts, Rhode Island, Connecticut)
207/874-6535 (voice & TDD)

Region II (New York, New Jersey, Puerto Rico)
609/392-4004 (voice) 609/392-7004 (TDD)

Region III (Pennsylvania, Delaware, Maryland,
District of Columbia, Virginia, West Virginia)
703/525-3268 (voice & TDD)

Region IV (Kentucky, Tennessee, North Carolina,
South Carolina, Georgia, Alabama, Mississippi,
Florida)
404/888-0022 (voice) 404/888-9098 (TDD)

Region V (Ohio, Indiana, Illinois, Michigan,
Wisconsin, Minnesota)
312/413-7756 (voice & TDD)

Region VI (Arkansas, Louisiana, Oklahoma, Texas,
New Mexico)
713/520-0232 (voice) 713/520-5136 (TDD)

Region VII (Iowa, Missouri, Nebraska, Kansas)
314/882-3600 (voice & TDD)

Region VIII (North Dakota, South Dakota,
Montana, Wyoming, Colorado, Utah)
719/444-0252 (voice & TDD)

Region IX (Arizona, Nevada, California, Hawaii,
Pacific Basin)
510/465-7884 (voice) 510/465-3172 (TDD)

Region X (Idaho, Oregon, Washington, Alaska)
206/438-3168 (voice) 206/438-3167 (TDD)

Addresses for ADA Information
U.S. Equal Employment Opportunity Commission
1801 L Street NW
Washington, DC 20507

U.S. Department of Justice
Civil Rights Division
Public Access Section
P.O. Box 66738
Washington, DC 20035-6738

U.S. Department of Transportation
400 Seventh Street SW
Washington, DC 20590

Architectural and Transportation Barriers
Compliance Board
1331 F Street NW
Suite 1000
Washington, DC 20004-1111

Federal Communications Commission
1919 M Street NW Washington, DC 20554

EEOC Recordkeeping Requirements

In general, employers must keep all personnel or employment records for one year. If an employee is involuntarily terminated, his/her personnel records must be retained for one year from the date of termination. If a claim of discrimination is filed, all relevant personnel records must be retained until final disposition of the matter.

Under *Age Discrimination in Employment Act* of 1967 (ADEA) recordkeeping requirements, employers must also keep all payroll records for three years. Additionally, employers must keep on file any employee benefit plan (such as pension and insurance plans) and any written seniority or merit system for the full period the plan or system is in effect and for at least one year after its termination.

Under *Fair Labor Standards Act* (FLSA) recordkeeping requirements applicable to the Equal Pay Act of 1963 (EPA), employers must keep payroll records for at least three years. In addition, employers must keep for at least two years all records (including wage rates, job evaluations, seniority and merit systems, and collective bargaining agreements) that explain the basis for paying different wages to employees of opposite sexes in the same establishment.

The EEOC requires larger employers to file an EEO-1 report each year, which provides a breakdown of the employer's work force by race, sex, and national origin. However, employers with fewer than 100 employees and federal contractors with fewer than 50 employees and contracts under $50,000 are exempt from this requirement.

Title VII of the Civil Rights Act of 1964

Title VII prohibits employers from discriminating against workers because of race, color, religion, sex, or national origin.

Sexual harassment —

Sexual harassment is a form of unlawful sex discrimination.

Sexual harassment includes unwelcome sexual advances, requests for sexual favors, and other verbal or physical conduct of a sexual nature that are made a condition of employment, that unreasonably interfere with work performance, or that create an intimidating, hostile, or offensive work environment.

Employers are responsible for maintaining a workplace free of sexual harassment, and they may be liable for the unlawful conduct of their agents, supervisory employees, employees, and, in certain circumstances, even non-employees who sexually harass employees at work.

Racial and ethnic harassment —

Harassment on the basis of an individual's race or national origin violates Title VII.

Racial or ethnic slurs, jokes, offensive or derogatory comments, or other verbal or physical conduct based on race or nationality are unlawful if the conduct creates an intimidating, hostile, or offensive work environment, or if it unreasonably interferes with an employee's work performance.

Employers are responsible for maintaining a workplace free of racial and ethnic harassment, and they may be liable for unlawful conduct by their agents, supervisory employees, employees, and, in certain circumstances, non-employees who harass employees at work.

Pregnancy discrimination —

Under Title VII, discrimination on the basis of pregnancy, childbirth, or related medical conditions is unlawful sex discrimination.

Title VII's prohibition against pregnancy discrimination applies to all terms and conditions of employment, including hiring, firing, promotion, leave, and benefits.

Religious accommodation —

An employer is required to provide an accommodation for employees' sincerely held religious observances or practices unless the accommodation would impose an undue hardship on the employer's business.

Undue hardship can be claimed if an accommodation imposes more than "de minimis" cost, generally meaning more than ordinary administrative costs.

Undue hardship can also be claimed if an accommodation requires violating the terms of a seniority system (for example, by denying another employee's job or shift preference).

Immigration Reform and Control Act (IRCA)

The Immigration Reform and Control Act of 1986 (IRCA) makes it unlawful for an employer to hire any person who is not legally authorized to work in the United States, and it requires employers to verify the employment eligibility of all new employees.

IRCA also prohibits discrimination in hiring and discharge based on national origin (as does Title VII) and on citizenship status.

IRCA's anti-discrimination provisions are intended to prevent employers from attempting to comply with the Act's work authorization requirements by discriminating against foreign-looking or foreign-sounding job applicants.

IRCA's anti-discrimination provisions apply to smaller employers than those covered by EEOC-enforced laws.

IRCA's national origin discrimination provisions apply to employers with between 4 and 14 employees (who would not be covered by Title VII).

IRCA's citizenship discrimination provisions apply to all employers with at least 4 employees.

IRCA is enforced by the U.S. Department of Justice. For information on IRCA's anti-discrimination provisions, contact:

> United States Department of Justice
> Office of Special Counsel for Immigration-Related Unfair Employment Practices
> (800) 255-8155 (employer hotline/voice)
> (800) 237-2515 (TDD)
> http://www.usdoj.gov/crt/osc

Age Discrimination in Employment Act (ADEA)

The ADEA prohibits age discrimination against older workers (persons 40 or older) in all aspects of employment, including hiring and benefits.

Stereotypical assumptions based on age —

To avoid violating the ADEA, employers should carefully avoid basing employment actions — particularly hiring, firing, and promotion decisions — on stereotypical assumptions based on age. Such beliefs include notions that older workers are inflexible, set in their ways, unable to learn new procedures, unable to perform certain jobs safely, unable to work for younger supervisors, and likely to retire.

Employment decisions regarding older workers — just as those regarding younger workers — should be based on their individual skills, abilities, and merit.

Job advertisements —

To avoid unlawfully deterring older job seekers from applying for advertised jobs, help-wanted notices and job advertisements should not include terms or phrases such as "young," "recent graduate," "boy," "girl," or "age 25 to 35."

Cost exception —

An employer is not required to provide equal health insurance, life insurance, or disability benefits to older workers if it costs more to do so.

An employer may provide older employees with lower health, life, and/or disability benefits as long as it spends the same amount on both older and younger workers.

Because of the ADEA's cost exception, small employers can hire older workers without concern about additional or undue expenses for such employee benefits.

Source: U.S. Department of Justice

The Occupational Safety and Health Act of 1970 (OSHA)

Source: U.S. Department of Labor

Who is Covered: In general, coverage of the Act extends to all employers and their employees in the 50 states, the District of Columbia, Puerto Rico, and all other territories under federal government jurisdiction. Coverage is provided either directly by the Federal Occupational Safety and Health Administration (OSHA) or through an OSHA-approved state occupational safety and health program.

As defined by the Act, an employer is any "person engaged in a business affecting commerce who has employees, but does not include the United States or any state or political subdivision of a State." Therefore, the Act applies to employers and employees in such varied fields as manufacturing, construction, longshoring, agriculture, law and medicine, charity and disaster relief, organized labor and private education. Such coverage includes religious groups to the extent that they employ workers for secular purposes.

The following are not covered by the Act:
Self-employed persons;

> Farms at which only immediate members of the farmer's family are employed;
>
> Working conditions regulated by other federal agencies under other federal statutes. This category includes most employment in mining, nuclear energy and nuclear weapons manufacture, and many segments of the transportation industries;
>
> Employees of State and local governments (unless they are in one of the States with OSHA-approved safety and health programs).

Other federal agencies are sometimes authorized to regulate safety and health working conditions in a particular industry; if they do not do so in specific areas, then OSHA requirements apply.

Basic Provisions/Requirements

The Act assigns to OSHA two principal functions: setting standards and conducting workplace inspections to ensure that employers are complying with the standards and providing a safe and healthful workplace. OSHA standards may require that employers adopt certain practices, means, methods or processes reasonably necessary to protect workers on the job. It is the responsibility of employers to become familiar with standards applicable to their establishments, to eliminate hazardous conditions to the extent possible, and to comply with the standards. Compliance may include ensuring that employees have and use personal protective equipment when required for safety or health. Employees must comply with all rules and regulations that are applicable to their own actions and conduct.

Even in areas where OSHA has not promulgated a standard addressing a specific hazard, employers are responsible for complying with the OSH Act's "general duty" clause. The general duty clause of the Act [Section 5(a)(1)] states that each employer "shall furnish . . . a place of employment which is free from recognized hazards that are causing or are likely to cause death or serious physical harm to his employees."

States with OSHA-approved job safety and health programs must set standards that are at least as effective as the equivalent federal standard. Most of the state-plan states adopt standards identical to the federal ones (two states, New York and Connecticut, have plans which cover only public sector employees).

Federal OSHA Standards

Standards fall into four major categories: general industry (29 CFR 1910), construction (29 CFR 1926), maritime - shipyards, marine terminals, longshoring (29 CFR 1915-19), and agriculture (29 CFR 1928).

Each of these four categories of standards imposes requirements that are targeted to that industry, although in some cases they are identical across industries. Among the standards that impose similar requirements on all industry sectors are those for access to medical and exposure records, personal protective equipment, and hazard communication.

Access to Medical and Exposure Records: This standard requires that employers grant employees access to any of their medical records maintained by the employer and to any records the employer maintains on the employees' exposure to toxic substances.

Personal Protective Equipment: This standard, included separately in the standards for each industry segment (except agriculture), requires that employers provide employees, at no cost to employees, with personal protective equipment designed to protect them against certain hazards. This can range from protective helmets to prevent head injuries in construction and cargo handling work, to eye protection, hearing protection, hard-toed shoes, special goggles (for welders, for example) and gauntlets for iron workers.

Hazard Communication: This standard requires that manufacturers and importers of hazardous materials conduct a hazard evaluation of the products they manufacture or import. If the product is found to be hazardous under the terms of the standard, containers of the material must be appropriately labeled and the first shipment of the material to a new customer must be accompanied by a material safety data sheet (MSDS). Employers, using the MSDSs they receive, must train their employees to recognize and avoid the hazards the materials present.

In general, all employers (except those in the construction industry) should be aware that any hazard not covered by an industry-specific standard may be covered by a general industry standard; in addition, all employers must keep their workplaces free of recognized hazards that may cause death or serious physical harm to employees, even if OSHA does not have a specific standard or requirement addressing the hazard. This coverage becomes important in the enforcement aspects of OSHA's work.

Other types of requirements are imposed by regulation rather than by a standard. OSHA regulations cover such items as recordkeeping, reporting and posting.

Recordkeeping: Every employer covered by OSHA who has more than 10 employees, except for certain low-hazard industries such as retail, finance, insurance, real estate, and some service industries, must maintain OSHA-specified records of job-related injuries and illnesses. There are two such records, the OSHA Form 200 and the OSHA Form 101.

The OSHA Form 200 is an injury/illness log, with a separate line entry for each recordable injury or illness (essentially those work-related deaths, injuries and illnesses other than minor injuries that require only first aid treatment and that do not involve medical treatment, loss of consciousness, restriction of work or motion, or transfer to another job). A summary section of the OSHA Form 200, which includes the total of the previous year's injury and illness experience, must be posted in the workplace for the entire month of February each year.

The OSHA Form 101 is an individual incident report that provides added detail about each individual recordable injury or illness. A suitable insurance or workers' compensation form that provides the same details may be substituted for the OSHA Form 101.

Unless an employer has been selected in a particular year to be part of a national survey of workplace injuries and illnesses conducted by the Department of Labor's Bureau of Labor Statistics (BLS), employers with ten or fewer employees or employers in traditionally low-hazard industries are exempt from maintaining these records; all employers selected for the BLS survey must maintain the records. Employers so selected will be notified before the end of the year to begin keeping records during the coming year, and technical assistance on completing these forms is available from the state offices which select these employers for the survey.

Industries designated as traditionally low hazard include: automobile dealers; apparel and accessory stores; furniture and home furnishing stores; eating and drinking places; finance, insurance, and real estate industries; and service industries, such as personal and business services, legal, educational, social and cultural services and membership organizations.

Reporting: In addition to the reporting requirements described above, each employer, regardless of number of employees or industry category, must report to the nearest OSHA office within 8 hours of any accident that results in one or more fatalities or hospitalization of three or more employees. Such accidents are often investigated by OSHA to determine what caused the accident and whether violations of standards contributed to the event.

Employee Rights

Employees are granted several important rights by the Act. Among them are the right to: complain to OSHA about safety and health conditions in their workplace and have their identity kept confidential from the employer, contest the time period OSHA allows for correcting standards violations, and participate in OSHA workplace inspections.

Anti-Discrimination Provisions

Private sector employees who exercise their rights under OSHA can be protected against employer reprisal, as described in Section 11(c) of the OSH Act. Employees must notify OSHA within 30 days of the time they learned of the alleged discriminatory action. This notification is followed by an OSHA investigation. If OSHA agrees that discrimination has occurred, the employer will be asked to restore any lost benefits to the affected employee. If necessary, OSHA can take the employer to court. In such cases, the worker pays no legal fees.

Copies of Standards

The *Federal Register* is one of the best sources of information on standards, since all OSHA standards are published there when adopted, as are all amendments, corrections, insertions or deletions. The *Federal Register*, published five days a week, is available in many public libraries. Annual subscriptions are available from the Superintendent of Documents, U.S. Government Printing Office (GPO), Washington, D.C. 20402. OSHA also provides copies of its Federal Register notices on its website.

Each year the Office of the *Federal Register* publishes all current regulations and standards in the Code of Federal Regulations (CFR), available at many public libraries and from GPO. OSHA's regulations and standards are collected in several volumes in Title 29 CFR, Parts 1900-1999. OSHA's regulations and standards are also available through the Internet on OSHA's page on standards. OSHA also has a compliance assistance section on its website. For a reasonable price, GPO offers a data text-retrieval package in CD- ROM format that contains all OSHA standards, compliance directives and standards interpretations.

Since states with OSHA-approved job safety and health programs adopt and enforce their own standards under state law, copies of these standards can be obtained from the individual states.

Training and Education

OSHA's field offices (more than 70) are full-service centers offering a variety of informational services such as publications, technical advice, audio-visual aids on workplace hazards, and lecturers for speaking engagements.

The OSHA Training Institute in Des Plaines, Illinois, provides basic and advanced training and education in safety and health for federal and state compliance safety and health officers; state consultants; other federal agency personnel; and private sector employers, employees and their representatives. Institute courses cover topics such as electrical hazards, machine guarding, ventilation and ergonomics. The Institute facility includes classrooms, laboratories, a library and an audio-visual unit. The laboratories contain various demonstrations and equipment, such as power presses, woodworking and welding shops, a complete industrial ventilation unit, and a noise demonstration laboratory. Sixty-one courses are available for students from the private sector dealing with subjects such as safety and health in the construction industry and methods of voluntary compliance with OSHA standards.

OSHA also provides funds to nonprofit organizations to conduct workplace training and education. OSHA annually identifies areas of unmet needs for safety and health education in the workplace and invites grant applications to address these needs. The Training Institute is OSHA's point of contact for learning about the many valuable training products and materials developed under such grants.

Organizations awarded grants use the funds to develop training and educational programs, reach out to workers and employers for whom their program is appropriate, and provide these programs to employers and employees.

Grants are awarded annually. Grant recipients are expected to contribute 20 percent of the total grant cost.

While OSHA does not distribute grant materials directly, it will provide addresses and phone numbers of contact persons from whom the public can order such materials for its use. However, OSHA does provide limited lending of grant-produced audiovisual training programs through the Resource Center Audiovisual Circulation Project. Contact the OSHA Training Institute at (708) 297-4810.

Consultation Assistance

Consultation assistance is available to employers who want help in establishing and maintaining a safe and healthful workplace. Largely funded by OSHA, the service is provided at no cost to the employer, and is available in every State and territory.

Primarily targeted for smaller employers with more hazardous operations, the consultation service is delivered by state government agencies or universities employing professional safety consultants and health consultants. On-site OSHA consultation assistance includes an opening conference with the employer to explain the ground rules for consultation, a walk through the workplace to identify any specific hazards and to examine those aspects of the employer's safety and health program which relate to the scope of the visit, and a closing conference followed by a written report to the employer of the consultant's findings and recommendations.

This process begins with the employer's request for consultation and the commitment to correct any serious job safety and health hazards identified by the consultant. Possible violations of OSHA standards will not be reported to OSHA enforcement staff unless the employer fails or refuses to eliminate or control worker exposure to any identified serious hazard or imminent danger situation. In such unusual circumstances, OSHA may investigate and begin enforcement action. Employers must also agree to allow the consultant to freely confer with employees during the on-site visit.

Additional information concerning consultation assistance, including a directory of OSHA-funded consultation projects, can be obtained by requesting OSHA publication No. 3047, Consultation Services for the Employer.

Information Sources

Information about state programs, VPP, consultation programs, and inspections can be obtained from the nearest OSHA regional, area, or district office. Area offices are listed in local phone directories under U.S. Government listings for the U.S. Department of Labor. OSHA's Public Service Plan, published in September 1994, is a good source for these phone numbers. Copies are available from the OSHA Publications Office, whose address, telephone and facsimile number in the paragraph below.

The OSHA Home Page contains information on other OSHA activities, statistics, media releases, technical assistance, and links to other safety and health Internet sites. OSHA has developed interactive software to assist employers in complying with OSHA's cadmium, confined spaces, and asbestos standards.

A single free copy of an OSHA catalog, OSHA 2019, "OSHA Publications and Audiovisual Programs," may be obtained by mailing a self-addressed mailing label to the OSHA Publications Office, Room N3101, U.S. Department of Labor, Washington, DC 20210; telephone (202) 219-4667; facsimile (202) 219-9266. Descriptions of and ordering information for all OSHA publications and audiovisual programs are contained in this catalog.

A variety of information is available on OSHA's Publications website , including on-line publication order forms, the OSHA poster, guidance on OSHA recordkeeping, and on-line access to several OSHA publications in PDF format.

Questions about OSHA programs, the status of ongoing standards-setting activities, and general inquiries about OSHA may be addressed to the OSHA Office of Information & Consumer Affairs, Room N3637, U.S. Department of Labor, Washington, DC 20210; telephone (202) 219-8151.

Penalties (Inspections and Citations)
Workplace Inspections

To enforce its standards, OSHA is authorized under the Act to conduct workplace inspections. Every establishment covered by the Act is subject to inspection by OSHA compliance safety and health officers (CSHOs) who are chosen for their knowledge and experience in the occupational safety and health field. CSHOs are thoroughly trained in OSHA standards and in the recognition of safety and health hazards. Similarly, states with their own occupational safety and health programs conduct inspections using qualified state CSHOs.

OSHA conducts two general types of inspections: programmed and unprogrammed. There are various OSHA publications and documents which describe in detail OSHA's inspection policies and procedures. Unprogrammed inspections respond to fatalities, catastrophes and complaints, the last of which is further detailed in OSHA's complaint policies and procedures.

The following are the types of violations that may be cited and the penalties that may be proposed:

Other-Than-⌐   ⌐us Violation: A violation
that has a dirє   ¹ationship to job safety and
health, but proι   vould not cause death
or serious physicɑ   ⌐n. A proposed penalty
of up to $7,000 for each violation is discre-
tionary. A penalty for an other-than-serious
violation may be adjusted downward by as
much as 95 percent, depending on the
employer's good faith (demonstrated efforts
to comply with the Act), history of previous
violations, and size of business. When the
adjusted penalty amounts to less than $50, no
penalty is proposed.

Serious Violation: A violation where there is
substantial probability that death or serious
physical harm could result and that the
employer knew, or should have known, of the
hazard. A mandatory penalty of up to $7,000
for each violation is proposed. A penalty for a
serious violation may be adjusted downward,
based on the employer's good faith, history
of previous violations, the gravity of the
alleged violation, and size of business.

Willful Violation: A violation that the
employer intentionally and knowingly commits. The employer either knows that what he
or she is doing constitutes a violation, or is
aware that a hazardous condition exists and
has made no reasonable effort to eliminate it.

The Act provides that an employer who willfully violates the Act may be assessed a civil
penalty of not more than $70,000 but not less
than $5,000 for each violation. A proposed
penalty for a willful violation may be adjusted

downward, depending on the size of the business and its history of previous violations. Usually no credit is given for good faith.

If an employer is convicted of a willful violation of a standard that has resulted in the death of an employee, the offense is punishable by a court-imposed fine or by imprisonment for up to six months, or both. A fine of up to $250,000 for an individual, or $500,000 for a corporation [authorized under the Comprehensive Crime Control Act of 1984 (1984 CCA), not the OSH Act], may be imposed for a criminal conviction.

Repeated Violation: A violation of any standard, regulation, rule or order where, upon reinspection, a substantially similar violation is found. Repeated violations can bring a fine of up to $70,000 for each such violation. To be the basis of a repeat citation, the original citation must be final; a citation under contest may not serve as the basis for a subsequent repeat citation.

Failure to Correct Prior Violation: Failure to correct a prior violation may bring a civil penalty of up to $7,000 for each day the violation continues beyond the prescribed abatement date.

Additional violations for which citations and proposed penalties may be issued are as follows:

Falsifying records, reports or applications can bring a fine of $10,000 or up to six months in jail, or both;

Assaulting a compliance officer, or otherwise resisting, opposing, intimidating, or interfering with a compliance officer in the performance of his or her duties is a criminal offense, subject to a fine of not more than $250,000 for an individual and $500,000 for a corporation (1984 CCA) and imprisonment for not more than three years.

Citation and penalty procedures may differ somewhat in states with their own occupational safety and health programs.

Appeals Process

Appeals by Employees: If an inspection was initiated as a result of an employee complaint, the employee or authorized employee representative may request an informal review of any decision not to issue a citation.

Employees may not contest citations, amendments to citations, penalties or lack of penalties. They may contest the time in the citation for abatement of a hazardous condition. They also may contest an employer's Petition for Modification of Abatement (PMA) which requests an extension of the abatement period. Employees must contest the PMA within 10 working days of its posting or within 10 working days after an authorized employee representative has received a copy.

Within 15 working days of the employer's receipt of the citation, the employee may submit a written objection to OSHA. The OSHA area director forwards the objection to the Occupational Safety and Health Review Commission, which operates independently of OSHA.

Employees may request an informal conference with OSHA to discuss any issues raised by an inspection, citation, notice of proposed penalty or employer's notice of intention to contest.

Appeals by Employers: When issued a citation or notice of a proposed penalty, an employer may request an informal meeting with OSHA's area director to discuss the case. Employee representatives may be invited to attend the meeting. The area director is authorized to enter into settlement agreements that revise citations and penalties to avoid prolonged legal disputes.

Notice of Contest: If the employer decides to contest either the citation, the time set for abatement, or the proposed penalty, he or she has 15 working days from the time the citation and proposed penalty are received in which to notify the OSHA area director in writing. An orally expressed disagreement will not suffice. This written notification is called a "Notice of Contest."

There is no specific format for the Notice of Contest; however, it must clearly identify the employer's basis for contesting the citation, notice of proposed penalty, abatement period, or notification of failure to correct violations.

A copy of the Notice of Contest must be given to the employees' authorized representative. If any affected employees are not represented by a recognized bargaining agent, a copy of the notice must be posted in a prominent location in the workplace, or else served personally upon each unrepresented employee.

Appeal Review Procedure

If the written Notice of Contest has been filed within the required 15 working days, the OSHA area director forwards the case to the Occupational Safety and Health Review Commission (OSHRC). The Commission is an independent agency not associated with OSHA or the Department of Labor. The

Commission assigns the case to an administrative law judge.

The judge may disallow the contest if it is found to be legally invalid, or a hearing may be scheduled for a public place near the employer's workplace. The employer and the employees have the right to participate in the hearing; the OSHRC does not require that they be represented by attorneys.

Once the administrative law judge has ruled, any party to the case may request a further review by OSHRC. Any of the three OSHRC commissioners also may individually move to bring a case before the Commission for review. Commission rulings may be appealed to the appropriate U.S. Court of Appeals.

Appeals in State-Plan States

States with their own occupational safety and health programs have a state system for review and appeal of citations, penalties, and abatement periods. The procedures are generally similar to Federal OSHA's, but cases are heard by a state review board or equivalent authority.

Relation to State, Local and Other Federal Laws

The agency covers all working conditions that are not covered by safety and health regulations of another federal agency under other legislation. Industries where such regulations frequently apply include most transportation industries (rail, air and highway safety are under the Department of Transportation), nuclear industries (covered either by the Department of Energy or the Nuclear Regulatory Commission) and mining (covered by the Department of Labor's Mine Safety and Health Administration, and discussed elsewhere in this publication). OSHA also has the authority to monitor the safety and health of federal employees. It is the goal of all federal agencies to make their requirements compatible with those of Federal OSHA and to avoid conflicts and duplication.

Fair Labor Standards Act of 1938, as Amended

(29 USC §201 et seq.; 29 CFR 510-794)

Source: U.S. Department of Labor

Who Is Covered

The Fair Labor Standards Act (FLSA) establishes minimum wage, overtime pay, record-keeping and child labor standards that affect over 100 million full- and part-time workers in the private sector and in federal, state and local governments.

The Act applies to enterprises that have employees who are engaged in interstate commerce, producing goods for interstate commerce, or handling, selling or working on goods or materials that have been moved in or produced for interstate commerce. For most firms, an annual dollar volume of business test of $500,000 applies (i.e., those enterprises under this dollar amount are not covered). The following are covered by the Act regardless of their dollar volume of business: hospitals, institutions primarily engaged in the care of the sick, aged, mentally ill or disabled who reside on the premises; schools for children who are mentally or physically disabled or gifted; preschools, elementary and secondary schools and institutions of higher education; and federal, state and local government agencies.

Employees of firms that do not meet the $500,000 annual dollar volume test may be individually covered in any workweek in which they are individually engaged in interstate commerce, the production of goods for interstate commerce, or an activity which is closely related and directly essential to the production of such goods. Domestic service workers, such as day workers, housekeepers, chauffeurs, cooks, or full-time babysitters, are also covered if they receive at least $1,000 (1995) in cash wages from one employer in a calendar year, or if they work a total of more than 8 hours a week for one or more employers.

An enterprise that was covered by the Act on March 31, 1990, and that ceased to be covered because of the increase in the annual dollar volume test to $500,000, as required under the 1989 amendments to the Act, continues to be subject to the overtime pay, child labor and recordkeeping requirements of the Act.

Some employees are exempt from the Act's overtime pay provisions or both the minimum wage and overtime pay provisions under specific exemptions provided in the law. Because these exemptions are generally narrowly defined, employers should carefully check the exact terms and conditions for each by contacting local offices of the Wage and Hour Division listed in most telephone directories under U.S. Government, Department of Labor, Wage and Hour Division.

The following are examples of employees exempt from both the minimum wage and overtime pay requirements:

> Executive, administrative and professional employees (including teachers and academic administrative personnel in elementary and secondary schools), outside sales employees, and certain skilled computer professionals (as defined in Department of Labor regulations);
>
> Employees of certain seasonal amusement or recreational establishments;
>
> Employees of certain small newspapers and switchboard operators of small telephone companies;

Seamen employed on foreign vessels;

Employees engaged in fishing operations;

Employees engaged in newspaper delivery;

Farm workers employed on small farms (i.e., those that used less than 500 "man-days" of farm labor in any calendar quarter of the preceding calendar year);

Casual babysitters and persons employed as companions to the elderly or infirm.

The following are examples of employees exempt from the Act's overtime pay requirements only:

Certain commissioned employees of retail or service establishments;

Auto, truck, trailer, farm implement, boat or aircraft salesworkers, or parts-clerks and mechanics servicing autos, trucks or farm implements, who are employed by non-manufacturing establishments primarily engaged in selling these items to ultimate purchasers;

Railroad and air carrier employees, taxi drivers, certain employees of motor carriers, seamen on American vessels, and local delivery employees paid on approved trip rate plans;

Announcers, news editors and chief engineers of certain non-metropolitan broadcasting stations;

Domestic service workers who reside in their employer's residence;

Employees of motion picture theaters;

Farmworkers.

Certain employees may be partially exempt from the Act's overtime pay requirements. These include:

Employees engaged in certain operations on agricultural commodities and employees of certain bulk petroleum distributors;

Employees of hospitals and residential care establishments which have agreements with the employees to work a 14-day work period in lieu of a 7-day workweek (if the employees are paid overtime premium pay within the requirements of the Act for all hours worked over 8 in a day or 80 in the 14-day work period, whichever is the greater number of overtime hours);

Employees who lack a high school diploma or who have not completed the eighth grade may be required by their employer to spend up to 10 hours in a workweek in remedial reading or training in other basic skills that are not job-specific, as long as they are paid their normal wages for the hours spent in such training. Such employees need not be paid overtime premium pay for their remedial training hours.

Basic Provisions/Requirements

The Act requires employers of covered employees who are not otherwise exempt to pay these employees a minimum wage of not less than $5.15 an hour beginning September 1, 1997. Youths under 20 years of age may be paid a minimum wage of not less than $4.25 an hour during the first 90 consecutive calendar days of employment with an employer. Employers may not displace any employee to hire someone at the youth minimum wage. Employers may pay employees on a piece-rate basis, as long as they receive at least the equivalent of the required minimum hourly wage rate. Employers of tipped employees, i.e., employees who customarily and regularly receive more than $30 a month in tips, may consider the tips of these employees as part of their wages, but must pay a direct wage of at least $2.13 per hour if they claim a tip credit. Certain other conditions must also be met.

The Act also permits the employment of certain individuals at wage rates below the statutory minimum wage under certificates issued by the Department:

> Student learners (vocational education students);

> Full-time students in retail or service establishments, agriculture, or institutions of higher education;

> Individuals whose earning or productive capacity is impaired by a physical or mental disability, including those related to age or injury, for the work to be performed.

The Act does not limit the number of hours in a day or days in a week an employee (at least 16 years old) may be required or scheduled to work, including overtime hours. The Act requires that covered employees, unless otherwise exempt, be paid not less than one and one-half times their regular rates of pay for all hours worked in excess of 40 in a workweek.

Employers are required to keep records on wages, hours and other items as set out in the Department of Labor's regulations. Most of this information is of the type generally maintained by employers in ordinary business practice.

Performance of certain types of work in an employee's home is prohibited under the Act unless the employer has obtained prior certification from the Department of Labor. Restrictions apply in the manufacture of knitted outerwear, gloves and mittens, buttons and buckles, handkerchiefs, embroideries, and jewelry (where safety and health hazards are not involved). Employers wishing to employ homeworkers in these industries are required to, among other things, provide written assurances to the Department that they will comply with the Act's wage and other requirements. The manufacture of women's apparel (and jewelry under hazardous conditions) is generally prohibited, except under special certificates that allow homework in these industries when the homeworker is unable to adjust to factory work because of age or physical or mental disability, or is caring for an invalid in the home.

Special provisions apply to state and local government employment.

It is a violation of the Act to fire or in any other manner discriminate against an employee for filing a complaint or for participating in a legal proceeding under the Act. The Act also prohibits the shipment of goods in interstate commerce which were produced in violation of the minimum wage, overtime pay, child labor, or special minimum wage provisions.

Assistance Available

More detailed information on the FLSA, including copies of explanatory brochures and regulatory and interpretative materials, may be obtained by contacting local Wage-Hour offices listed in most telephone directories under U.S. Government, Department of Labor, Wage and Hour Division.

Penalties

Enforcement of the Act is carried out by Wage and Hour Division investigators stationed throughout the country. A variety of remedies is available to the Department to enforce compliance with the Act's requirements. When investigators encounter violations, they recommend changes in employment practices in order to bring the employer into compliance and request the payment of any back wages due employees. Willful violations may be prosecuted criminally and the violators fined up to $10,000. A second conviction may result in imprisonment. Employers who willfully or repeatedly violate the minimum wage or overtime pay requirements are subject to civil money penalties of up to $1,000 per violation. When a civil money penalty is assessed, employers have the right, within 15 days of receipt of the notice of such penalty, to file an exception to the determination. When an exception is filed, it is referred to an administrative law judge for a hearing and determination as to the appropriateness of the penalty. If an exception is not filed, the penalty becomes final.

The Secretary of Labor may also bring suit for back pay and an equal amount in liquidated damages and obtain injunctions to restrain persons from violating the Act. Employees may also bring suit, where the Department has not done so, for back pay and liquidated damages, as well as attorney's fees and court costs.

Relation to State, Local and Other Federal Laws

State laws also apply to employment subject to this Act. When both this Act and a state law apply, the law setting the higher standards must be observed.

Employee Retirement Income Security Act (ERISA)

Source: U.S. Department of Labor
29 USC §1001 et seq., 29 CFR 2509 et seq.)

Who Is Covered

The provisions of Title I of ERISA cover most private sector employee benefit plans. Employee benefit plans are voluntarily established and maintained by an employer, an employee organization, or jointly by one or more such employers and an employee organization. Pension plans—a type of employee benefit plan—are established and maintained to provide retirement income or to defer income until termination of covered employment or beyond. Other employee benefit plans are called welfare plans and are established and maintained to provide health benefits, disability benefits, death benefits, prepaid legal services, vacation benefits, day care centers, scholarship funds, apprenticeship and training benefits, or other similar benefits.

In general, ERISA does not cover plans established or maintained by governmental entities or churches for their employees, or plans which are maintained solely to comply with applicable workers compensation, unemployment or disability laws. ERISA also does not cover plans maintained outside the United States primarily for the benefit of nonresident aliens or unfunded excess benefit plans.

Basic Provisions/Requirements

ERISA sets uniform minimum standards to assure that employee benefit plans are established and maintained in a fair and financially sound manner. In addition, employers have an obligation to provide promised benefits and satisfy ERISA's requirements for managing and administering private

pension and welfare plans. The Department's
Pension and Welfare Benefits Administration
(PWBA), together with the Internal Revenue
Service (IRS) , carries out its statutory and regulatory authority to assure that workers receive the
promised benefits. The Department has principal
jurisdiction over Title I of ERISA, which requires
persons and entities who manage and control plan
funds to:

> Manage plans for the exclusive benefit of par-
> ticipants and beneficiaries;

> Carry out their duties in a prudent manner
> and refrain from conflict-of-interest transac-
> tions expressly prohibited by law;

> Comply with limitations on certain plans'
> investments in employer securities and
> properties;

> Fund benefits in accordance with the law and
> plan rules;

> Report and disclose information on the oper-
> ations and financial condition of plans to the
> government and participants;

> Provide documents required in the conduct
> of investigations to assure compliance with
> the law.

The Department also has jurisdiction over the
prohibited transaction provisions of Title II of
ERISA. However, the IRS administers the rest of
Title II of ERISA, as well as the vesting, participa-
tion, nondiscrimination and funding standards of
Title I of ERISA.

Reporting and Disclosure

Any individual or organization affected by ERISA
may request an advisory opinion or information

letter regarding the interpretation or application of the statutory provisions (or the implementing regulations, interpretive bulletins or exemptions) within the Department's jurisdiction. *ERISA Procedure 76-1,* 41 Federal Register 36281 (August 27, 1976), sets forth the procedures governing the advisory opinion process.

Part 1 of Title I requires the administrator of an employee benefit plan to furnish participants and beneficiaries with a summary plan description (SPD), describing in understandable terms, their rights, benefits and responsibilities under the plan. Plan administrators are also required to furnish participants with a summary of any material changes to the plan or changes to the information contained in the summary plan description. Copies of these documents are not required to be automatically filed with the Department, but must be furnished to the Department on request.

In addition, the administrator generally must file an annual report (Form 5500 Series) each year containing financial and other information concerning the operation of the plan. Plans with 100 or more participants file the Form 5500. Plans with fewer than 100 participants file the Form 5500-C/R; the form 5500-C at least every third year and the Form 5500-R, an abbreviated report, in the two intervening years. Plan administrators must furnish participants and beneficiaries with a summary of the information in the annual report.

Certain pension and welfare benefit plans may be exempt from the requirement to file an annual report. For example, welfare benefit plans with fewer than 100 participants that are fully insured or unfunded within the meaning of the Department's regulation at 29 CFR 2520.104-20 are not required to file an annual report.

The Department's regulations governing these reporting and disclosure requirements are set forth beginning at 29 CFR 2520.101-1.

Fiduciary Standards

Part 4 of Title I sets forth standards and rules governing the conduct of plan fiduciaries. In general, persons who exercise discretionary authority or control over management of a plan or disposition of its assets are "fiduciaries" for purposes of Title I of ERISA. Fiduciaries are required, among other things, to discharge their duties solely in the interest of plan participants and beneficiaries and for the exclusive purpose of providing benefits and defraying reasonable expenses of administering the plan. In discharging their duties, fiduciaries must act prudently and in accordance with documents governing the plan, to the extent such documents are consistent with ERISA. Certain transactions between an employee benefit plan and "parties in interest," which include the employer and others who may be in a position to exercise improper influence over the plan, are prohibited by ERISA and may trigger civil monetary penalties under Title I of ERISA. Most of these transactions are also prohibited by the Internal Revenue Code ("Code"). The Code imposes an excise tax on "disqualified persons" — whose definition generally parallels that of parties in interest — who participate in such transactions.

Exemptions

Both ERISA and the Code contain various statutory exemptions from the prohibited transaction rules and give the Departments of Labor and Treasury, respectively, authority to grant administrative exemptions and establish exemption procedures. Reorganization Plan No. 4 of 1978 transferred the authority of the Treasury Department over prohibited transaction exemptions, with certain exceptions, to the Labor Department.

The statutory exemptions generally include loans to participants, the provision of services necessary for operation of a plan for reasonable compensation, loans to employee stock ownership plans, and investment with certain financial institutions regulated by other State or Federal agencies. (See ERISA section 408 for the conditions of the exemptions.) Administrative exemptions may be granted by the Department on a class or individual basis for a wide variety of proposed transactions with a plan. Applications for individual exemptions must include, among other information:

> A detailed description of the exemption transaction and the parties for whom an exemption is requested;
>
> Reasons a plan would have for entering into the transaction;
>
> Percentage of assets involved in the exemption transaction;

The names of persons with investment discretion;

> Extent of plan assets already invested in loans to, property leased by, and securities issued by parties in interest involved in the transaction;
>
> Copies of all contracts, agreements, instruments and relevant portions of plan documents and trust agreements bearing on the exemption transaction;

Information regarding plan participation in pooled funds when the exemption transaction involves such funds;

Declaration, under penalty of perjury by the applicant, attesting to the truth of representations made in such exemption submissions;

Statement of consent by third-party experts acknowledging that their statement is being submitted to the Department as part of an exemption application.

The Department's exemption procedures are set forth at 29 CFR 2570.30 through 2570.51.

Enforcement

ERISA confers substantial law enforcement responsibilities on the Department. Part 5 of ERISA Title I gives the Department authority to bring a civil action to correct violations of the law, gives investigative authority to determine whether any person has violated Title I, and imposes criminal penalties on any person who willfully violates any provision of Part 1 of Title V.

Health Insurance Portability and Accountability Act of 1996

The Health Insurance Portability and Accountability Act of 1996 (HIPAA), Pub. L. 104- 191,was enacted on August 21, 1996. HIPAA amended ERISA to provide for, among other things, improved portability and continuity of health insurance coverage provided in connection with employment. The HIPAA portability provisions relating to group health plans and health insurance coverage offered in connection with group health plans are set forth under a new Part 7 of Subtitle B of Title I of ERISA. These provisions include rules relating to preexisting conditions exclusions, special enrollment rights, and prohibition of discrimination against individuals based on health status- related factors.

Consolidated Omnibus Budget Reconciliation Act of 1985 (COBRA)

Source: U.S. Department of Labor

Continuation of Health Coverage

Continuation of health care provisions were enacted as part of the Consolidated Omnibus Budget Reconciliation Act of 1985 (COBRA) and are codified in Part 6 of Title I of ERISA. These provisions apply to group health plans of employers with 20 or more employees on a typical working day in the previous calendar year. COBRA gives participants and beneficiaries the right to maintain, at their own expense, coverage under their health plan that would be lost due to a triggering event, such as termination of employment at a cost that is comparable to what it would be if they were still members of the employer's group. Plans must give covered individuals an initial general notice informing them of their rights under COBRA and describing the law. The law also places notification obligations upon plan administrators, employers, and qualified beneficiaries with regard to certain "qualifying events." In most instances of employee death, termination, reduced hours of employment, entitlement to Medicare, or bankruptcy, it becomes the employer's responsibility to provide a specific notice to the plan administrator. The plan administrator must then notify the qualified beneficiaries the opportunity to elect continuation coverage.

The Department's regulatory and interpretive jurisdiction over the COBRA provisions is limited to the COBRA notification and disclosure provisions.

Jurisdiction of the Internal Revenue Service

The IRS has regulatory and interpretive responsibility for all provisions of COBRA not under the

Department's jurisdiction. In addition, ERISA provisions relating to participation, vesting, funding and benefit accrual, contained in parts 2 and 3 of Title I, are generally administered and interpreted by the Internal Revenue Service.

Assistance Available

PWBA has numerous general publications designed to assist employers and employees in understanding their obligations and rights under ERISA. A list of PWBA booklets and pamphlets is available by writing to: Publications Desk, PWBA, Division of Public Affairs, Room N-5656, 200 Constitution Ave., NW, Washington, DC 20210. Many of these documents are available via PWBA's homepage.

Penalties

PWBA has authority under ERISA Section 502(c) to assess civil penalties for reporting violations and prohibited transactions involving a plan. A penalty of up to $1,000 per day may be assessed against plan administrators who fail or refuse to comply with annual reporting requirements. Section 502(I) gives the agency authority to assess civil penalties against parties in interest who engage in prohibited transactions with welfare and nonqualified pension plans. The penalty can range from five percent to 100 percent of the amount involved in a transaction. A parallel provision of the Code directly imposes an excise tax against disqualified persons, including employee benefit plan sponsors and service providers, who engage in prohibited transactions with tax-qualified pension and profit sharing plans. Finally, the Department is required under Section 502(l) to assess mandatory civil penalties equal to 20 percent of any amount recovered with respect to fiduciary breaches resulting from either a settlement agreement with the Department or a court order as the result of a lawsuit by the Department.

Relation to State, Local and Other Federal Laws

Part 5 of Title I provides that the provisions of ERISA Titles I and IV supersede State and local laws which "relate to" an employee benefit plan. ERISA, however, saves certain state and local laws from ERISA preemption, including state insurance regulation of multiple employer welfare arrangements (MEWAs). MEWAs generally constitute employee welfare benefit plans or other arrangements providing welfare benefits to employees of more than one employer, not pursuant to a collective bargaining agreement.

In addition, ERISA's general prohibitions against assignment or alienation of pension benefits do not apply to qualified domestic relations orders. Plan administrators must comply with the terms of orders made pursuant to State domestic relations law and award all or part of a participant's benefit in the form of child support, alimony, or marital property rights to an alternative payee (spouse, former spouse, child or other dependent). In addition, group health plans covered by ERISA must provide benefits in accordance with the applicable requirements of qualified medical child support order issued under State domestic relations laws.

DEPARTMENT OF COMMERCE TABLE OF OFFENSES AND PENALTIES

Here is how one federal government department, the Department of Commerce, deals with employee problems. You might use these as a model for your own business.

Relationships with the Public

Offense: Failure to obtain any required clearance of official speech or article (See DAO 219-1)

Penalty for First Offense: Written Reprimand to Removal

Penalty for Second Offense: 5 days suspension to removal

Penalty for Subsequent Offense: 30 days suspension to removal

Security Regulations

Offense: Violation of a Security Regulation

Penalty for First Offense: Oral Admonishment to Removal

Penalty for Second Offense: 5 days suspension to removal

Penalty for Subsequent Offense: 30 days suspension to removal

Outside Employment and Interests

Offense: Engaging in private business activities of a prohibited or unethical nature

Penalty for First Offense: Written Reprimand to Removal

Penalty for Second Offense: 5 days suspension to removal

Penalty for Subsequent Offense: 30 days suspension to removal

Offense: Acceptance of improper dual employment or dual compensation by the U.S. Government

Penalty for First Offense: Written Reprimand to Removal

Penalty for Second Offense: 5 days suspension to removal

Penalty for Subsequent Offense: 30 days suspension to removal

Offense: Acceptance by an employee of gratuity which might reasonably be interpreted as tending to affect the performance of official duties

Penalty for First Offense: Written Reprimand to Removal

Penalty for Second Offense: 5 days suspension to removal

Penalty for Subsequent Offense: 30 days suspension to removal

Offense: Acceptance of foreign employment without prior authorization

> Penalty for First Offense: 5 days suspension to removal

> Penalty for Second Offense: 30 days suspension to removal

> Penalty for Subsequent Offense: Removal

Political Activity

Offense: Improper Political Activities

> Penalty for First Offense: Suspension or removal as determined by the Merit Systems Protection Board or the Department of Commerce

Conduct on the Job

Offense: Unauthorized absence from the job during working hours or on any scheduled day of work

> Penalty for First Offense: Oral admonishment to 3 days suspension

> Penalty for Second Offense: Written reprimand to 5 days suspension

> Penalty for Subsequent Offense: 5 days suspension to removal

Offense: Tardiness

> Penalty for First Offense: Oral admonishment to 1 day suspension

> Penalty for Second Offense: Written reprimand to 5 days suspension

> Penalty for Subsequent Offense: 5 days suspension to removal

Offense: Improper use of sick leave

> Penalty for First Offense: Written reprimand to 10 days suspension

> Penalty for Second Offense: 5 days suspension to removal

> Penalty for Subsequent Offense: 30 days suspension to removal

Offense: Intoxication while on duty which impairs the ability to perform duties properly

> Penalty for First Offense: 5 days suspension to removal

> Penalty for Second Offense: 30 days suspension to removal

> Penalty for Subsequent Offense: Removal

Offense: Selling intoxicants on premises occupied by the Department

    Penalty for First Offense: Removal

Offense: Unauthorized possession or use of intoxicants on premises of the Department

    Penalty for First Offense: 3 days suspension to 30 days suspension

    Penalty for Second Offense: 10 days suspension to removal

    Penalty for Subsequent Offense: 30 days suspension to removal

Offense: Promotion of gambling or lotteries on Government premises or while in duty status

    Penalty for First Offense: 5 days suspension to removal

    Penalty for Second Offense: 30 days suspension to removal

    Penalty for Subsequent Offense: Removal

Offense: Gambling on Government premises or while in duty status

    Penalty for First Offense: Written reprimand to 10 days suspension

    Penalty for Second Offense: 5 days suspension to removal

    Penalty for Subsequent Offense: 30 days suspension to removal

Offense: Borrowing money or obtaining co-signature from subordinates

    Penalty for First Offense: Written reprimand to removal

    Penalty for Second Offense: 5 days suspension to removal

    Penalty for Subsequent Offense: 30 days suspension to removal

Offense: Lending of money to other employees at usurious rates

    Penalty for First Offense: 5 days suspension to 10 days suspension

    Penalty for Second Offense: 30 days suspension to removal

    Penalty for Subsequent Offense: Removal

Offense: Creating a disturbance in the work place or on premises of the Department

    Penalty for First Offense: Written reprimand to 10 days suspension

    Penalty for Second Offense: 5 days suspension to removal

    Penalty for Subsequent Offense: 30 days suspension to removal

Offense: Fighting

>Penalty for First Offense: Written reprimand to removal

>Penalty for Second Offense: 5 days suspension to removal

>Penalty for Subsequent Offense: 30 days suspension to removal

Offense: Conduct which violates common decency or morality, including use of improper or obscene language

>Penalty for First Offense: Written reprimand to 10 days suspension

>Penalty for Second Offense: 5 days suspension to removal

>Penalty for Subsequent Offense: 30 days suspension to removal

Offense: Making vicious, malicious or knowingly false statements concerning another officer or employee of the Government

>Penalty for First Offense: Written reprimand to removal

>Penalty for Second Offense: 5 days suspension to removal

>Penalty for Subsequent Offense: 30 days suspension to removal

Offense: Negligent or intentional injury to person or property of other employees

>Penalty for First Offense: Written reprimand to removal

>Penalty for Second Offense: 5 days suspension to removal

>Penalty for Subsequent Offense: 30 days suspension to removal

Offense: Safety (non-motor vehicle): Violation of safety regulations, instructions, or prescribed safe practices, including failure to report accident or injury

>Penalty for First Offense: Oral admonishment to 3 days suspension

>Penalty for Second Offense: Written reprimand to 5 days suspension

>Penalty for Subsequent Offense: 5 days suspension to removal

Offense: Safety (Government motor vehicle operation): Violation of traffic laws, safety regulations or instructions, or safe driving practices, including failure to report accident or injury

>Penalty for First Offense: Written reprimand to removal

>Penalty for Second Offense: 5 days suspension to removal

>Penalty for Subsequent Offense: 30 days suspension to removal

Offense: Willful or negligent damage or defacement of Government property

Penalty for First Offense: Written reprimand to removal

Penalty for Second Offense: 5 days suspension to removal

Penalty for Subsequent Offense: 30 days suspension to removal

Offense: Use of or allowing the use of Government motor vehicles, aircraft, or watercraft for other than official purposes

Penalty for First Offense: 30 days suspension (mandatory) to removal

Penalty for Second Offense: Removal

Offense: Act of negligence or careless workmanship in performance of duty resulting in waste of public funds or inefficiency

Penalty for First Offense: Oral admonishment to 3 days suspension

Penalty for Second Offense: Written reprimand to 5 days suspension

Penalty for Subsequent Offense: 5 days suspension to removal

Offense: Use of or allowing use of Government funds, property, personnel, or other resources for unauthorized purposes

Penalty for First Offense: 5 days suspension to removal

Penalty for Second Offense: 30 days suspension to removal

Penalty for Subsequent Offense: Removal

Offense: Conducting personal affairs while in duty status

Penalty for First Offense: Written reprimand to removal

Penalty for Second Offense: 5 days suspension to removal

Penalty for Subsequent Offense: 30 days suspension to removal

Offense: Loafing, willful idleness, wasting time

Penalty for First Offense: Oral admonishment to 3 days suspension

Penalty for Second Offense: Written reprimand to 5 days suspension

Penalty for Subsequent Offense: 5 days suspension to removal

Offense: Sleeping on duty where safety of persons or property is not endangered

> Penalty for First Offense: Written reprimand to 10 days suspension

> Penalty for Second Offense: 5 days suspension to removal

> Penalty for Subsequent Offense: 30 days suspension to removal

Offense: Sleeping on duty where safety of persons or property is endangered

> Penalty for First Offense: 5 days suspension to removal

> Penalty for Second Offense: 30 days suspension to removal

> Penalty for Subsequent Offense: Removal

Offense: Failure or excessive delay in carrying out orders or assignments

> Penalty for First Offense: Written reprimand 10 days suspension

> Penalty for Second Offense: 5 days suspension to removal

> Penalty for Subsequent Offense: 30 days suspension to removal

Offense: Insubordination

> Penalty for First Offense: Written reprimand to removal

> Penalty for Second Offense: 5 days suspension to removal

> Penalty for Subsequent Offense: 30 days suspension to removal

Offense: Improper use of official credential card

> Penalty for First Offense: 3 days suspension to 30 days suspension

> Penalty for Second Offense: 10 days suspension to removal

> Penalty for Subsequent Offense: 30 days suspension to removal

Offense: Unethical use of official authority or information

> Penalty for First Offense: 30 days suspension to removal

> Penalty for Second Offense: Removal

Offense: Acceptance of voluntary services for the Government contrary to statute

> Penalty for First Offense: Removal (required by statute - 31 USC 665)

Offense: Attempted use of influence or pressure to secure favor in the appointment, transfer, advancement, or retention of a relative in the Department

> Penalty for First Offense: 5 days suspension to removal

> Penalty for Second Offense: 30 days suspension to removal

> Penalty for Subsequent Offense: Removal

Offense: Violation of "no strike" affidavit

> Penalty for First Offense: Removal

Offense: Unauthorized canvassing, soliciting, or peddling on Department premises

> Penalty for First Offense: Oral admonishment to 3 days suspension

> Penalty for Second Offense: Written reprimand to 5 days suspension

> Penalty for Subsequent Offense: 5 days suspension to removal

Offense: Deliberate or grossly negligent violations of merit principles or procedures with a demonstrable adverse effect on one or more persons

> Penalty for First Offense: Written reprimand to 10 days suspension

> Penalty for Second Offense: 5 days suspension to removal

> Penalty for Subsequent Offense: 30 days suspension to removal

Offense: Harassing, threatening, or raking reprisal action against an employee as a result of or in anticipation of a grievance, appeal, complaint, or other exercise of rights

> Penalty for First Offense: 5 days suspension to removal

> Penalty for Second Offense: 30 days suspension to removal

> Penalty for Subsequent Offense: Removal

Offense: Misappropriation of funds

> Penalty for First Offense: Removal

Offense: Inefficiency

> Penalty for First Offense: Demotion or separation (as authorized by Chapter 43 of 5 USC)

Offense: Soliciting contributions for gifts or presents to those in superior official positions, accepting gifts or presents from Government employees receiving lower salary, or making donations as a gift or present to official supervisors

> Penalty for First Offense: Removal (required by 5 USC 7351)

Offense: Misconduct generally — criminal, infamous, dishonest, or notoriously disgraceful conduct

Penalty for First Offense: Written reprimand to removal

Penalty for Second Offense: 5 days suspension to removal

Penalty for Subsequent Offense: 30 days suspension to removal

Offense: Misrepresentation, falsification, or omission of material fact in connection with application, employment, or any record, report, investigation or other proceeding

Penalty for First Offense: Written reprimand to removal

Penalty for Second Offense: 5 days suspension to removal

Penalty for Subsequent Offense: 30 days suspension to removal

Offense: Certification to the accuracy of a position description containing substantial inaccuracies which may be grade controlling

Penalty for First Offense: Written reprimand to removal

Penalty for Second Offense: 5 days suspension to removal

Penalty for Subsequent Offense: 30 days suspension to removal

Offense: Conduct demonstrating untrustworthiness or unreliability

Penalty for First Offense: Written reprimand to removal

Penalty for Second Offense: 5 days suspension to removal

Penalty for Subsequent Offense: 30 days suspension to removal

Offense: Discrimination. As used in this table, discrimination refers to specific acts taken by an employee in the performance of his/her official duties which discriminates against one or more individuals on the basis of race, color, religion, sex, national origin, age, physical or mental disability, or sexual orientation

Penalty for First Offense: Written reprimand to removal

Penalty for Second Offense: 5 days suspension to removal

Penalty for Subsequent Offense: 30 days suspension to removal

Offense: Refusal to answer appropriate interrogation in properly authorized inquiry

Penalty for First Offense: Written reprimand to removal

Penalty for Second Offense: 5 days suspension to removal

Penalty for Subsequent Offense: 30 days suspension to removal

Offense: Failure to pay a just financial obligation in a proper and timely manner

>Penalty for First Offense: Written reprimand to removal

>Penalty for Second Offense: 5 days suspension to removal

>Penalty for Subsequent Offense: 30 days suspension to removal

*Violation of any administrative regulation which
does not provide a penalty*

Offense: Minor offense

>Penalty for First Offense: Oral admonishment to 3 days suspension

>Penalty for Second Offense: Written reprimand to 5 days suspension

>Penalty for Subsequent Offense: 5 days suspension to removal

Offense: Major offense

>Penalty for First Offense: 5 days suspension to removal

>Penalty for Second Offense: 30 days suspension to removal

>Penalty for Subsequent Offense: Removal